# Cinematic Geopolitics

In recent years, film has been one of the major genres within which the imaginaries involved in mapping the geopolitical world have been represented and reflected upon.

In this book, one of America's foremost theorists of culture and politics treats those aspects of the "geopolitical aesthetic" that must be addressed in light of both the post-Cold War and post-9/11 world and contemporary film theory and philosophy. Beginning with an account of his experience as a juror at film festivals, Michael J. Shapiro in *Cinematic Geopolitics* analyzes the ways in which film festival space and both feature and documentary films function as counter-spaces to the contemporary "violent cartography" occasioned by governmental policy, especially the current "war on terror."

Influenced by the cinema–philosophy relationship developed by Gilles Deleuze and the politics of aesthetics thinking of Jacques Rancière, the book's chapters examine a range of films from established classics like *The Deer Hunter* and *The Battle of Algiers* to contemporary films such as *Dirty Pretty Things* and *The Fog of War*. Shapiro's use of philosophical and theoretical works makes this cutting-edge examination of film and politics essential reading for all students and scholars with an interest in film and politics.

**Michael J. Shapiro** is a Professor in the Department of Political Science, University of Hawai'i at Mānoa, USA. His research and teaching are in the areas of political theory, global politics, and cultural studies. Among his publications are: *Methods and Nations: Cultural Governance and the Indigenous Subject* (Routledge, 2004) and *Deforming American Political Thought: Ethnicity, Facticity and Genre* (University Press of Kentucky, 2006).

**GLOBAL HORIZONS**
Series Editors

*Richard Falk, Princeton University, USA
and R.B.J. Walker, University of Victoria, Canada*

We live in a moment that urgently calls for a reframing, reconceptualizing, and reconstituting of the political, cultural and social practices that underpin the enterprises of international relations.

While contemporary developments in international relations are focused upon highly detailed and technical matters, they also demand an engagement with the broader questions of history, ethics, culture and human subjectivity.

GLOBAL HORIZONS is dedicated to examining these broader questions.

# Cinematic Geopolitics

Michael J. Shapiro

Routledge
Taylor & Francis Group

LONDON AND NEW YORK

First published 2009
by Routledge
2 Park Square, Milton Park, Abingdon, Oxon, OX14 4RN

Simultaneously published in the USA and Canada
by Routledge
270 Madison Avenue, New York, NY 10016

*Routledge is an imprint of the Taylor & Francis Group, an informa business*

© 2009 Michael J. Shapiro

Typeset in Times New Roman by
Swales & Willis Ltd, Exeter, Devon
Printed and bound in Great Britain by
CPI Antony Rowe, Chippenham, Wiltshire

*British Library Cataloguing in Publication Data*
A catalogue record for this book is available from the British Library

*Library of Congress Cataloging in Publication Data*
A catalog record for this book has been requested

ISBN 10: 0–415–77635–X (hbk)
ISBN 10: 0–415–77636–8 (pbk)
ISBN 10: 0–203–89200–3 (ebk)

ISBN 13: 978–0–415–77635–6 (hbk)
ISBN 13: 978–0–415–77636–3 (pbk)
ISBN 13: 978–0–203–89200–8 (ebk)

To the memory of my cousin, Malcolm Greenberg,
1930–2004

# Contents

# Figures

# Acknowledgments

I am especially indebted to Jochen Peters of the Center for Peace Studies at the University of Tromsø for inviting me to serve as a juror at two Tromsø International Film Festivals and to the jurors with whom I served (see Introduction). I want also to thank those who invited presentations of prototypes of the various chapters, commented on them, or inspired and supported aspects of my thinking and analyses: Jane Bennett, Peter Burgess, Bill Connolly, Mick Dillon, Jason Frank, Jon Goldberg-Hiller, Bianca Isaki, Sankaran Krishna, Debbie Lisle, Nizar Messari, Daniel Bertrand Monk, Joao Nogueira, Rob Walker, Cindy Weber. I also owe special thanks to the students in Rio who took my seminar on cinematic geopolitics and edified me on the subject of Brazilian films: Daniel Mauricio Aragao, Moema Viera Correa, Andrea Freitas da Conceicao, Carlos Frederico Pereira da Silva Gama, Fabiano Mielniczuk, Marcello Mello Valenca, and Roberto Vilchez Yamato. My greatest debt is to my wife and film-watching partner, Hannah Tavares, whose compassion and critical thinking accompany me everywhere. This book is dedicated to the memory of my late cousin, Malcolm Greenberg, who took me to see one of my first war films, the Fred Zinnemann film version of James Jones's novel *From Here to Eternity*. Malcolm and his friend Alan provided the first film commentary I had ever heard. Watching the film as a 13-year-old, I had my attention on heroes and bad guys, and my primary emotion was fear, in reaction to the brutality of Sgt. James R. ('Fatso') Judson (played convincingly by Ernest Borgnine). As I regained my composure while Malcolm drove us home from the film, I listened while he and Alan translated a war film drama into a complex story about the ways in which characters are shaped by circumstances. Then, as always, Malcolm displayed both a critical and a generous view of humanity's diverse personae. I profited from being exposed to both of his dispositions.

# Introduction

Two historical events, one in which I participated and one that I merely witnessed, supplied the initiating impetus for this book. First, during the third week of January 2005, while President George W. Bush was using his second inaugural address to rally support for his "war on terror," deployed at home and abroad, I was with over five thousand people attending the Tromsø International Film Festival (the TIFF). Up in the Arctic Circle in Norway, in a nation that has often played a mediating role in a world of intra- and inter-state violence, I was performing as a necessarily judgmental viewer. I served on a five-person jury charged to select one among ten films for *Den Norske Fredsfilmprisen* (The Norwegian Peace Film Award). Along with four other jurors, I watched the films and engaged in deliberations about both their artistic merits and their relevance to the contested concept of a "peace film." In addition, I participated in a panel discussion on the concept of a "peace film" and interacted with our audience, containing both festival attendees and students from the University of Tromsø.

Thus situated in a "cinematic heterotopia," I began the reflections on the relationship of film to the geo- and bio-politics of war and peace and to other aspects of violence versus sympathy and interpersonal generosity that are the foci of investigations and analyses in this book.[1] Thanks to our jury coordinator, Jochen Peters, who administers the University of Tromsø's Center for Peace Studies, and the jurors with whom I served—Eva Gran, the director of the Tromsø branch of Norway's UN information agency, Margreth Olin, a Norwegian filmmaker and director, Ola Lund Renolen, the cultural director for the municipality of Trondheim, Norway, and Alberto Valiente Thoresen, a student in the Peace Studies program at the University of Tromsø—my views were contested, edified, and often changed. During the course of a week, I was led to confront the limits of my own film viewing in particular and to the ways in which critically oriented films can challenge the limits of perception in general.

The film we selected for the prize, the Iranian director Asghar Farhadi's *Beautiful City*, was timely as well as complex and thought-provoking. The film narrative begins with a revelation during a birthday celebration at a youth prison for Akbar, who has just turned 18 and can therefore be executed unless the plaintiff, the father of the girl he murdered when he was 16, forgives him. His sister and his friend Ala, a fellow inmate out on furlough, seek to convince the father, who seems implacable in his desire for revenge, to forgive Akbar. As the plot unfolds, the viewer is treated to the complex cultural and economic patterns of an Iranian city, as well as to the array of personae who influence personal and cultural judgments. Much of the film's *mise en scène* is often more edifying than its dramatic plot. Indeed, apart from the plot as a whole, which never reaches a definitive resolution, one scene stood out for all of us jurors. After Ala and Akbar's sister bring their cause to the attention of the imam of the mosque where the victim's father attends, the imam engages the father in conversation about his refusal to forgive. The father asserts, "Doesn't the Koran mention my right to revenge?" The imam replies that indeed it does but then goes on to say that there are more places in the Koran that encourage forgiveness. Viewers are thus invited into a highly complex, text-based value negotiation at the center of an Islamic culture, at a time when many have regarded Islam's "faithful" as monomaniacally violent.

The experience at that festival and the historical moment within which it transpired encouraged me to think about how special film festival space is when a segment of it is given over to peace-oriented themes and to explore the cinema–violence and cinema–peace relationships deployed across the geopolitical world more extensively. After I learned that the first Norwegian Peace Film Award was given at the TIFF in 2004 to Michael Winterbottom's docudrama *In This Time*, I watched this film, which also won the top prize at the Berlin Film Festival in 2003. Using "real people" rather than actors, the film employed a road movie genre to follow two refugees, Jamal and his older cousin Enayat, headed to London to escape the hopeless lives they would otherwise lead in the Afghan refugee camps, which date back to the Russian invasion and have since been augmented after the disorder following the U.S. post-9/11 invasion. Like Winterbottom's more recent docudrama, co-directed with Mat Whitecross, *The Road to Guantanamo* (which I treat in chapter 1), *In This Time* gives the viewers an up-close experience of a smaller world of adversity within the larger, geopolitical world, where antagonisms lead to violent policies in places that most of the world grasps only with remote abstractions. Lodged between documentary and fictional genres, the film enjoyed a recognition at festivals that suggests that we might view film festivals as counter-spaces to the violent ones generated by inter- and intra-state antagonisms. Heeding the nature of that film and Winterbottom's *The Road to Guantanamo* (a prize winner at the 2006 Berlin Film Festival), while also reflecting on my 2005 experience at the TIFF, led me to sign on as a juror for the Peace Film Award at TIFF 2007, in order to explore more deeply the ways in which film festivals articulate a challenge to global violence in the post-9/11 world.

At TIFF 2007, where I served on a jury (again assisted by Jochen Peters), along with Rashid Masharawi, a Palestinian filmmaker from Gaza (living in Paris) and Silje Ryvold, a Norwegian graduate student in the University of Tromsø's Center for Peace Studies, we awarded the Peace Film Prize to Linda Hattendorf for her documentary *The Cats of Mirikitani*. It's a film that, among other things, articulates a historical case of both foreign civilian deaths and domestic oppression—the bombing of Hiroshima and the detention of America's Japanese Americans during World War II respectively—with the post-9/11 war on terror. I reserve my discussion of that film for chapter 3, in which I treat another notable prize-winning documentary, Erroll Morris's *The Fog of War*.

The second provocation for my turn toward cinema is a perverse occasion of cinema viewing, the widely reported screening of Gillo Pontecorvo's *The Battle of Algiers* (another film festival award winner—Grand Prize, Venice, 1966) for a group of officers and civilian "experts" employed by the Pentagon. In 2003 it was reported in the *New York Times* that the flier used to invite the viewers read, "How to win a battle against terrorism and the war of ideas."[2] Of special interest to those viewers was the effectiveness of the French "interrogation" techniques (the euphemism used by the commanding lieutenant colonel for torture). Pontecorvo's film is in an Italian neo-realist style. It uses non-actors in a vernacular setting and a Rossellini-inspired newsreel style—in black and white with documentary-type editing—to demonstrate, with close-up looks at Algerian insurgents (while in most scenes the French colonialists are shot from distances that render them as remote and unsympathetic), a people seeking to control their political destiny. As one writer notes, "Pontecorvo has penetrated our Western self-absorption and let in the harsh light of reality" and adds that "the true heirs of *Algiers* have been the numberless filmmakers from Brazil, Argentina, Bolivia, Cuba, Senegal, Mali, Tunisia, Morocco, Palestine and Algeria itself—inspired by Pontecorvo's supreme empathy to tell their own stories of nationalist striving."[3]

In contrast, the Pentagon's viewers were encouraged to watch the film to explore "the advantages and costs of resorting to torture and intimidation in seeking human intelligence about enemy plans."[4] What they were able to see, given their instructions, was tortures which include electric shock, near drowning, blowtorch burning, and upside-down hanging. Could this provide lessons for U.S. invaders of Iraq, involved in what they have called "Operation Iraqi Freedom"? What might they have seen were they able to place the scenes in the context of the anti-colonial struggle that the film's *mise en scène* foregrounds—a situation of curtailed freedom in which (in Jean-Paul Sartre's words during the actual rebellion) "the riches of the one are built on the poverty of the other"?[5]

On reading about the episode, I was reminded of an earlier attempt at perverse cinema appropriation, Hitler's propaganda minister Josef Goebbels's complimentary response in the German press to Sergei Eisenstein's *The Battleship Potemkin*, and his suggestion that National Socialist films should seek to emulate Eisenstein's techniques. Eisenstein's reaction, in an open letter, is memorable. Reminiscent of Walter Benjamin's famous remark that fascism has no use for the arts employing mechanical reproduction is Eisenstein's remark that Goebbels's "suggestion that Fascism can give birth to a great German cinema is profoundly mistaken." After asserting that "National Socialism has not produced a single work of art that is in the least bit digestible,"[6] Eisenstein goes on to state that "*truth and National Socialism are incompatible*" (283), and ends with the following:

> *Get back to your drums, Herr drummer in chief!* Don't play the tune of National Socialist realism in cinema on your magic flute . . . . Stick to the instrument you're used to—the axe. Make the most of it. *Burn your books.*

*Burn your Reichstags.* But don't imagine that a bureaucratic art fed on all this filth will be able to "set the hearts of men on fire with its voice" (284).

The Goebbels–Eisenstein exchange cannot be dismissed as a matter of the opposing ideologies of two propagandists. Although many have seen Eisenstein's films as propaganda in behalf of the (then) new Soviet experiment, Jacques Rancière makes a compelling contrary case. Eisenstein's films (for example *The General Line*), he suggests, are aesthetic, and thus political in a critical sense, rather than ideological, because they are "about what we see" and, most significantly:

> A propaganda film must give us a sense of certainty about what we see, it must choose between the documentary that presents what we see as a palpable reality or the fiction that forwards it as a desirable end, all the while keeping narration and symbolization in their respective places. Eisenstein systematically denies us this sense of certainty.[7]

Although it's tempting to respond to the Pentagon in the style with which Eisenstein engaged Goebbels, I am adopting a more theoretical stance in order to locate the perverse screening event in an aesthetic, rather than a polemical, context. Pontecorvo's characters, wrought from Algerian non-professionals, are aesthetic and thus highly political subjects. To follow their movements is less to interrogate their psychology than it is to watch "history-a-transpiring" (to enlist a Thomas Pynchon phrase).[8] Instead of merely condemning the Pentagon's film enthusiasts, I want to introduce an analytic (which I apply more extensively in chapter 5) to suggest that we can use the contrast between Pontecorvo's cinematic efforts and the Pentagon viewer's project to think about a politics that crosses geopolitical boundaries. In the canonical political theory literature, which foregrounds the social contract (John Locke's treatises are exemplars), the primary political problem is one of translating egotism into sociality. This leaves the outside of national societies in the cold, because, as many theorists of international relations insist, there is no global society and thus no international contract but rather a situation of normative anarchy (as some put it), or at least a normativity that is less than contractual (as others note). However, if we turn to David Hume instead of the various contract theorists, we are encouraged to consider the role of partialities rather than contracts, because for Hume passion precedes perception. Within the Humean frame, the political problem is one of how to stretch the passions into commitments that extend beyond them, how, as Gilles Deleuze puts it in his gloss on Hume, "to pass from a 'limited sympathy' to an 'extended generosity,'"[9] for, as Hume insists, "the qualities of the mind are *selfishness* and *limited generosity*."[10]

The two initiating experiences I have described have prompted me to investigate the ways in which cinema, when viewed critically in order to think rather than perversely to pursue a particular interest, can be used to extend generosity and thus to challenge the episodes of the violence deployed in official war policy and other modes of coercion and abjection. Accordingly the studies in this book are illustrations of cinema's contributions to sympathetic as well as critical political thinking about the modern world. And crucially, contrary to the dominant presumption in the social sciences, *thinking* as I will be emphasizing it is not a matter of systematically achieving representations of experience by using reliable (that is, repeatable) techniques of observation. Rather, thinking involves resistance to the dominant modes of representing the world, whether those representational practices function as mere unreflective habit or as intentionally organized, systematic observation.

Cinema, as it has functioned in the hands of certain directors, is a vehicle for animating and encouraging such thinking. For Gilles Deleuze cinema is a technology that produces signs, which, in their encounter with the body, provide for a new "image of thought."[11] Yet many academics tend to dismiss the epistemic significance of cinema. More than one reviewer of essays I have written on film for social science journals have offered remarks to the effect that this or that essay is just about "movies" (enough said). And, when I have presented prototypes of the chapters in this book to university audiences, composed mostly of those who are more attuned to the reliability of representations than to the provocations of critical genres, some have reacted by wondering what one can derive from examining films, which they see as mediated, fictional renderings of human experience. For them, the mediating effects of measurement devices aimed at static data are less problematic with respect to access to "empirical reality" than are films, which restore the process through which such "empirical reality" emerges.

Against such a "trained incapacity" (thank you, Thorstein Veblen), a variety of philosophers and social theorists whose writings influence my analyses have argued that cinema provides superior access to empirical veracity than other forms of managed perception. Among these, Friedrich Kracauer tellingly subtitled his mid-twentieth-century film book *The Redemption of Physical Reality*. Cinema, according to Kracauer, allows us "the experience of things in their concreteness"; it restores what scientific abstractions remove. Science's "objects are stripped of the qualities which give them 'all their poignancy and preciousness.'"[12] Similarly Walter Benjamin saw film technology, still in its early realizations, as a mechanism that makes the real more apparent than mere vision, by among other things allowing "the audience to take the position of a critic" as it "takes the position of the camera." It is a perspectival position that "reactivates the objects produced" to comport with the viewer's contemporary situation rather than articulating "the traditional value of the cultural heritage." In addition the kind of vision offered by cinema contrasts with the perspectives of its actors because the way the camera presents the actor to the public is such that the viewer "need not respect the performance as a whole."[13]

More recently, in a gloss on the film-philosophy writings of Deleuze, Rancière has noted that cinema achieves what vision obscures by undoing the "ordinary work of the human brain." It "puts perception back in things because its operation is one of restitution" of the reality that the brain has "confiscated," in part because it disrupts the human tendency to place oneself at "the center of the universe of images."[14] Space and positionality are crucial aspects of Deleuze's contribution to the analysis of cinema's critical capacity because cinema deprivileges the directionality of centered commanding perception; it allows the disorganized multiplicity that is the world to emerge. In his words, "Instead of going from the acentered state of things to centered perception, [we] could go back up towards the acentered state of things and get closer to it."[15]

To pursue the epistemic and political significance of recovering the "acentered state of things," I want to elaborate Deleuze's remark by turning to Thomas Mann, who provides a similar insight in his epic tetralogy *Joseph and His Brothers*. Not surprising, the style of this set of novels is strikingly cinematic; Mann explicitly formulated a principle of montage, which he applied in his writing.[16] The third book, *Joseph in Egypt*, begins with Joseph's remark "Where are you taking me?" to a group of nomadic Ma'onites who have pulled him from the pit where his brothers had left him to die. After deflecting this and subsequent queries with which Joseph expresses the presumption that the Ma'onites are part of *his* story, Kedema, whose father is the group's patriarch, says, "You have a way of putting yourself in the middle of things," and goes on to disabuse him of his privileged location: "Do you suppose . . .that we are journeying simply so that you may arrive somewhere your god wants you to be?"[17] Like Kedema, who contests Joseph's conceit that his spatio-temporal location commands all relevant perception, cinema effects a decentering mode of creation and reception.

Those who have recognized cinema's decentering effects are in debt to Henri Bergson's philosophy of embodiment. Bergson saw the body as a center of perception, but crucially the Bergsonian centered body is a center of indetermination in that its perceptions are always partial. To perceive is to subtract in order to come up with *a* sense of the world, selected from all possible senses. Inasmuch as each body, as a center of indetermination, selects an aggregate of images from the totality of the world's images, the question for Bergson becomes:

> How is it that the same images can belong at the same time to two different systems [for example Joseph's and Kedema's]: one in which each image varies for itself and in a well defined measure that it is patient of the real action of surrounding images; and another in which all images change for a single image [for Bergson each *body* is a single image] and in varying measure that they reflect the eventual action of this privileged image?[18]

As is well known Bergson's answer is that each single image or body subtracts in its own interest-based way, its way of isolating some aspects of the aggregate of images rather than others. Hence the Joseph–Kedema interchange is quintessentially Bergsonian.

For Bergson, the brain is a particularizing and evacuating mechanism. Edified by Bergson's insights on perception, Deleuze offers a *cinematic* body as a center of indetermination by noting how a film's cuts and juxtapositions generate perspectives that depart from the control exercised by individual embodiment. Subjective perception is not cinema's primary model for Deleuze, who insists that "cinema does *not* have natural subjective perception as its model . . . because the mobility of its centers and the variability of its framings always lead it to restore vast acentered and deframed zones."[19] For Deleuze, as for Bergson, perception is a moment of arrest; it is an interval that sits suspended between a sensation and an action. That the interval is a matter of "indetermination" reflects the multiple possibilities for response as the subject oscillates, "going backwards between the plane of action and that of pure memory."[20] And cinema, inasmuch as it lacks a stable center (contrary to mind-based models of meaning production such as phenomenology, which privileges "natural perception"), has an "advantage" according to Deleuze: "just because it lacks a center of anchorage and of horizon, the sections which it makes would not prevent it from going back up the path that natural perception comes down."[21] It is a superior screen to the brain-as-screen because it allows for a recovery of what perception evacuates.

Kracauer offers a similar insight. For him, cinema "provides a critique of the sovereign subject."[22] And Rancière puts it another way; he notes that cinema's operation is such that space "loses privileged directions"; cinematic spaces, he asserts, "have lost the character of spaces oriented by our will."[23] It is in this sense that Mann's novel is cinematic. Joseph's interlocutors help move him toward an appreciation of the limits of a single locus of perception. Prompted by their resistance to his grammatical constructions, Joseph (at first grudgingly) avows that "the world has many middle points," his and Kedema's, among others, and each, he suggests, provides an alternative locus of enunciation ("whether spoken from your middle or from mine"). Yet Joseph maintains nevertheless that he stands in the center of *his* circle.[24]

Other aspects of Mann's understanding of the critical capacity of his Joseph novels comports well with critical approaches to cinema. Similar to Kracauer's statement that film allows us "the experience of things in their concreteness" is Mann's remark that his compendious, novelistic treatment of the short and very reportorial version of the Joseph story in the Hebrew bible allowed him "to carry out in detail what has been briefly reported [to] . . . draw into proximity something very remote and vague."[25] The world of the biblical Joseph that Mann recreates in rich detail is one that he saw as an emerging totality, a world reflecting movement toward the kind of unity he perceived as part of his present, one in which "all sovereignties have to abdicate."[26] To articulate the merging of the many into a one, Mann has his tetralogy feature a multi-cultural soundscape (effectively anticipating film director Robert Altman's soundtracks). Describing the distribution of lyricisms in his texts, he notes that "all that is Jewish, throughout the work, is merely foreground, only one style element among others, only *one* stratum of its language which strangely fuses the archaic world and the modern, the epical and the analytical." And he adds that the poem in the last book, "the song of annunciation" which the musical child sings for the aged Jacob, is an odd composition of psalter recollections and little verses of the German romantic type. This musical fusion:

> is an example of the character of the whole work, which seeks to blend a great many things, and because it imagines everything human as a unity, it borrows its motives, memories, allusions, as well as linguistic sounds from many spheres.[27]

Mann's ecumenical approach to political modernity aside, the decentering effect that he achieves at the level of language—exemplified in both dialogic encounters and inter-articulated linguistic rhythms—operates in his imagery as well. While Mann does not eschew psychological characterization, his characters are best understood as *aesthetic* rather than psychological subjects. In Mann's terms Joseph is:

> a transparent figure, changing with the illumination in vexatory fashion: he is, with a great deal of consciousness, an Adonis—and Tamuz figure; but then he perceptibly slides into a Hermes part, the part of the mundane businessman and the intelligent profit producer among the gods, and in his conversations with Pharaoh the mythologies of the world, the Hebraic, Babylonian, Egyptian and Greek are mingled so thoroughly that one will hardly be aware of holding a biblical Jewish story in one's hands.[28]

What is an aesthetic as opposed to a psychological subject (a distinction I offered earlier)? To approach this question one has to appreciate that subjects are best understood not as static entities—as for example tinkers, tailors, soldiers, and spies (to borrow from a le Carré title)—but as beings with multiple possibilities for becoming. Such an assumption deflects attention from the motivational forces of individuals—away from "psychic subject-hood"—and toward the "aesthetic" subject.[29] For example, in Leo Bersani and Ulysse Dutoit's treatment of Jean-Luc Godard's *Contempt* (1963), a film in which a couple becomes estranged as the wife, Camille (Bridget Bardot), has her feelings for her husband, Paul (Michel Piccoli), turn from love to contempt, they note that Godard's focus is not on "the psychic origins of contempt" but on "its effects on the world," which in the context of cinema is conveyed by "what contempt does to cinematic space . . . how it affect[s] the visual field within which Godard works, and especially the range and kinds of movement allowed for in that space."[30] As Bergson insisted, the interval constituted as perception brings into proximity multiple points in space that connect with the subject's motor responses. Accordingly, in Godard's *Contempt*, the dynamics of changing interpersonal perception are reflected in the ways that the spatial trajectories are constructed through linked cinematic frames, which, as a whole, convey implications beyond those that the estranged couple explicitly perceive and acknowledge.

Another telling illustration of the epistemic and political value of the aesthetic as opposed to psychological subject is apparent in Sean Penn's *The Pledge* (2001). Much of the film involves close-up shots of the face of Jerry Black (Jack Nicholson), a retired police detective who becomes obsessed with solving a series of murders (all of young school girls) in the Reno–Lake Tahoe vicinity. While many of the film's shots, especially close-ups of faces, convey the film's psychological drama (it is never clear whether the evidence of a serial killer reflects actual occurrences or is a result of Jerry's obsessions and struggle to manage a post-retirement malaise), there are also depth-of-focus, and wide-angle and framing

*Figure I.1* Jerry Black
Courtesy of Warner Home Video

shots throughout, which supplement the personal drama with imagery that conveys both the timeless aspects of the landscape and aspects of its regional past. Ultimately, the film's *mise en scène* is more telling than its storyline. The landscape shots usher in historical time as they locate the viewers in "spatial and temporal positions" that are "distinct from those of the characters."[31] As a result, to follow Jerry's investigation—his encounters and movement through space—is to map an area that was once inhabited by Native American peoples.

Thus although much of the film focuses on the character Jerry Black, who is situated in time, first as an aging retiree, then as one partially stymied by the temporal rhythms of police investigations (once a suspect is selected, there is enormous pressure to close the case), and finally as one whose investigative opportunities are affected by seasonal changes (there are several seasonal tableaux that are interspersed in the imagistic mechanisms of the storyline), Jerry can also be viewed aesthetically rather than psychologically, because his movements in the institutionalized spaces of Reno–Tahoe reveal the existence of different dimensions of ethnic and geopolitical time. The area of the drama, now a white-dominated region of the West, is shown to be firmly linked to the U.S. nation in, for example, an Independence Day parade scene. However, there are also signs of the region's ethnohistorical past.

*Figure I.2* Landscape
Courtesy of Warner Home Video

Signs of the process of whitening are shown continually—in scenes that include Native Americans, in some of the landscape scenes (which include both panoramas and depth-of-focus shots), and in scenes that focus on a white icon; a plump pink and white adolescent appears at key moments, once as a witness of a Native American running through a snow field toward his truck, and once at the Independence Day parade. While all these scenes implicate Jerry Black's personal drama, they also function outside of the psychological story. Jerry's perceptual responses to images are dictated by his deeply motivated interest in finding clues to a series of crimes. As a result, he does not isolate the historical dimensions of the landscape within which he is acting.

But the film reveals that to which Jerry is inattentive. When the land- and ethnoscape shots are shown, often in contrast to Jerry's perceptions, Jerry becomes effectively a transparent figure whose movements point to a historical, politically fraught trajectory. As I have put it elsewhere:

> Ultimately, despite the intensity of its foregrounded, psychological drama and the suspense it generates around its crime story, the haunted land- and ethnoscape that *The Pledge* presents, primarily with images that are

*Figure I.3* The plump white adolescent

Courtesy of Warner Home Video

often disjunctive with the psychological and crime narratives, reflects a historical crime, the violence attending the Euro American continental ethnogenesis.[32]

In short, a focus on the aesthetic rather than the psychological subject places an emphasis on images rather than the film narrative, and turns the analysis of a film away from personal drama and toward the changing historico-political frame within which the drama takes place.

My turn to cinema in order to map the contemporary violent global cartography therefore has a strong epistemic encouragement. Cinema is an exemplary aesthetic whose implications derive from the way it produces and mobilizes images. In Rancière's terms, its effect is to "wrench the psychic and social powers of *mimesis* from the grip of the mimetic regime of art," the regime within which the narrative flow was organized to provoke "the audience's identification with the characters."[33] The post-mimetic aesthetic that cinema animates inter-articulates and mobilizes images to provoke thinking outside of any narrative determination. In a gloss on Michelangelo Antonioni's *L'Avventura*, the film director Martin Scorsese expresses well how a critical film articulates a world rather than merely a specific drama within it:

*Figure I.4* The Native American
Courtesy of Warner Home Video

> The more I saw *L'Avventura*—and I went back many times—the more I
> realized that Antonioni's visual language was keeping us focused on the
> rhythm of the world: the visual rhythms of light and dark, of architectural
> forms, of people positioned as figures in a landscape that always seemed
> terrifying and vast.[34]

Scorsese's observations call to mind the enactment of a more recent cinematic
visual language, constituted as the *mise en scène* in writer–director Ivan Sen's
dramatic rendering of ethnic alienation in his *Beneath Clouds* (2002). The plot is
easily summarized:

> *Beneath Clouds* is the story of Lena, the light-skinned daughter of an
> Aboriginal mother and Irish father and Vaughn, a Murri boy doing time in a
> minimum security prison in North West NSW. Dramatic events throw them
> together on a journey with no money and no transport. To Lena, Vaughn
> represents the life she is running away from. To Vaughn, Lena embodies the
> society that has rejected him. And for a very short amount of time, they
> experience a rare true happiness together.[35]

However, Sen's dynamic imagery transcends the plot. His camera delivers up the emotionally charged and complex ethnic mix of Australia by focusing alternatively on eyes and landscape. Close-ups of eyes, some blue (for example belonging to a mixed Irish–Aboriginal teenage girl) and some dark brown (for example belonging to a Murri teenage boy), serve to map the complexity of Australia's ethnoscape. Cuts from eyes to landscape shots, some of which show vast expanses devoid of enterprises, some of which show industrial interventions into the landscape, and one of which shows a looming mountain, filtered in a way that spiritualizes it, demonstrate the multiplicity of ways in which the land is occupied and symbolically experienced. And shots taken from the viewpoints of the different characters, mixed, by dint of cuts and juxtapositions, with images that often contradict the expressed viewpoints, show that subjective perception is not what commands meaning. While delivering up the multiplicity that is Australia, Sen's film is at the same time realistic in a way that enables the kind of rendering of film–space relationships that are at the center of my investigations. With his depth-of-focus shots of the landscape and his panning shots that locate his characters and interactions in spatial contexts, Sen lends "spatial expression" to his drama to develop political implications that exceed the particular moments experienced by the bodies moving across the landscapes.[36]

*Figure I.5* Lena

Courtesy of Magna Pacific

*Figure I.6* Vaughn
Courtesy of Magna Pacific

From the outset, Sen's film "establishes a geography."[37] And throughout, by cutting away from the drama of the two young people on the road, Sen makes it evident that the landscape is not merely a domain of sensations to which the characters are meant to react. The sensations reflect, in Deleuze's terms, "environments with which there are now only chance relations" and "the viewer's problem becomes 'What is there to see in the image?' (and not now 'What are we going to see in the next image?')."[38] Although there is a drama involving motion and choices, Sen's *Beneath Clouds* is best thought of as a cinema of seeing rather than of action, for, in Deleuze's terms, "The seer [*voyant*] has replaced the agent [*actant*]."[39] The difference is articulated in a critical experience for the viewers. Unlike films that trade in what Kracauer calls "corroborative images," "intended to make you believe, not see," Sen's film offers visuals in a way that reveals the contemporary "flow of material life" among other things.[40]

All the chapters in this investigation turn in varying degrees to cinema in order to take advantage of both its critical and its epistemic advantages in order to map and bring into focus spaces of coercion and violence in a changing, geopolitical world. I begin in chapter 1 with reflections and analysis provoked by a photographic image of a lone U.S. soldier taking refuge in a partially destroyed building in the midst of an Afghan land/war-scape. Exploring the "flow of material life" that extends from the scene captured in the photo, the chapter treats the contemporary spaces of militarization and securitization. The analysis in this chapter has two critical moments. First, the focus is on the way in which diverse institutions and agencies have been historically implicated in military and security policies and have generated the contemporary war on terror at home and abroad. Second, the analysis turns to film festival space as increasingly a domain for the critique of violence by summarizing a film festival award docudrama, Michael Winterbottom and Mat Whitecross's *The Road to Guantanamo*, which dramatizes the experiences of innocent young men, detained at the Guantanamo prison, after being picked up in Afghanistan and charged as "enemy combatants." The subsequent chapters, 2 through 6, contain film readings designed to illuminate a variety of aspects of contemporary geopolitics and, as is the case in chapter 1, are designed to oppose a politics of aesthetics to the dominant geo-strategic modes of analysis.

# 1    The new violent cartography

## Introduction: "A U.S. soldier mounts guard"

When viewed with a historical sensibility, this war photo (Figure 1.1) migrates almost irresistibly into two frames of reference. One is a history of images that juxtapose interior sanctuaries and exterior loci of danger. The other is a long trajectory of violent engagements in diverse global venues. One belongs to media history, while the other is situated in a history of inter-state hostilities. However, the two frames of reference have tended to merge since the advent of the mass-produced and disseminated image. In the case of inter-state wars, photographic and cinematic technology bring remote battle venues into view all over the globe. Accordingly, as Allen Feldman notes, while observing the media portrayals of contemporary U.S. wars in Afghanistan and Iraq, the danger that "eludes everyday sensory perception becomes socially available as a cinematic structure."[1] It has become evident that the way we experience war history is inextricably linked to the forms it has taken on in media representations. Nevertheless, despite the evocative historical summonses it delivers, the photo's accompanying description belongs to a temporal present; it references political after-effects of the United States *et al.*'s 2002 invasion of Afghanistan, a U.S. "policy" reaction to the 9/11 destruction of the World Trade Center:

> A U.S. soldier mounts guard in a tower of the village of Mangal Khan, the main village of the Khakeran Valley, Zabul province, Afghanistan, June 27, 2005. From the U.S. and U.N. officials down to Afghan villagers, there is growing fear that this country may be at a seminal moment with three years of state-building in danger of succumbing to the barrage of violence.[2]

Doubtless the moment that the photographer, Tomas Munita, has captured will live on into a more pacific future, for, as Ernst Jünger's classic observation on the role of war photography puts it, war photographs, "as instruments of a technological consciousness, preserve the image of [the] ravaged landscapes which the world of peace has long reappropriated." And, he adds (in a remark that inspires much of the analysis in this chapter), they also speak to:

*Figure 1.1* Tomas Munita's photo of a soldier
Courtesy of AP

the life of the soldier on leave, in the reserves, and in the combat zones; the types of weaponry, the look of destruction they inflict on human beings and on the fruits of their labor, on their dwellings and on nature; the face of the battlefield at rest and at the peak of activity, as seen by the observers in the trenches or bomb craters, or from the altitude of flight—all this has been captured many times over and preserved for later ages in a fashion that complements written descriptions.[3]

In its present articulation, much of the semiotic urgency of the photo is owed to its composition, which is "the key," as Munita puts it. Providing, in his terms, a "relation between the destroyed interior with the soldier hiding in it and the square luminous landscape," the image evokes a disquieting mood: "Outside is the light of what can be a peaceful environment, but the soldier, hidden in his own dark watchtower brings a sense of terror." Moreover, "since the tower is tilted, [it] suggest[s] imbalance, instability and obscurity."[4] In sum, in addition to conveying the emotional resonances of the particular historical moment to which Munita refers, the image evokes and preserves an instance that is part of a visually captured and thus enduring history (as Ernst Jünger famously observed[5]). Given Munita's composition, the history to which this photo contributes is a history of vulnerable bodies seeking temporary refuge and a place for safe observation in hostile landscapes that seem both benign, because they are temporarily devoid of hostile engagement, and threatening, because their encompassing scale appears to thwart human attempts to manage them securely.

In what follows, I pursue the two correlated frames of reference to which I refer at the outset, first locating instances in the aesthetic patrimony of the image's stark juxtaposition of sequestered interior and expansive exterior landscape, and then examining its related historical evocation of a changing cartography of violent encounters. With respect to this latter dimension of the image, I treat the spatial trajectories that the photograph implies, in order to map what is historically singular about the contemporary "violent cartography" that the United States' post-9/11 war on terrorism (displaced on state venues) has created.[6] The most immediate spatial implication of the image is contained within it; it is the juxtaposition between the inside, a temporary sanctuary, and the immense outside that encompasses the interior. However, beyond the image's historical immediacy—its specific reference to the conflict in Afghanistan—are its deeper historical trajectories. My turn to the image's aesthetic patrimony, its sharp juxtaposition between interior sanctuary and exterior expanse, has a counterpart in a film history that operates most famously in a set of very similar juxtapositions in John Ford's cinematic rendering of an earlier violent cartography.

## Conceptual strategies

The two primary conceptions driving my analysis require elaboration before I treat that Ford rendering. First, what is a "violent cartography"? In my original approach to the concept, I suggested that the bases of violent cartographies are the "historically developed, socially embedded interpretations of identity and space" that constitute the frames within which enmities give rise to war-as-policy.[7] Violent cartographies are thus constituted as an articulation of geographic imaginaries and antagonisms, based on models of identity–difference. Since the Treaty of Westphalia (1648), a point at which the horizontal, geopolitical world of nation-states emerged as a more salient geographic imaginary than the theologically oriented vertical world (which was imaginatively structured as a separation between divine and secular space), maps of enmity have been framed by differences in geopolitical location, and (with notable exceptions) state leaders have supplanted religious authorities. Moreover— yet also with notable exceptions—geopolitical location has since been a more significant identity marker than spiritual commitment.

During the Cold War, the coincidence between enmity and nation-state and nation-state bloc affiliation tended to coincide. And since that period, the geopolitical imaginary has been so persistent that, although the most violent contemporary enmities involve states versus networks, war-as-policy-response continues to function largely within the old geopolitical frame. Why refer to the cartographies as imaginaries? Michel Foucault supplies an ontological justification: "We must not imagine that the world turns toward us a legible face which we would have only to decipher."[8] How we receive the world (or, in Heideggerian terms, how we world) is a matter of the shape we impose on it, given the ideational commitments and institutional practices through which spatio-temporal models of identity–difference are practiced. Resistance to the geographies of enmity that drive war and security policy therefore requires one to offer "an approach to maps that provides distance from the geopolitical frames of strategic thinkers and security analysts" because, as I put it in my first approach to violent cartographies, geography is inextricably linked to "the architecture of enmity." As a result, to understand and challenge modern security practices requires one to first map and then supply alternative imaginaries to "the security analysts way of constructing global problematics."[9] However, the mapping of a contemporary violent cartography that I provide here goes beyond geographic imaginaries. Part of that mapping involves the forces, institutions, and agencies that move bodies into the zones of violent encounter (realized, for example, in the process of military recruitment), and it involves the forces, institutions, and agencies that identify the domestic spaces where bodies are judged to be dangerous because they are associated with foreign antagonists. Necessarily, then, my analysis is deployed on both the distant and the home fronts in the United States' pervasive war on terror, which began after 9/11, 2001.

Second, to elaborate the concept of aesthetic patrimony, I want to show how the photo's interior–exterior juxtaposition is reminiscent of several of Ford's scenes in his treatment of the violent Euro American–Native American encounter in the West, in what is arguably his most complex and politically acute western, *The Searchers* (1956). An image's "aesthetic patrimony" is the legacy of its form and implications from earlier images in similar media. To pursue that legacy is to provide a comparative frame that helps to isolate what is singular about the context of the current image. Accordingly, I am suggesting that Munita's photo calls Ford's film to mind because, in several scenes in *The Searchers*, the camera is positioned in "a place of refuge, a dark womb like space,"[10] in interiors of refuge not unlike that in which Munita's soldier is sitting. Here, I am working with two of them (Figures 1.2 and 1.3).

The opening scene of *The Searchers* (Figure 1.2) is both cinematically powerful and narratively expansive. It is shot from inside the cabin of Ethan Edwards's (John Wayne) brother's cabin, providing a view of a vast, expansive prairie, from which Edwards is approaching. Edwards, a loner who is headed west after having fought on the Confederate side in the Civil War, is part of a historical migration. He represents one type among the many kinds of bodies that flowed westward after Euro America emerged from the fratricidal conflict of the Civil War and was then free to turn its attention to another venue of violence, the one involved in the forced displacement of indigenous America. Edwards's approach is observed by his sister-in-law from her front porch, which, architecturally, plays a role in designating the house as a refuge from outer threats. In a lyrical soliloquy by a character in an Alessandro Baricco novel, the porch is aptly described as being:

inside and outside at the same time . . . it represents an extended threshold. . . . It's a no man's land where the idea of protected place—which every house, by its very existence, bears witness to, in fact embodies—expands beyond its own definition and rises up again, undefended, as if to posthumously resist the claims of the open. . . . One could even say that the porch ceases to be a frail echo of the house it is attached to and becomes the confirmation of what the house just hints at: the ultimate sanction of the protected place, the solution of the theorem that the house merely states.[11]

Thus, as is the case with the scene in Afghanistan, viewed by the lone soldier, the valley and Edwards's approach to the house cannot be discerned simply through the objects observed. One needs to recognize the historical space of observation and the ways in which the observer (Edwards's sister-in-law) is connected to that space. Shortly after the opening shot, we are taken inside the cabin of the resident Edwards family. They are part of an earlier movement westward that established what Virginia Wexman identifies as part of an American "nationalist ideology," the Anglo couple or "family on the land."[12] The couple (Edwards's brother and his wife) and their children are participants in the romantic ideal of the adventurous white family, seeking to spread Euro America's form of laboring domesticity westward in order to settle and civilize what was viewed from the East as a violent, untamed territory, containing peoples or nations unworthy of participating in an American future.

*Figure 1.2* Ethan Edwards arrives

Courtesy of Warner Home Video

*Figure 1.3* Ethan and Martin
Courtesy of Warner Home Video

The second image (Figure 1.3) from *The Searchers* participates in a referential montage. It reproduces and extends the implicit warning in the first. Here, the encompassing landscape is lent threatening bodies. At this stage of the film narrative, Ethan and his nephew, Martin, are taking refuge in a cave as they hold off a Comanche attack, led by Scarface, who, with his band of warriors, had murdered Ethan's brother, wife, and eldest daughter and carried off the younger one, Debbie. Rescuing Debbie and enacting revenge for the destruction of a family, which at a symbolic level stands for white domestic settlement as a whole, had become the object of Ethan and Martin's long search, which constitutes most of the film narrative. Apart from the complications attending the motivations for the search—Ethan, a (not unredeemable) racist, had sworn that he would kill Debbie because her long captivity had rendered her unfit to rejoin white society, while Martin was bent on rescuing her—I want to focus on the rearticulation of domestic coherence versus external threat that this scene effects.

While the adventures associated with the five-year search are proceeding, a domestic drama is unfolding. Early in the film Ethan expresses contempt for Martin's part-Indian heritage (at their first meeting he says, "Fellow could mistake you for a half-breed," even though Martin is, by his account, only one-eighth Cherokee). However, by the time they are sequestered in the cave, Ethan has come, ambivalently, to accept his family bond with Martin, even though he continues to insist that Martin is not his kin. Given Ethan's change in attitude, the scene in the cave becomes an instance of family solidarity. The implication seems to be that Native America can be part of Euro America if it is significantly assimilated and domesticated. Ethan effectively supports that domestication by ultimately bequeathing Martin his wealth. He has apparently discovered that part of himself that craves a family bond, a part that has been continuously in contention with his violent, ethnic policing. And on his side, Martin fulfills all of the requirements of a family-oriented, assimilated Indian. He becomes affianced to the very white daughter of Swedish Americans, after he has rejected an Indian spouse he had inadvertently acquired while trading goods with Comanches.

By becoming part of a white family, Martin is involved in a double movement. He is participating in one of Euro America's primary dimensions of self-fashioning, its presumption that a Christian marriage is the most significant social unit (that such "legal monogamy benefitted the social order"[13]), and he is distancing himself from the Native American practices of which the nuclear family was often not a primary psychological, economic, or social unit (and was often viewed by settlers as a form of "promiscuity"[14]).

## Visual analytics

How then can we read this Afghan photo (Figure 1.1) in the context of this specific part of *its* aesthetic patrimony? The attack on Afghanistan's incumbent Taliban regime, however distant its territory from the United States, was sold to the American public as a legitimate reaction to the continuing threat to domestic America that was initiated by Al Qaeda's attack on American soil, the first time in modern American history in which a domestic vulnerability has been experienced as a result of an attack by adversaries in league with forces outside the continent. Certainly the spatial and biopolitical aspects of the historical situations to which Ford's film and the photo refer are vastly different.[15] The Ford images reference an expanding frontier, as settlers and their armed protectors move in and push Native American nations westward after the Civil War. In this period, the (Euro) American military effectively had to defend a form of domestic life that existed on the same terrain as the battlefield. By contrast the current "forward position" (to use a phrase that is part of the discourse of the U.S. military) is very far from American domestic life, in whose behalf the attack on Afghanistan (and subsequently Iraq) allegedly took place. Among other things, the Munita image reflects the current preemptive policy of a nation displacing a domestic security problem on foreign turf. To access that domestic life, in behalf of which this lone soldier sits on a dangerous vigil, from within the space of immediacy framed by the photo, we need an analytic that allows us to escape the confinement of the frame and effectively connects an element in the picture to parts of the absent world it can be seen to evoke.

Two related options suggest themselves. The first derives from Roland Barthes's well-known distinction between a photograph's *studium* and its *punctum*. Munita himself has testified to the former, because a photo's *studium*, according to Barthes, registers the photographer's intentions. In this case, it is showing the radical separation of outer light and internal darkness and the instability that the soldier's situation entails.[16] Thus, what can be clearly seen—the contrasts of light and darkness, the momentarily peaceful exterior and the destroyed interior, and the tilted angle, which is a visual code for instability—constitutes the image's *studium*, which, Barthes notes, is always coded in a way that allows us to "enter into a harmony with the photographer's intentions."[17] Unlike the *studium*, the *punctum* is uncoded; it is "a prick," something that breaks or punctuates the *studium*."[18] It is an element in the image that does not contribute to the image's displayed or intended meaning. To access this aspect of the photo, we have to seek elements that escape the control of its intended meaning.

The second option articulates well with the first. Influenced by Barthes's *studium–punctum* distinction in photographs, Georges Didi-Huberman has developed an anti-iconographic reading of paintings by focusing on patches of color that do not constitute the details that contribute to the painting's referential meaning. He treats such patches as symptoms of the process of painting that, like the prick of Barthes's *punctum*, disrupt the image's coding within the frame. As he points out, what we can see does not exhaust what we can know, because "knowing and looking have utterly different modes of being."[19] The patch in a painting plays the same role as Barthes's *punctum* because, lacking definitive contours, it disrupts depiction or, in Didi-Huberman's hyperbolic terms, it creates a "catastrophic commotion."[20] It disturbs representation by being an "intrusion" that exists "as a result of not seeing well."[21] Failing a clear participatory role in the referential register of the image, the patch, like the *punctum*, sends us toward other zones of intelligibility. In the case of Barthes's *punctum*, the disruption points us to the world outside the photo, while, in the case of Didi-Huberman's patch, the disruption is a symptom that sends us away from the image's reference and toward the painting subject or the dynamic of painting.[22]

If we heed Didi-Huberman's point about not seeing well and, at the same time, acknowledge the Barthean effect of being sent out into the world, we can reflect first on what cannot be seen well in the image of the soldier in an Afghan landscape and then on where, as a result, it sends us. Despite the almost pervasive clarity of the details in the image, what cannot be clearly seen is the soldier's ethnicity. Doubtless he is a U.S. soldier, but from what part of the U.S. ethnoscape does he come? What kind of "ethnic" American is the vulnerable body in this photo, and what are the forces involved in expediting his arrival on the scene? To the extent that we are now forced to *think* because mere looking will not avail, we can ask about the trajectories of recruitment that are producing disproportionate levels of vulnerability for various ethnic Americans and, beyond that, about the trajectories leading back from this particular landscape of violence to the overall network of securitization and militarization that effectively legislates the problematic within which "terrorism," the presumed global object of the war/policy that is visited upon the Afghanistan terrain, among others, is apprehended.

## Locating the spaces of securitization

Ultimately the biopolitical dimensions of the U.S.'s anti-terrorism initiatives (the decisions about what lives to waste and what ones require exclusion or containment) are deployed on particular bodies, both those that are the targets and those that are the ones that must confront those bodies on dangerous terrains. But it is the structured nature of the gaze on those bodies that situates the elaborate dynamic of the post-9/11 securitization. To locate and conceptualize the current anti-terrorism policies, I turn to one of Michel Foucault's older, archaeological investigations, his treatment of medical perception, and apply his notion of the spatialization of disease to the spatialization of terrorism. At the outset of his investigation of the history of the medical gaze, Foucault discerns three levels of spatialization. At the primary level, disease exists in a classification (in "an area of homologies"[23]). At a secondary level, it is located in "the space of the body"; it is focused on an assemblage of individuals. And finally, and perhaps most relevant to the current intensification of surveillance of potential terrorism, when medicine becomes a "task for the nation," it is located in an administrative structure. For example, with the development of a "medicine of epidemics," a policing "supplement" is enjoined and doctors and patients are subject to "supervision."[24] Displacing the old encounter between doctor and patient is an increasing institutionalization involving, for example, "a jurisprudence of the medical state," as medical consciousness becomes linked to a life beyond individual lives; it is deployed on "the life of the nation."[25]

Analogously, to treat the tertiary spatialization of terrorism is to note the increasing, officially sanctioned rapport among political, administrative, judicial, and military agencies, especially those agencies, organizations, and professions that have heretofore had seemingly more benign roles with respect to violence (for example the EPA, the university, and various entertainment industries). This broad, political, administrative, and professional collusion is deployed through an elaborate expansion of the primary and secondary spatializations of terrorism. In terms of the primary or classificatory space, many more acts have been recruited into the designation of terrorism—for example attending seminars or summer camps in "terrorist" venues or making a charitable donation to a mosque whose subsequent allocations are along money trails that lead to "enemies." This latter example can locate the donor in the category of one who has lent "material support" to terrorists.

Importantly, there are more than mere homologies between the tertiary spatialization of disease and that of terrorism. For example, analyzing the first known case of the African Ebola virus in North America (brought in by an immigrating African, Colette Matshimoseka, to Toronto), Jorge Fernandes points out that the event highlights the interconnections between anxieties about "the body's integrity and anxiety about the nation-state's decreased viability as a stable cultural and linguistic site."[26] And, tellingly, the case provoked a meeting between the Royal Canadian Mounted Police and immigration officials and, thereafter, produced a conversation between both these agencies and representatives of Canada's "health system."[27] As Fernandes goes on to demonstrate, the resulting "'community discourse' engendered by the fear of viral pandemics is a productive terrain for analyzing the mechanisms by which the nation-state codes bodies and arrests their flows to protect the nation-state's locus of qualified bodies."[28]

In the contemporary period, in which we can observe an inter-articulation between pandemics and terrorism, the qualifications applied to bodies have achieved a high level of complexity. Thus, the secondary spatialization of terrorism (like that of disease), its location in the body, has resulted in a body that is expanded well beyond its corporeal existence. As A. R. Stone puts it, "[t]he socially apprehensible citizen . . . consists of a collection of both physical and discursive elements." It is a "legible body" whose "textually mediated physicality" extends to its paper [and electronic] trail.[29] Hence, for example, the militarized, surveilling agencies connected with the war on terror treat the body's phone, e-mail, credit card, and library borrowing records, and, in some cases, phone conversations. Bodies inside and outside, citizen and non-citizen, thus have enlarged silhouettes, shapes that extend to their financial, communicational, and informational prostheses. Just as, in Foucault's terms, there are spatializations of disease beyond the confines of the individual body to include "other distributions of illness," the location of a contemporary political pathology goes beyond directly implemented ideologies, beyond the desires and drives in the individual terrorist body, to networks and cells with a global distribution.[30]

To connect this newly produced and expanded terrorist and/or terrorist-supporting body to the relationships emerging between political initiatives and institutional structures (the tertiary spatialization of terrorism) we can return momentarily to Foucault's insights about the nineteenth-century convergence that developed between "the requirements of *political ideology* and those of *medical technology*."[31] As the space of medicine shifted to hospitals, whose function was not only to care for patients but also to provide a venue in which the medical gaze could aid and abet the state's developing concern with the vitality of its population as a whole, medical authorities and state-directed policing authorities developed a working rapport. Given the increasingly militarized state's concern with the recruitment of an army (as well as with the mobilization of a labor force), "medical knowledge," assisted by developments in "probabilistic thought," became collectively inflected; the locus of medical knowledge turned away from the peculiar maladies of individuals and toward "the collective life of the nation."[32] Disease was increasing observed in terms of "frequency."[33]

Analogously, if we fast-forward two centuries, we can observe a similar political and institutional rapport as health officials as well as environmental and other surveilling agencies associated with anti-terrorism policy collaborate. Confirming Foucault's insight about the co-development of medical and state ideologies, the modern agency responsible for directing the medical gaze, the public health service, is one among many involved in restructuring its agenda to adjust to anti-terrorism policy. The recent publication *Terrorism and Public Health* applies the venerable medical strategies of epidemiology, a mode of medical knowledge that has for over a century produced an inter-articulation of medical and policing authorities, to the threat of terrorist biological warfare strategies. Agencies such as the Council of State and Territorial Epidemiologists (CSTE), the Centers for Disease Control (CDC), and the National Electronic Disease Surveillance System (NEDSS) are being configured to, in the author's terms, respond to the "challenges posed by terrorism."[34]

While using health agencies as defensive strategies against the intentional spread of disease may not be very politically contentious (except for those whose movement across borders is impeded by yet another surveillance agency), other components of the "institutional ecologies" produced by the contemporary, anti-terrorism militarization are more broadly controversial.[35] For example, when intelligence gathering by FBI agents after 9/11 began creating a pervasive climate of intimidation, even extended to surveillance of people's library borrowing, they attempted to enlist the support of librarians and booksellers, many of whom resisted and continue to resist the recruitment of their services into the war on terror. Thus unlike previous wars, the contemporary war on terror is deployed not only on a distant front but also on a home front. As a result, a mapping of the current violent cartography requires an exploration of its dual spatial deployment.

## The distant front

Given the elaborate network of agencies involved in the war on terror, it is clear that the home front is as much a target as are the distant ones. Moreover, on both home and distant fronts, there are technology-aided instances of hysterical perception. Turning first to a telling instance in a distant front: in the fall of 2001, shortly after the U.S.-led invasion of Afghanistan, it was reported that there was a lethal episode of mistaken identity. A remote operator, controlling a Predator Drone (a pilotless "weaponized" aircraft), killed three non-combatants. When first employed, the Predator Drone was an unarmed surveillance technology. But, as a commentator on the episode notes, "[B]ack in 2000, when the CIA thought it had Osama bin Laden under live aerial surveillance in Afghanistan, it pressed for a weaponized version of the Predator." The Defense Department followed through; they purchased a fleet of armed Predator Drones from General Atomics Aeronautical Systems, and, as the story goes, one of them, operated in accordance with the pretext for arming the Predators, "was . . . involved in at least one bombing in Afghanistan, in which a 'tall man' was presumed by a remote operator to be bin Laden." The time-gap between "seeing" and shooting from the air has become almost instantaneous since the beginning of the war–cinema articulation, which began during World War I when "general staffs began to take aviation seriously [and] aerial reconnaissance, both tactical and strategic, became chronophotographic and then cinematographic."[36] But, as Paul Virilio adds, at this early stage it took "considerable time . . . to analyze the photographic information" before the photo- and cinematographic results could be transmuted into "military activity."[37]

In the episode in the Afghanistan desert, the fates of the tall man and his two companions, who were civilians foraging for scrap metal, were decided in a matter of seconds; "he and two companions were killed."[38] The commentator reporting the episode was not writing a human interest story, even though, ironically, the makers of the Predator Drone regard themselves as (in their words, with apparently no irony intended) "committed to improving the human condition."[39] He was writing a military technology story, pointing out, among other things, that, in addition to being prone to surveillance errors, the Drone's airworthiness is questionable; it often crashes. Undeterred by the "perception" errors to which such technologies are prone, the air force commissioned an updated unmanned aerial vehicle (UAV) from General Atomics, the Reaper, aka the "hunter-killer," which, at the time of this writing, is deployed in Iraq. "The name Reaper captures the lethal nature of this new weapon system," says General T. Michael Moseley, the air force chief of staff, in September 2006.[40] As is now evident, non-combatants in Afghanistan have born the brunt of the "lethality" of the United States' remotely guided weapons.[41] In addition to the tragedies that the stories of innocent victims of the vaunted lethality of weapons such as the Predator Drone and the Reaper represent, the tales about the vagaries of accident-prone military technologies are pregnant with political significance.

For example, the story about the Predator's killing of the tall man and his companions reflects a remarkable shift in the deployment of warring violence. Whereas the industrialization of warfare, which peaked during the twentieth century, involved complex organizational decision making to shape the delivery of force on battlefields, contemporary infowar resembles some aspects of the historical trajectory of industrial production; the recottagization of production witnessed in such concerns as the Benetton corporation, which collects the products of many individual producers rather than relying on a factory system, is also apparent in the move to infowar structures. As Friedrich Kittler observes, "Information Warfare can begin on any desk equipped with a PC."[42] In the case of the new Reaper, the PCs running them are mobile; the Reaper is designed to be controlled by ground troops equipped with laptops. Taken as a whole, the UAVs represent a "shift from weaponry to computers that the military analysts call 'the revolution in military affairs' or RMA," which, according to some, was initiated with the NATO bombings in Kosovo in 1999.[43]

However, the shift from the foundry (where weapons of steel are forged) and the mechanized battlefield (where they are put to use by a massed army) to the PC-equipped desks or mobile ground troops reflects more than a mere dispersal of the production and delivery of lethality. Historical developments in weapons technology speak to a history of nation-state policy and, in particular, to a genealogy of sovereignty and sovereignty-related practices: productions of political space, epistemological orientations, and the biopolitical designation of qualified versus unqualified (or dangerous versus benign) bodies, especially those belonging to the friends and enemies of political entities. Discourses on weapons therefore extend well beyond technological issues. Doubtless, we can learn as much about the biopolitics of contemporary sovereignty-as-decision-making by heeding the minutiae of ballistics and delivery systems as we can from the pronouncements of "defense intellectuals" about what lives are at stake, where danger lies, and who are the enemies. Weapons design is, among other things, an implementation of the state's approach to valuing, excluding, and sustaining versus eliminating forms of life. Among other things, the anticipated new weapons designs, developed as a reaction to an enemy that cannot be confronted on a fixed or demarcated battlefield, reflect the United States' planning for a new cartography of violence. As before, weapons design articulates the spaces of encounter.

As a case in point, the American navy has announced a plan for a different kind of fleet. During the Cold War, the aircraft carrier and Polaris submarine patrolled in the spaces around the Soviet bloc. Now the plan is to resort to smaller craft with shallow draft. A report in the *New York Times* describes the design:

> The plan calls for 55 small, fast vessels called littoral combat ships, which are being designed to allow the navy to operate in shallow coastal areas where mines and terrorist bombings are a growing threat. The plan calls for building 31 amphibious assault ships, which can be used to ferry marines ashore or support humanitarian operations.[44]

Thus despite the hi-tech weapons that can be aimed and launched from a remote computer-equipped desk, some soldiers, like the one in Munita's photo, will be in close proximity with the "enemy." And where the enemy is to be found is reflected in the Pentagon's new map of danger, which, as current strategic thinking would have it, disproportionately includes states that are "disconnected," insofar as they exist outside of globalization's frontier.[45] From the point of view of the U.S. executive branch's geography of enmity, if you are not an intimate in the global exchange of resources—for example being an Iran rather than a Saudi Arabia—it increases your chances of becoming a "rogue state" or part of the "axis of evil" and thus a potential target. But while those who draw the new maps remain safely outside of the line of fire, others have to implement the cartography of enmity "on the ground." Moreover, in addition to the vulnerable bodies abroad are those "at home," who are vulnerable to the war on the domestic front, carried out by a militarization that comprehends numerous agencies involved in either recruiting bodies to send abroad or identifying dangerous ones to isolate. It is primarily the involvement of recruiting agencies that raises the question of the home front, the space from which vulnerable bodies will be drawn and, increasingly, the space within which domestic counterparts of external enemies are sought.

## The home front

As Paul Virilio points out, in an analysis he undertook during the first Gulf War, the militarized state looks inward as well as outward, manifesting a "panicked anticipation of internal war."[46] In the case of the post-9/11 war on terror, the same preemption involved in assaults on states has been turned inward. A state of siege mentality is effacing the inside–outside boundary. Achille Mbembe puts it succinctly, "The *state of siege* is itself a military institution."[47] Although in contrast with the firefights deployed on distanced terrains, the weapons used internally are surveillance technologies and extra-juridical modes of detention. For example, as an instance of hysterical perception, an FBI fingerprinting laboratory identified a lawyer in Oregon as one whose fingerprints were found among the detritus of the train bombings in Madrid in 2004. And the FBI pressed its perceptions for some time, despite a rejection of their fingerprint data by their counterparts in Madrid.

The technologies deployed in the war on terror, which have been developed for the distant front, are sometimes operating on the home front as well. Thus the Drone, which was "weaponized" for use on a distant battlefield, is being employed in its spare, observational version in the United States–Mexico border areas to help prevent illegal entry of immigrants from Mexico. As was reported in the *New York Times*, on June 25, 2004, unmanned planes known as Drones, which use thermal and night vision equipment, were used in the U.S. southwest to catch illegal immigrants attempting to cross into the United States from Mexico. The Drones are part of the domestic front in the United States' war on terror; specifically, they are part of "the Department of Homeland Security's 'operational control' of the border in Arizona."[48] However, while one agency involved in the war on terror is diverting its technology to help exclude Latino bodies, another is actively recruiting them for duty on the external war fronts. As was shown in Michael Moore's documentary *Fahrenheit 9/11*, military recruiters are most in evidence in poorer and disproportionately "ethnic" neighborhoods and venues—for example the parking lots of discount department stores.

Ironically, given the participation of southwestern border patrol agencies within the Homeland Security network, much of the recruiting is aimed at those Hispanics who live on the margins of the national economy. This item about recruitment in the Denver area tells much of the story:

> In Denver and other cities where the Hispanic population is growing, recruiting Latinos has become one of the Army's top priorities. From 2001 to 2005, the number of Latino enlistments in the Army rose 26 percent, and in the military as a whole, the increase was 18 percent. The increase comes at a time when the Army is struggling to recruit new soldiers and when the enlistment of African-Americans, a group particularly disillusioned with the war in Iraq, has dropped off sharply, to 14.5 percent from 22.3 percent over the past four years.[49]

Where are the recruiters searching? The story continues:

> Sgt. First Class Gavino Barron, dressed in a crisp Army uniform, trawls the Wal-Mart here for recruits, past stacks of pillows and towers of detergent, he is zeroing-in on one of the Army's "special missions": to increase the number of Hispanic enlisted soldiers.[50]

## Elaborated militarization

The military's domestic initiatives go beyond collecting bodies. They also involve militarizing other agencies. As the author of *The Pentagon's New Map* points out, "a whole lot more than just the Defense Department" is actively pursuing the "war on terror."[51] One aspect of that broadened participation is evident in a recent collaboration between three kinds of institutions: Hollywood filmmaking, the military, and the university, all of which share participation in the University of Southern California's Institute for Creative Technologies. The collaboration belongs to what I have termed "the tertiary spatialization of terrorism" inasmuch as it is located in the sector of the institutional ecologies of militarization that involve relations among military, entertainment, and university agencies. Leaving aside the historical development of the film industry (which, like the Internet, has borrowed much of its technology from innovations in the military's information technologies[52]), USC's involvement can be located in a long history of the university's role in national policy.[53]

The modern university began, at least in part, as an ideological agency of the state. It was intellectually shaped as a cultural institution whose task was to aid and abet the production of the nation-state, a coherent, homogeneous cultural nation contained by the state. Bill Readings describes a paradigmatic example, the University of Berlin, for which Alexander von Humboldt was primarily responsible: "Humboldt's project for the foundation of the University of Berlin is decisive for the centering of the University around the idea of culture, which ties the University to the nation-state." And, he adds, the project is developed at the moment of the emergence of the German nation-state. In addition to being "assigned the dual task of research and teaching" it is also involved in "the production and inculcation of national knowledge."[54] Although, as Readings points out, in recent decades, the "university of culture" has been transformed into more of a corporate-type entity, a bureaucratically run "university of excellence" (where "'Excellence' . . . functions to allow the University to understand itself solely in terms of the structure of corporate administration"[55]), there are nevertheless key periods in which its faculties have participated in shaping and reproducing the dominant discourses of national policy. Certainly the colonial period is significant. The university, like weapons technology, helped to consolidate colonial empires. Just as the repeating rifle and machine gun were instruments used in the European nations' expansive/violent sovereignty in the nineteenth century (as John Ellis puts it, it was used to "consolidate their nation's empires"[56]), even the so-called literary canon, both a governmental and an academic production, served as a pacifying instrument. For example, it was invented in Britain as part of a colonial pedagogy to subdue the Indian subcontinent culturally.[57]

Certainly in the twentieth century, the Cold War stands out as a period in which a wide variety of disciplines participated in creating the geopolitical imaginary that dominated European and American national policies. In political science, the sub-discipline of comparative politics, especially the segment that overlapped with "area studies," developed its still-enduring orientation during the Cold War. It articulated the idioms of political science with those of other social science disciplines, and partook of an undisguised, geopolitical partisanship. For example, an analysis of key area studies methods texts reveals that, "just as the humanities were meant to cultivate a self that was authorized to transmit the legacy of the past, area studies would develop a body of elite scholars capable of producing knowledge about other nations to the benefit of our nation."[58] Of course, no discipline was more actively complicit with American military strategy during the Cold War than "operations research," a quantitative, decision calculus-oriented discipline. Beginning as a military-sponsored set of research teams, the national security state shaped the field, which soon migrated into academia, while nevertheless retaining its defense department and military funding. As one historian of the field points out, "by the mid 1950's, several universities . . . began offering master's and doctoral programs in operations research [and] by the end of the 1950's . . . operations researchers . . . began mass producing publications."[59]

At the same time, the CIA was recruiting practitioners of the arts and humanities as part of a cultural Cold War being staged in postwar Germany:

> In consultation with American academics, playwrights and directors, a massive theater programme was . . . launched. Plays by Lillian Hellman, Eugene O'Neill, Thornton Wilder, Tennessee Williams, William Saroyan, Clifford Odets and John Steinbeck were offered . . . and a vast books programme was launched, aimed primarily at "projecting the American story before the German reader in the most effective manner possible."[60]

But even on their own, the humanities often failed to maintain their presumed scholarly disinterest during this period. Some humanities scholars helped to make university space a supplement to Cold War geopolitics. For example, William Epstein has shown how eighteenth-century studies in the mid-twentieth century articulated with "Cold-War American culture."[61] Various "eighteenth-century and other literary scholars" served as cold warriors in both "the American intelligence community and the American academic community."[62] While the "American academic recolonizing of the post-war world" was certainly led by area specialists who "divided the world into geopolitical spheres of influence contested by the two great powers," there were fellow recolonization travelers among eighteenth-century and other literary scholars.[63] Quite aside from whether academics actually engaged in intelligence operations, scholars in a wide variety of disciplines affirmed and reinforced aspects of national policy while presuming to be mere "realists." Among these, perhaps the most noteworthy "intellectual" cadre is the sub-discipline of international studies/international relations known as "strategic studies," but many mainstream international relations theorists cleave to a dominant power-legitimating and violence-supporting frame of analysis as well.

While there are other noteworthy periods in which one can discern an academic–militarization/securitization connection, my main interest here is the new twenty-first century relationship between the academy and infowar strategies. This connection, best exemplified in the University of Southern California's Institute for Creative Technologies (ICT), is not historically unique. While it can be argued that the 2003 war in Iraq is the first true infowar (Brzezinski states that "Iraq . . . may be remembered as the first true war of the information age, when command-and-control technology took over the battlefield"[64]), an infowar prototype can be found in Napoleon's war strategy. As Friedrich Kittler points out, it is "[a] likely assumption that the coupling of general staff and engineering education, which was institutionalized by the French Revolution," was supported "through the founding of the Ecole Polytechnique in 1794, [which] made information systems conceivable as weapons systems."[65] But the university–militarization relationship is far more elaborate now than in earlier periods. To appreciate the extent of the collaboration it is worth scrutinizing the USC program, which assembles the military, the Hollywood entertainment industry, and the university into a cooperative enterprise.

In their description of their mandate, the ICT states:

> For the Government, the ICT provides the ability to focus these technologies [those of their computer facilities and those used in Hollywood's film industry] toward learning and training in the civilian sector with far reaching implications for revolutionizing education in our country and the world. For Hollywood, it is a form for filmmakers to contribute their knowledge and expertise to the daunting challenges of anti-terrorism and national defense.[66]

Having indicated that they are a vehicle to articulate Hollywood entertainment technologies with the technological service they render for the army, the ICT justifies its role in the anti-terrorism infowar by noting that it addresses two constituencies, military and academic; their "Experience Learning System" (ELS) "will teach soldiers and students about the future by having them 'virtually' go there." Many of the prototexts for this dual pedagogy are provided by past Hollywood feature films. For example, in describing "the hub of the ICT's research," its "Experience Learning System," they liken it to "the Holodeck in Star Trek," which they see as a model that allows one to "'virtually' go there." This "virtual reality" thematic pervades the ICT's educational strategy. For example, in the graphics lab, the goal is "to achieve 'virtual reality,' absolute realism in geometry, reflectance, lighting, dynamics and animation. The lab [they note] is doing groundbreaking research in active range sensing, global illumination, reflectometry, dynamic simulation, human and facial animation, and real-time rendering."

However, entertainment media constitutes a small part of the articulation of the military with information and entertainment agencies. Recently, for example, investigative journalists discovered that the U.S. army was paying Iraqi journalists to write favorable articles about the U.S. role in the reconstitution of an Iraqi political system. But of course many dimensions of domestic journalism celebrate the post-9/11 securitization and military initiatives on their own initiative. Part of the new violent cartography is to be found in the pages of many daily newspapers, often in feature sections rather than national and international news reports. For example, the *Honolulu Advertiser*'s "Military Briefing" section reports episodes of "heroism under fire" and features human interest vignettes about brave soldiers missing their families but remaining dedicated to their missions. Nevertheless, in recent months some of the independent media is asserting itself, rather than allowing its space to be incorporated within the new violent cartography. For example, in 2006, the Associated Press, under the Freedom of Information Act, forced the release of documents—"hearing transcripts and evidentiary statements from the two types of military panels that evaluate whether the detainees should remain at Guantanamo."[67] Such reports, along with an increasing number of editorials attacking the implementation of a detainee status, a series of violent spaces of interrogation and torture, contest some of the most hidden and extra-legal parts of the new violent cartography, where "detainees" exist in what Giorgio Agamben calls "a space devoid of law, a zone of anomie in which all legal determinations—and above all the very distinction between public and private—are deactivated."[68]

## Conclusion: contesting the new violent cartography

Where are the other counter-spaces to the new violent cartography (in addition to various segments of the news media)? The violence that has emerged from contemporary practices of securitization and militarization is being contested in display spaces that function outside of the governmental controls that were exercised in earlier historical periods. The fate of Édouard Manet's painting *The Execution of the Emperor Maximilian* provides an apt illustration of a former governmental suppression. France installed the Austrian archduke Maximilian as the puppet monarch of Mexico in 1863. By 1866, Napoleon decided that funding the French forces required to keep him in his position—in the faced of an armed, republican insurrection—was too costly and withdrew his troops. Being left without sufficient protection, Maximilian, who had in fact behaved for the most part as a humane and enlightened monarch, was captured and executed by a firing squad, along with two of his loyalist generals in 1867.

Shortly after the event, Manet completed his first of four historical paintings of the execution. However, because it was politically controversial, inasmuch as it displayed, graphically, one of the lethal consequences of the French foreign policy, visited on what many regarded as an innocent victim, it was denied entry into the Paris Salon, year after year. A picture that was perhaps a nineteenth-century equivalent to the images of a helicopter on the roof of the U.S. embassy in Saigon, leaving many South Vietnamese to their postwar fates, did not appear in public until it was shown in Boston, seven years after the execution. In contrast, not long after media publicity revealed the torture and humiliation of prisoners in Abu Ghraib prison in Iraq, the Colombian artist Fernando Botero executed a series of paintings of the atrocities committed against the Iraqis held there. Shortly after they were finished, the paintings began traveling around the world, appearing first in Rome at the Palazzo Venezia (beginning in mid-June 2005) and heading thereafter to art museums in Germany, Greece, and Washington, D.C.[69]

There is another kind of display space that is available and increasingly used by those who supply images that contest militarization, securitization, and violence. As I note in the Introduction, contemporary film festivals provide a venue for films with significant anti-violence and anti-war themes and cinematic styles. For example, at the 2006 Berlin Film Festival the trend was "definitely political," whereas at the previous year's festival political themes were matched by emphases on sex and football.[70] Similarly, the same year at Cannes, politically oriented films continued to displace Cannes's historical emphasis on the "beautiful," continuing the trend that brought Michael Moore's anti-war documentary *Fahrenheit 9/11* Cannes's top prize, the Palme d'Or. And, as I point out in the Introduction, every year at the Tromsø (Norway) International Film Festival, there is a category for the prize for the best "peace film."[71] A panel of scholars, among whom are those involved in peace and conflict studies, those who organize film festivals, and those who make feature films and documentaries, deliberates about the anti-war, anti-violence merits of films from all over the planet and brings those deliberations into public dialogue with sizable audiences. Significantly, many of the films shown at all these festivals find their way into chain theaters and thus expose them to mass audiences (as was the case with Moore's *Fahrenheit 9/11*).

I want to call particular attention to one of the films showing at the Berlin Film Festival in 2006, *The Road to Guantanamo*, directed by Michael Winterbottom and Mat Whitecross. The film, which like Botero's series of paintings about the abuses at Abu Ghraib provides stark images of atrocities visited on prisoners/detainees, features "three British Muslims who traveled to Afghanistan just as the United States was embarking on its military campaign."[72] These men, who are played by actors in the film, report that after being "captured by the pro-American Northern Alliance . . . they are hooded, beaten, transported with other prisoners in a packed truck and eventually turned over to the Americans who beat them during interrogation and fly them to Guantanamo, Cuba." Specifically the Winterbottom/Whitecross film starts out as a road movie, as shortly after 9/11 a young Brit of Pakistani heritage, Asif Iqbal (Arfan Usman), heads to Pakistan to meet a young woman whom his mother has arranged for him to marry. Because his first choice of a best man cannot come along, Asif recruits another English friend as best man, Ruhel (Farhad Harun). The two are joined by two other friends, Shafiq Rasul (Rizwan Ahmed) and Monir Ali (Waqar Siddiqui). However, what begins as a road film turns into a war film that provides close-up images of some of the arbitrary processes through which bodies move into one of the most disturbing loci of the contemporary violent cartography, the detention camp at Guantanamo, Cuba, a space "devoid of law," one which, from the point of view of those interested in American institutions, participates in the process by which "America," in reaction to the threat of terrorism, decided to "dismantle the structures that made America what it is."[73] From the points of view of the detainees, which are what are primarily in focus in the film, it's a space of undeserved and violent mistreatment. Mixing a staged drama of the young men, who are picked up while visiting Afghanistan and shipped to Guantanamo, with interviews of the actual victims, the docudrama powerfully contests the Bush administration's reassurances about the guilt of the detainees (there's archival footage with Bush remarking, "These are bad men") and reassurances about human treatment (there's an insert with such a remark by Defense Secretary Rumsfeld).

How does the film achieve its effective challenge to the U.S. Gulag at Guantanamo? It does so by confronting lies with truth. As the film editor and

*Figure 1.4* Bush, "These are bad people"
Courtesy of Sony Pictures

documentary analyst Dai Vaughan puts it, "for those who bewail its absence, honesty is a moral problem. For those who try to achieve it, it is a technical one."[74] He goes on to point out that filming a process of interaction fails to convey what is going on. There is a need for some degree of simulation.[75] The significance of the events being filmed is effectively created by the editing. In the case of *The Road to Guantanamo*, what produces the truth of the injustice of the detention and abuse of those who have come to be known as "the Tipton Three" is the cuts and juxtapositions from recreations of the staged mobile life worlds of the protagonists (which point to their innocence) as they move from their homes to Pakistan and Afghanistan and thence, under coercion, to Guantanamo, to shots that recreate the abusive interrogations and forms of incarceration, to interviews with the actual victims.

"Truth" for the Bush administration and the operatives running its detention, torture, and incarceration policies harks back to the system of medieval justice. The only recourse allowed those identified as "enemy combatants"—who are always already guilty once apprehended—is to say what their interrogators/ torturers demand that they say, that is, to condemn themselves. In contrast, the film articulates truth with "image facts."[76] The viewer observes juxtapositions between the bizarre, hostile environments of capture—interrogation/torture and

*Figure 1.5* One of the "bad people"

Courtesy of Sony Pictures

incarceration—and the mundane daily lives of young men, who are engaged in such innocent tasks as brushing their teeth and packing for a trip, and are doing so in the context of exchanges of familial affection: a mother caressing her departing son, a younger brother tearfully begging his older sibling to come back home. And as the drama reaches Pakistan, the juxtapositions are between the hostile moments of capture versus the forms of sympathy and affection afforded by extended families and village communities.

As it turns out the film's main actant in its title, "road," has an effective double resonance which articulates well with the film's challenge to the United States' detention policy. A road movie is a genre of innocent movement, while the "road to Guantanamo" conveys a perversion, a turning of innocent movement into oppressive counter-movement.

The truth-effect of *The Road to Guantanamo*'s approach to the war on terror has been validated by its many awards: the Silver Bear Award at the 2006 Berlin Film Festival, among several others at smaller festivals. At a minimum, the recognition the film has achieved testifies to the role of film festival space, which is opening itself to images that disclose the violence and abuses of rights that constitute much of the new violent cartography that has been effected during the war on terror. Such films, which have opened the way to cinematic challenges to U.S. war

*Figure 1.6* Detainees
Courtesy of Sony Pictures

policy, suggest that film festival space is a counter-space (what I refer to as a "cinematic heterotopia" in the Introduction) to the violence-congeniality of USC's militarization–complicit university–Hollywood–military connection at its Institute for Creative Technologies. However, perhaps the success of the art house-oriented anti-war films at festivals have had an effect on Hollywood. At the same time that some of its practitioners are aiding and abetting militarization and securitization, others are challenging the United States' war policy, for example the 2007 Hollywood feature films *Shooter*, *The Bourne Ultimatum*, *Lions for Lambs*, *In the Valley of Elah*, *Rendition*, and *Redacted*, all of which have plots that involve either governmental complicity in illicit violence and/or its cover-up.

Ultimately, cinema's increasingly political and anti-militarization impetus, evident at international film festivals and in Hollywood's feature films, raises important epistemic and political issues about realism, given the technologies through which cinema presents the reality of policy-as-violence. As Michael Dillon points out, the governing associated with the war on terror has produced a legitimating account of the "real," a soliciting of fear and an enframing of danger that is "beginning to transform the cultural and political codes of security—civil and military."[77] As I noted, the military dimension of that transformation is focused on the "realism" that Hollywood film technologies can add to the military's simulations of battlefield experiences. But film offers a version of realism that is also critical rather than merely warrior-vocational. As I note in the Introduction, during an early epoch of film history Walter Benjamin suggested that, because of its ability to "reactivate the object," film offers an intimacy with reality that was unavailable before the "work of art" was transformed in "the age of mechanical reproduction."[78] Film, he noted, "permits the audience to take the position of the critic . . . [because the audience] takes the position of the camera."[79] Insofar as the spaces of contemplation and exchange on the reality of the violence associated with recoded modes of security are increasingly activated at film festivals and in Hollywood feature films, screened for mass audiences, both film festival space and movie theaters in general articulate resistance to the new violent cartography. They counter the state's "truth weapon" with a form of critique, a juxtaposition with which I begin chapter 2.

# 2 Preemption up close

## Film and pax Americana

Truth, in this new world order, is by nature retroactive. Fact grows conditionally in the soil of an indeterminately present futurity. It *becomes objective* as that present reflexively plays out as an *effect* of the preemptive action taken.

Brian Massumi[1]

When are you going to believe what your eyes see and not what military intelligence tells you to believe?

Richard Boyle (James Woods) in *Salvador*

## Introduction: the "truth weapon" and the role of critique

At one point in his lectures on the war–society relationship, Michel Foucault poses the question "What is the principle that explains history [and right]?" The answer, he suggests, is to be found in "a series of brute facts" such as "physical strength, force, energy," in short in "a series of accidents, or at least contingencies." But governments have tended to dissimulate the events of global violence by interpolating the use of raw force into the implementation of rationality and right. Accordingly, Foucault refers to:

> the rationality of calculations, strategies, and ruses; the rationality of technical procedures that are used to perpetuate the victory, to silence . . . the war . . . [and adds that] given that the relationship of domination works to their advantage, it is certainly not in their [government's] interest to call any of this into question.[2]

Yet while segments of the media and academia (for example major television networks in the case of the former and such disciplines as "area studies" and "strategic studies" in the case of the latter) perpetuate what Foucault calls a "truth weapon"[3] by collaborating with policy makers and, like them, producing abstract rationalities that turn deadly conspiracies into rational self-interest and situation-provoked necessity, some filmmakers and many scholars in the humanities have turned to genres that provide realistic (close-up, in the language of cinema) access to the victims of those rationalities and "truths."

From Foucault's perspective, the answer to the "truth weapon" is "critique," which he identifies as "the movement by which the subject gives himself the right to question truth on its effects of power and question power on its discourses of truth."[4] In this sense, critique serves as a defense against the kind of official persuasion that for example has led to the nearly 4,000 U.S. soldiers killed in Iraq (by the summer of 2007). "War," as John Johnston points out, "depends not only on a communications structure of command and control . . . but on strategies of persuasion in the art of getting other people to die for you."[5] The Iraq war has also produced a rapidly mounting Iraqi civilian death toll—approximately one million by the summer of 2007. What was the "truth weapon" that accompanied the military weapons in the attack on Iraq? It was a series of publicly offered, duplicitous rationales for an invasion by a government that went to war against nation-states when their actual antagonists were from violent extra-state networks. Those in power had created their own version of truth. Reflecting on Foucault's concern with the power–truth relationship, Gilles Deleuze asks, "If power is constitutive of truth, how can we conceive of a 'power of truth' which would no longer be the truth of power, a truth that would release transversal lines of resistance and integral lines of power?"[6] As noted, Foucault's response is critique.

In addition to its role in opposing the "truth" of power, critique stands as a defense against the dissimulation of harm, for the main objective of war's operation, where it takes place, is to destroy or injure bodies (as the literary theorist Elaine Scarry pointed out more than two decades ago). But injury, she writes, is conjured away, allowed to "recede from view," through the use of tropes and redescriptions that displace the damage to human bodies with abstract imagery of weapons, space, and strategy.[7] Curiously, Scarry, who begins her investigation by noting that bodily pain is difficult to bring into discourse, because it is anterior to language, pays relatively little attention to film. Of course, Scarry's investigation precedes some of the contemporary war films—for example the Gulf War film *Three Kings* (1999), in which there is a "nearly clinical imaging of the effects of bullets entering bodies"[8]—but some of Hollywood's World War II films of the 1940s had already focused on bodily violence, even though in much of their visual grammar the depiction of violence is indirect, for example "cross-cutting between close-ups . . . long shots . . . [and] slanted camera angles rather than agonizing long takes or gruesome special effects."[9]

Apart from occasional mention of feature films and painting, Scarry's emphasis is on literary artists, who, she says, must necessarily "fall silent" in the face of pain.[10] While she does recognize, with occasional reference to Bergman's films, that human suffering can be depicted and dramatized cinematically, she fails to make effective use of the film genre, which would have helped her to develop a mode of counter-intelligibility to her objects of critique, the strategic and technical discourses of war. If, with Gilles Deleuze, we recognize that a linguistically oriented approach to film is inadequate to the moving image, we can attribute Scarry's perfunctory treatment of the genre to her fixation on language rather than images as the basis of intelligibility. An emphasis on linguistic meaning, which Scarry shares with some semiotic approaches to film, impoverishes the significance of the film image "by subtracting its most visible characteristic: movement."[11] Among the antidotes to the discourse of the abstract adversary, which abounds in the writings of defense and security analysts (among others), who focus on the rationalities of geopolitical antagonists, are both film, which turns "antagonists" into complex and vulnerable lives which become intelligible as a series of interconnected images deployed in a changing and fraught life-world, and those critical film analyses that elaborate the political implications of such cinematically rendered lives. Moreover, film articulates well with Foucault's suggestion that critique involves the "the movement by which the subject gives himself the right to question truth," because it is the genre that is constituted through movement.

It is also important to recognize that film, and its extension in critical analysis, provides a political pedagogy that exceeds the dramas of individual lives. As many critics have pointed out, feature films, which invariably foreground the experiences of individuals and bring into view the individual consequences of violent collective dynamics, also articulate spaces and historical moments that transcend the events of individual encounter. Accordingly, in his *The Geopolitical Aesthetic*, which treats the "geopolitical unconscious" lurking in conspiracy thrillers, Fredric Jameson treats films "with a view towards an unsystematic mapping or scanning of the world system itself."[12] Because he selects the feature film, a genre that almost invariably dramatizes the experiences of individual characters, he must necessarily ask "under what circumstances can a necessarily individual story with individual characters function to represent collective processes?"[13] Using the analytic of the allegory, Jameson points out that the "motif of conspiracy" provides a "narrative structure" that brings into focus both collective relations and epistemological issues,[14] and reveals, among other things, "the incommensurability between an individual witness—the individual character of a still anthropomorphic narrative—and the collective conspiracy which must somehow be exposed or revealed through these individual efforts."[15]

## Updating the geopolitical aesthetic

Jameson's focus on individual–world system relationships in his film readings is applicable to a film that post-dates his analysis, Wim Wenders's *The End of Violence* (1997), to which I turn briefly here in order to address some of the injuries resident in a contemporary "world system," a "violent cartography" that is subsequent to the Cold War object-world toward which Jameson's film readings are allegorically aimed.[16] In *The End of Violence*, the primary individual story features Mike Max (Bill Pullman), a Hollywood producer whose wealthy, ocean-front-estate lifestyle is a result of the commercial success of his violent films, which seemingly pander to a public that savors that genre. However, his films put him in danger because they disturb an authoritarian anti-violence policing institution. As a result, he is compelled to drop out of sight after surviving a murder-for-hire plot against him. But the drama surrounding Mike Max, who abandons his former life and hides by joining a more or less invisible group (from the vantage point of his past lifestyle), the Mexican groundskeepers of his former estate, is only intermittently in focus. There are frequent cuts to a parallel drama involving Ray Bering (Gabriel Byrne), a computer scientist running the official anti-crime surveillance system from Los Angeles's Griffith Observatory. The drama involving Bering, who ends up being killed by a sniper because he discovers privileged information, results from his being under surveillance by his superiors in the anti-crime program, which is ironically aimed at "ending violence as we know it." And there is yet a third narrative thread that explores violence-related policing–entertainment industry connections, a developing relationship between one of Mike Max's former actresses and a Hollywood film-obsessed police detective.

Although the various stories in Wenders's Altmanesque, multi-focused film are loosely tied together from the point of view of the relationships among the individuals, the film's persistent question, verbalized and foregrounded, about how to define violence makes the film's coherence similar to that identified in the conspiracy films that Jameson treats. Wenders's *The End of Violence* provides an articulation between collective patterns and epistemological issues. But there is a significant difference in the structure of Wenders's film. It does not render itself readily available to the allegorical analytic applied by Jameson to Cold War-era conspiracy films, because its structure resists traditional narrativity. It is perhaps best characterized by what Jacques Rancière identifies as the contemporary "aesthetic regime of the arts," which has adopted "a fragmented or proximate mode of focalization, which imposes raw presence to the detriment of the rational sequences of the story."[17]

For purposes of my analysis, there is one "raw presence" in *The End of Violence* that undermines the conceits behind the official policy of ending violence as we know it. Mathilda (Marisol Padia Sanchez), a Central American refugee, is placed in Ray Bering's employ, ostensibly as a "domestic," as a cleaning woman assigned to the Griffith Observatory. However, her cleaning woman status is a cover for her actual job; she is employed by the anti-violence policy officials to spy on Bering. It is implied that it is her testimony that causes his death. However, Mathilda's relationship with Bering exceeds her official job description. Before she turns over the information that Bering is pursuing his discovery of a murder—an event of the violence undertaken by those involved in the policy to end violence—their relationship becomes sexual. At one point in their intimacies, Bering discovers, while removing Mathilda's blouse, that she is scarred from having been tortured. Her surveillance role is clearly suborned. Working for the violent anti-violence officials is the quid pro quo for her protection from being sent back to her official enemies elsewhere.

If we assume that Mathilda is Salvadoran (the most likely origin of Central American political refugees in the 1980s), she would clearly need such protection. For example, in her autobiographical treatment of her experiences in El Salvador, Joan Didion reports the dire warnings about the dangers in El Salvador from *her* Salvadoran domestic employee:

> She spoke with considerable vehemence, because two of her brothers had been killed in Salvador in August of 1981, in their beds. The throats of both brothers

*Figure 2.1* Bering, "I never noticed"
Courtesy of MGM

had been slashed. Her father had been cut but stayed alive. Her mother had been beaten. Twelve of her other relatives, aunts, uncles, and cousins had been taken from their houses one night the same August, and their bodies had been found some time later, in a ditch.[18]

It is ironic that Mathilda is a vulnerable (foreign) domestic, because her situation reveals that the domestic anti-violence policy network feeds on a history of foreign policy violence. This singular, suborned body is a legacy of U.S. support of violent regimes that officially sponsored death squads in Latin and Central America during the Cold War. In effect, therefore, it is a Central American cleaning woman who extends Wenders's drama, both spatially and historically, beyond the dystopic Los Angeles (seen mostly on computer screens and through glass partitions, and represented in the stories of the technology-obsessed Mike Max and technology-employed Ray Bering) to a historical, violence-complicit foreign policy relationship that has produced palpable injury. Mathilda is the vehicle for what Jameson would call the film's geopolitical unconscious. As was the case with Jameson's reading of Cronenberg's *Videodrome* (1983), in *The End of Violence* "a host of political readings . . . compete for the surface of the text."[19] Two related political readings, both of which have historical depth, occupy my attention.

First, the panoptic all-seeing vantage point that Ray Bering operates in the Griffith Observatory, in order to facilitate a war on crime, reflects two dimensions of the nature of contemporary warfare. As Rey Chow points out, in her reflection on the future implications of the bombs dropped on Hiroshima and Nagasaki at the end of World War II, seeing the world as a pervasive target and, as a result, eliminating or at least diminishing "tactual physical warring activities had the effect not of bringing war to an end but instead of promoting and accelerating terrorism . . . the so-called terrorism of 'deterrent' weaponry."[20] Once that form of state-run terrorism was shared by the United States and the Soviet Union, these main Cold War antagonists targeted each other with weapons that have a capacity for what deterrence theorists call "mutual assured destruction." Because that mutual threat inhibited direct, U.S.–Soviet confrontation, direct engagement gave way to a global competition for political allegiance among non-superpowers (those unable to target the globe). From the U.S. perspective, which was dominated by a conception of "the Soviet threat," even in situations of ambiguous allegiance, when revolutionary forces sought to displace authoritarian regimes, U.S. policy makers saw a larger geopolitical stake involved.

The preemptive dimension of the contemporary war on terror has a well-known external dimension, realized in the preemptive attacks on Afghanistan and Iraq. Less well known, but increasingly publicized, is a preemptive dimension of violence prevention on the domestic front, an issue central to the Wenders film. Contemporary preemptive violence prevention operates not with a panoptic gaze over a city but with a nation-wide wiretapping technology, coupled with the use of agents provocateurs. For example, in June 2003, after the Defense Department got a hold of a notebook from an "enemy" safe house in Iraq with evidence of phone calls to an imam in the United States, Yassin M. Aref, federal agents set up a sting. They used a suborned informant to ask Mr. Aref and a friend to launder money being used to buy shoulder-launch missiles, allegedly to assassinate a Pakistani diplomat in New York. Aref and his friend have been jailed ever since.[21] However, the political reading I want to pursue is the second one prompted by Wenders's *The End of Violence*. It takes us to the death and destruction rendered in the U.S. Cold War-motivated proxy wars in Central America.

## Law and space: a vulnerable Salvadoran body

Assuming that the specific country of Mathilda's origin is El Salvador, the country that experienced the most extensive U.S. strategic attention during the post-Vietnam stage of the Cold War, as a political refugee without legal status she is an exemplar of what Giorgio Agamben refers to as "bare life," a form of mere existence that is abandoned to violence, as opposed to legally and politically qualified life. Bare life is vulnerable to injury and death; it can be killed without the killing being recruited under the rubric of homicide. Specifically (and ironically), Mathilda is a person devoid of legal protection, an expendable pawn in an organization involved in eliminating violence.[22] At the end of the film, when Mathilda refuses to offer further services and plans to leave, she is threatened with death. Agents of the anti-crime unit, sent to kill her, pull back at the last moment.

Apart from the irony of the violence of an anti-violence policy, there is a further, historical irony involved in Mathilda's vulnerability to the whims of governmental officials. That irony becomes evident if we inquire into the historical trajectory of the modern state's monopolizing of violence. The Icelandic sagas teach us that medieval Iceland had a singular way of identifying political affiliation and allocating legal protection. An individual's political identity was not spatial in the modern sense; rather than being territorial, for example being based on being a member of an Icelandic political territory as a whole, it was primarily biopolitical. It was a function of family and hereditary attachment. However, legal identity *was* spatial. In medieval Iceland, a person was either inside or outside the law. The process of transition, of going from inside to outside, was juridically determined. At a yearly meeting of the clans at the Icelandic Althing, one could be outlawed for failure to pay compensation to a victim's family or clan after a killing. Once declared an outlaw, the killer could be killed with impunity. In Agamben's sense, the Icelandic outlaw, like Mathilda, became "bare life" as opposed to being politically qualified life, a status within which one can be killed without having the killing criminalized. As a result, to read the various sagas is to encounter historically based characters with varying relationships to juridical space—those securely inside of it, those who are in danger of being forced outside of it (for example well-intentioned warrior Gunnar Hamundarson in *Njal's Saga*, whose unavoidable confrontations eventually push him across the boundary), and those whose persistently ill-intentioned behavior guarantees outlaw status (for example the notorious Killer Hraap, who appears in several sagas). At a minimum, the part-time administration of justice at the medieval Icelandic Althing functioned to allocate bodies to a space "devoid of law" (to invoke another of Agamben's concepts).[23]

Recalling the juridico-political system of medieval Iceland in the present provides for reflection on the historical trajectory of relationships between bodies and legal spaces. Certainly, to be outlawed in Iceland was unrelated to a security problematic, such as that preoccupying the contemporary state. It was a penalty designed to disconnect wealth and violence as well as to regulate inter-clan violence. The almost certain consequence of being placed outside the law was death at the hands of one's enemies. But there was no centralized system of revenge. Retaliation for the alleged crime was strictly freelance; it was in the hands of the aggrieved parties and their allies. As a result, it was common for cycles of retaliation to develop and engulf almost the entire social order. The justice system of the modern state was designed in part to avoid the escalating cycles of violence that have occurred in pre-state political systems. By monopolizing retaliation, the state monopolizes revenge.

There are various ways to characterize the advantages and disadvantages of centralized state power. Certainly there have been salutary effects of juridical systems that have developed protections for those with territorial identities that fall within state protection, among which are the rights of those accused of crimes. And much of the corpus of political theory and analysis testifies to the way the state system is an improvement over the anarchy of systems in which individuals and groups were in charge of retaliation, and legal protection was relatively absent. *Njal's Saga*, the most famous of the family sagas, affirms this insight. The narrative describes such a system and testifies to a society that was torn apart by an escalating cycle of retaliatory violence that respect for the law could not contain. However, as we witness the post-9/11 version of pax Americana, we see the alleged advantages of state centralization of violence dissipating. At a collective level there is a displacement of the U.S. attempts to apprehend "terrorist networks" by invoking the law of war and targeting nation-states and, at an individual level, there is a proliferation of spaces "devoid of law," for example Gitmo (Guantanamo Bay, Cuba), where "enemy combatants" are held, and hidden spaces of incarceration, and client states (where legal restraints on torture are either non-existent or are routinely ignored) to which individuals identified as terrorist threats or terrorist-complicit supporters are outsourced. After years of official denial, the existence of these "black sites" has been well documented.[24]

In medieval Iceland the protected juridical space was small, while the larger outside space, which was devoid of law, was enormous. It comprised the rest of the known world. Now that imbalance is reappearing. As the juridical space within which the accused have protections against arbitrary arrest and injury shrinks, the spaces of incarceration and physical abuse proliferate. As a result, we witness a post-9/11 security state that turns back the clock and substitutes arbitrary power for the rule of law. The anarchic violence of the pre-state system has returned as part of the exercise of state power. In Judith Butler's terms, the extra-legal attack on individuals by the state:

> returns the operation of power from a set of laws (juridical) to a set of rules (governmental) . . . rules that are not binding by virtue of established law or modes of legitimation, but fully discretionary, even arbitrary, wielded by officials who interpret them unilaterally and decide the condition and form of their invocation.[25]

There is another, crucial difference between the contemporary U.S. and medieval Icelandic versions of law and space. Whereas the Icelandic outlaw was perforce a nomadic wanderer who existed in an unprotected extra-legal status on the margins of the social order, the status of the contemporary U.S. "outlaw" goes a long way toward corroborating Agamben's claim that "today it is not the city but rather the camp that is the fundamental biopolitical paradigm of the West."[26] As the U.S.-sponsored detention camps proliferate, where detainees are outsourced to other countries, they, along with the ones held in Guantanamo and in the U.S.-run detention camps in Afghanistan and Iraq, reflect a "state of exception" that has devolved into an ecology of encampments. The contemporary U.S. outlaw is contained and interrogated rather than left to his fate in a lawless outside. As a result, there exists a contemporary version of Foucault's famous take on the disciplinary society in which the imprisonment, as a zone of power-knowledge, is expanded into a global context.

The consequences of arbitrary, extra-legal detention become increasingly evident. On June 11, 2006, after three "detainees" at the Guantanamo Bay, Cuba, detention camp committed suicide, an editorial in the *New York Times* stated the obvious:

> The news that three inmates at Guantanamo Bay hanged themselves should not have surprised anyone who has paid attention to the twisted history of the camp that President Bush built for selected prisoners from Afghanistan and antiterrorist operations. It was the inevitable result of creating a netherworld of despair beyond the laws of civilized nations, where men were to be held without any hope of decent treatment, impartial justice or, in so many cases, even release.[27]

How should one describe the violence of the conditions at Gitmo that preceded those acts of desperation? Jean-Luc Nancy provides an appropriate answer when he writes, "violence does not transform what it assaults; rather, it takes away its form and meaning. It makes it into nothing other than a sign of its own rage."[28] What kinds of media can make the consequences of the arbitrary exercise of violence evident to a broad and largely fear-distracted audience (a fear programmatically instigated by, among other things, the U.S. government's color-coded domestic terror alerts)?[29] At a minimum, we have to assume that any medium or genre that seeks to promote a critical interpretation of the violent episodes of pax Americana has to heed the ongoing phenomenology of everyday life, a situation in which people are always already trying to insert themselves into a complicated, highly mediatized and globalized world, while at the same time coping with their ongoing individual problems. One's relationship with a medium is therefore not a matter of engaging in an interpretation *ex nihilo*. Everyone is perpetually engaged in acts of interpretation. They are busy interpolating themselves as, for example, citizen subjects, threatened species, guilty fathers, unappreciated working mothers, disappointed professionals, and so on. They are screening options well before they experience what is, for example, on-screen in a film. As a result, as Vivian Sobchack has emphasized, the phenomenology of the film experience unites the dynamic motions of both on-screen and off-screen bodies.[30]

While often the effect of filmic work on what Sobchack calls "the cinesthetic subject" has been to shape the body politic by encouraging the same moral conversion in the audience that transpires for characters on-screen, some films have a more politically disruptive effect. The impact of a critical film is a matter of its ability to disturb that already-initiated interpretive work rather than reinforce it, so that viewers can apprehend the extent to which they have labored within an anachronistic imaginary, an officially promoted illusion, or a merely partial mapping of a sinister world. Jameson makes a relevant point in his reading of the film *Dog Day Afternoon* when he refers to our inability to grasp "the truth about our world as a totality."[31] While I would resist the notion that there is *a* totality, the point remains cogent, namely that we are in a condition in which critical genres will show that "we will no longer be able to maintain an imaginative relation to it [the 'totality']."[32]

Certainly Michael Moore's *Fahrenheit 9/11* (2004), which among other things contains graphic clips of civilian casualties, is, in some of its footage, an exemplar of the critically disruptive film, in that it shows the extraordinary violence inflicted on a civilian population by a war that is officially represented at the more abstract and benign level of "regime change." And, as I pointed out in chapter 1, the Winterbottom/Whitecross docudrama *The Road to Guantanamo* has a critical, counter-official effect. However, the critically oriented war film, aimed at indicting official culture, while showing the on-the-ground effects of war, began much earlier, primarily with Oliver Stone's Vietnam War films and his film *Salvador* (1986), a dramatic version of the effects of the proxy war conducted by the United States on behalf of the murderous regime in El Salvador. I turn to a treatment of that film here, both to illustrate how a critical film functions to disrupt officially encouraged political imaginaries and to offer a version of the U.S. preemptive violence in El Salvador that has contemporary relevance. While addressing the historical episode that is condensed in Wenders's character Mathilda, the film offers a significant contrast with the contemporary mode of U.S.-implicated preemptive war.

The question of how realistic Stone's film is does not admit of an answer based solely on attention to the cinematic object, even though a reality effect is enhanced by Stone's inclusion of documentary footage. As Sobchack has insisted, "our viewing experiences are best described as containing both documentary and fictional moments co-constituted by a dynamic and labile spectatorial engagement with all film images." Moreover, although these moments are "cued" by "conventional cinematic practices . . . it is our embodied experience and knowledge that governs how we first take up the images we see on the screen and what we make of them."[33] What I want to emphasize here is that both film history and the contemporary version of American security policy (especially as the latter is unfolding in Iraq as I write) influence what I make of Stone's images. Ironically, evidence of conversations in the Pentagon about a "Salvador Option" in 2005 effectively preempts (while affirming) the phenomenology of Stone's film, as it emerges in my treatment of *Salvador*, which is framed by a conceptual connection with the U.S. direct and sponsored violence in Iraq. Although the United States' support of death squads in El Salvador in the 1980s remains an official secret, it emerged in the Pentagon's Iraq war policy discussions. The January 8, 2005, issue of *Newsweek Magazine* reported that:

> the Pentagon is intensely debating an option that dates back to a still-secret strategy in the Reagan administration's battle against the leftist guerilla insurgency in El Salvador in the early 1980's. Then, faced with a losing war against Salvadoran rebels, the U.S. government funded or supported "nationalist" forces that allegedly included so-called death squads directed to hunt down and kill rebel leaders and sympathizers.[34]

Although the evidence is not in as to whether U.S. policy actually implemented "the Salvador Option" in Iraq, the *Newsweek* report noted that "the interim government of Prime Minister Ayad Allawi is said to be among the most forthright proponents of the Salvador Option." And significantly, since then, a virtual civil war has ensued between (largely Sunni) insurgents and what appear to be officially sponsored Shiite death squads that attack not only insurgents but also Sunni individuals and Sunni religious and civic gatherings. As one post–Salvador Option analysis points out, "It should come as no surprise . . . that sectarian death squads *tied directly to the Iraqi Interior Ministry* are running rampant in Iraq." Significantly on March 3, 2006, the head of the Baghdad morgue "fled the country in fear for his life after reporting that the units have *killed more than 7,000 people since last summer.*"[35] That episode has strong resonances with Joan Didion's 1982 visit to a San Salvador morgue, at a time when a conservative estimate numbered the death squad victims at just under 7,000. The entries in that day's log showed "seven bodies, all male, none identified, none believed older than twenty-five," and all had been shot.[36] Clearly, it is a propitious time to revisit Oliver Stone's *Salvador* and interpret its disruptive impetus within the present "policy" context.

### *Salvador*: sometimes a cigar is more than just a cigar

Stone's *Salvador*, when understood within its historical space, had a disruptive effect on a dominant political imaginary that was already under pressure. Walter LaFeber expresses well the agonistic historical moment within which the film was inserted:

> The 1986 film *Salvador*, resembling the actual U.S. policy in El Salvador between 1979 and 1991, resulted when the historical memories and corrupted idealism of the 1960's confronted the Central American revolutions of the 1980's. Above all, those memories revolved around the tragedy of the U.S. war in Vietnam.[37]

In general, the American involvement in El Salvador throughout the 1980s "occasioned the most bitter domestic political debate since Vietnam." And Stone, a decorated and disillusioned Vietnam veteran, was an exemplary carrier of "the historical memories and corrupted idealism of the 1960's [that] revolved around the tragedy of the U.S. war in Vietnam."[38] His film articulated his personal historical experience with the U.S. policy in El Salvador. However, my turn to Stone's film here is aimed at a political encounter with the present—the U.S.'s twenty-first-century war on terror, which includes the invasions of Afghanistan and Iraq, rather than with the Vietnam memory–El Salvador connection. A comparison between that foreign policy intervention and the current one in Iraq is therefore worth elaborating, not only because, in today's dollars, the degree of military-logistical support that was part of the U.S. intervention in the civil war in El Salvador is comparable to the investment involved in the U.S. "regime change" and subsequent war in Iraq, but also because both cases reveal the reasons why preoccupations with security problems have produced egregious inattention to violations of human rights. While in the case of Iraq the justification for the ongoing violence encounter is democratization, in El Salvador it was "nation-building" (propping up regimes that would resist left-leaning opponents, whether or not they had affinities with the communist bloc nations). Benjamin Schwarz effectively summarizes that latter project:

> With the exception of its involvement in South Vietnam, America had never been so deeply and intimately involved in attempting to transform a foreign society that it had not defeated in war and hence did not control. . . . Whether the geopolitical stakes demanded that involvement and whether letting events take their own course would have resulted in even more atrocities can be debated. What is indisputable is that for a decade American policymakers in Washington and American civilian and military personnel in El Salvador consorted with murderers and sadists.[39]

In the war on terror, which, as noted, has proliferated a global patchwork of gulags, zones of incarceration in Afghanistan and Iraq, where prisoners are held, and outsourced spaces of incarceration and interrogation for "detainees" worldwide, the United States has not simply consorted with murderers and sadists; some of its own personnel, who have operated with positive official sanction, fit that description.[40] It should be noted, however, that violence-by-proxy has not been wholly displaced by direct intervention in the historical trajectory from the Cold War to the war on terror. As Fernand Braudel put it, in his treatment of the historical shift from barter to money economies, history is "conjunctural" rather than linear. Early forms persist rather than being completely displaced by later ones.[41] What is the case in the history of economy, in which barter systems continue to exist alongside money forms, holds for U.S. military policy. After 9/11, in connection with the perception that all Islamicist political initiatives are enemies because they are Al Qaeda connected, the United States' Central Intelligence Agency began covertly financing Somali warlords in their fight against an Islamic political front for control of Mogadishu. The United States thus engaged in a proxy war—its signature mode of warfare during the Cold War—at the same time that it was involved directly in wars in Afghanistan and Iraq:

> Officials said that the C.I.A. effort, run from the agency's station in Nairobi, Kenya, had channeled hundreds of thousands of dollars over the past year to secular warlords inside Somalia with the aim, among other things, of capturing or killing a handful of suspected Al Qaeda believed to be hiding there.[42]

Stone's *Salvador* provides an intimate picture of the consequences of an earlier proxy war, the U.S. political and military involvement in El Salvador. The film stands as a counter-historical text to the attempt by policy makers to conjure away their complicity with one of the worst episodes of official murder and other violations of human rights. In contrast with the cinematic recreations of Tom

Clancy's hero Jack Ryan, for example, who personifies a heroic version of U.S. counter-intelligence fighters who battle evil enemies in Latin America (among other venues) in *Clear and Present Danger* (1994), Stone's characters are anti-heroes.[43] In addition to providing a telling look at one of the most odious episodes in U.S. military policy, the film (as was the case with Stone's earlier *Platoon*) also challenges a cinematic history of war films.

To return momentarily to the epigraph "When are you going to believe what your eyes see and not what military intelligence tells you to believe?" I want to note that, although it reflects an important political becoming of Stone's Richard Boyle (James Woods), it belies the effectiveness of Stone's cinematic work. The truth value of cinema exists outside of what its characters say or see because it can achieve what mere human looking tends to obscure.[44] Cinema, as Rancière, in his treatment of Deleuze's philosophy of cinema, puts it (as I noted in the Introduction), restores relations that the operation of the eyes and brain confiscates. While human sight tends to be ideological—for example turning the bizarre into the expected[45]—the movements and interrelations of images in films works to:

> put perception back in things because its operation is one of restitution. Intentional artistic activity renders unto the events of sensible matter the potentialities the human brain had deprived them of in order to constitute a sensory-motor universe adapted to its needs and subject to its mastery.[46]

To conceptualize how Stone's cinematic strategy works, we can borrow the perspective that Gilles Deleuze offers in his analysis of the canvases of the painter Francis Bacon.[47] Deleuze insists that it is wrong to assume that the artist "works on a white surface." Rather, "everything he has in his head or around him is already on the canvas, more or less virtually, before he begins his work."[48] To resist what Deleuze calls "psychic clichés" and "*figurative givens*," the artist must "transform" or "deform" what is "always already on the canvas."[49] This is as much the case with the silver screen as it is with the painter's canvas. In his deformation of the classic heroic war story, Stone exchanges the grimly determined, morally unambiguous intelligence types such as the Clancy/Noyce Jack Ryan (exemplified in close-ups of Harrison Ford's clenched jaw and in family scenes that show a conventional father and husband) with the morally questionable, liar and hustling journalist Richard Boyle (exemplified in close-ups of James Woods's shifty eyes and in scenes that express his unconventional, extramarital sexual behavior).

However, at the same time that Stone is deforming the "psychic clichés" and "figurative givens" of the heroic war film genre, he is also enlisting film clichés. He draws in his audience by mimicking Hollywood's familiar genres. For example, *Salvador* begins as a combination road movie and buddy film, as Boyle and Dr. Rock (James Belushi), Boyle's unemployed disc jockey friend, drive down to El Salvador. Although some of the film's reviewers criticized the presence of the Dr. Rock character, who whines and complains much of the time about being exposed to danger, Dr. Rock is an important part of the film's realism. Invoking another of Deleuze's insights in his study of Francis Bacon, we can designate Dr. Rock as an

*Figure 2.2* Ryan
Courtesy of MGM

"attendant" (the role I ascribe to Guo in my treatment of *Dirty Pretty Things* in chapter 4). In his illustration of the attendant function, Deleuze refers to the presence in some of Bacon's canvases of a figure or figures that have no narrative relationship to the central figure. An attendant serves as "a constant or point of reference," a "spectator," but not in the ordinary sense. The attendant is a "kind of spectator" who "seems to subsist, distinct from the figure."[50] Deleuze's attendant provides the basis for determining the facticity of the scene, or, in his words, "the relation of the Figure to its isolating place," or "what takes place."[51] As I have noted elsewhere, the Deleuzian attendant function is robust enough to apply to other visual media such as film.[52] In the case of *Salvador*, the naive and complaining Dr. Rock, who is more or less accidently in El Salvador with Boyle and is unused to seeing violence, is the one who continually verbalizes directly, and without mediating and legitimating concepts, the pervasive and uninhibited violence that he and Boyle witness.

In contrast with Dr. Rock, who in many scenes asks "What's going on?," Boyle is one who "has seen it all." He travels with a can of mace, a knife, fake watches for bribing potential antagonists, and cyanide pills, in case all else fails, because he knows what to expect from the violent characters they encounter. And, at least at the outset, he is a self-interested cynic, trying to make a journalistic score. He

*Figure 2.3* Boyle
Courtesy of MGM

is seemingly indifferent to the operation of the death squads with U.S. support. Nevertheless, although a very different type from Dr. Rock, Boyle is also an effective witness to the violence. That Boyle is an inveterate liar and hustler produces a powerful and instructive irony in Stone's drama of the U.S. support of a murderous repression of dissent during the civil war in Salvador in the 1980s. It is a liar who delivers the truth of the events in Salvador.

To summarize briefly: Rick Boyle heads back to El Salvador, which is in a state of civil war, because his life is in shambles. He has drinking and drug problems, he is without work, he has been evicted from his apartment, his wife has left him, his reporter's credential has expired, and he has had to be bailed out of jail (after being arrested for multiple traffic fines) by his equally dissipated and unemployed disc jockey friend, Dr. Rock. We first encounter Boyle's character in scenes in San Francisco, where he lies to his wife, to a former employer, and to an arresting police officer—all in vain. But once the drama unfolds, Boyle-the-liar, whose manipulative behavior is aimed at personal survival, becomes the one who speaks the truth about the conduct of right-wing death squads and their official support by both the U.S. and the Salvadoran government. During a debriefing with a U.S. military and diplomatic official, after he had spent time taking pictures of insurgents in the mountains, Boyle argues against the official line about a global communist attempt to take over all of Central America and beyond. He refers to the insurgency as a peasant revolution about which numerous lies are being told and goes on to refer to the U.S. policy of helping to repress the revolution as equivalent to the Vietnam War debacle.

Here Stone's Boyle contrasts sharply with the subsequent mainstream Hollywood tendency to overcome the Vietnam War stigma with a return to what is generally regarded as the morally unambiguous World War II (as in Spielberg's *Saving Private Ryan* (1998) and the Spielberg/Hanks made-for-television *Band of Brothers* (2001)). Stone's Boyle is a very different kind of character from the morally upright Spielberg heroes. At the outset of *Salvador*, Boyle seems oblivious to the violence, while Dr. Rock is the one who is jarred by the savage realities they encounter. When the two of them see a burning body as they drive into El Salvador, Dr. Rock exclaims, "They kill people here," and the cynical Boyle, fixated on achieving a journalistic stake at this point, responds, "It's just some guy." At the same time, however, Boyle never accepts the official Cold War line about communist expansion. From the outset, he sees the violence as an over-reaction to the encounter between the leftist/peasant revolution and the wealthy, oligarchy's government and military and paramilitary death squads, supported by the United States. This truth-telling aspect of Boyle is contrasted with another character who has a different, vocation-related relationship to truth. Pauline Axelrod (Valerie Wildman), a television journalist whose major credential is being photogenic, is unambivalently committed to accepting and reporting official statements as the truth. For example, when a Salvadoran military unit rapes and kills a group of nuns, she espouses the official line that perhaps they had run a road block and drawn weapons.

There is yet another contrast, which is played out in the film's most disturbing scene, when Boyle and his old acquaintance, the fellow photojournalist John Cassady (John Savage), visit *El Playon*, a garbage dump, where the death squads leave their victim's bodies out in the open for vultures to devour. As Boyle and Cassady photograph bodies, some with hands tied behind their backs, Cassady utters two of the film's most significant approaches to the truth of the war in El Salvador: "You've got to get close to get the truth" and "If you get too close you die." The film presents close-ups of, first, the death squad's murder victims and, subsequently, the abject misery of family members, who search the photos from *El Playon* to try to find the "disappeared." The bizarre difference between these realities and official geopolitical pronouncements is rendered throughout with Stone's cuts and juxtapositions—for example from *El Playon* to the center city where a human rights group is providing the photos of death squad victims and then to documentary footage where President Reagan is giving a Cold War-obsessed speech that is very distant from the actualities in El Salvador. Reagan refers to "infiltrators into the Americas, terrorists from the outside," who threaten not only Central America but ultimately all of South and North America as well.

Although Boyle is well aware that this kind of legitimation for the U.S. proxy war is ideologically obscene, given the effect of U.S. involvement, which he describes during his debriefing with the military and diplomatic characters as merely

*Figure 2.4* El Playon
Courtesy of MGM

exacerbating the people's suffering, he is never represented as one who totally abandons his old manipulative and self-centered ways to take a moral stand. Although Boyle is repulsed by the circumstances that have yielded the bodies he and Cassady photograph at *El Playon*, professional survival and recognition remain among his strongest motivations. For example, while they are photographing the *El Playon* bodies, they get into a discussion of Robert Capa's famous photo of a dying Spanish soldier during the Spanish civil war. Each of them imagines achieving the same degree of celebrity by finding an equivalent shot. Thus Boyle and Cassady, like all the other Americans on the scene, screen the war not merely through right-versus-left versions of ideological commitment but also through their vocational practices. Diplomats, military advisers, and journalists, among others— Boyle included—"see" the war in terms of the opportunities it delivers to them personally. Only the Catholic sisters appear to engage with the victims selflessly (but, of course, selflessness is also a vocational commitment in their case). And Dr. Rock, who understands little of either the historical background or the present stakes but is continually shocked by both the violence and the way it is exploited by all parties, is the only one who offers disinterested statements about what is going on.

Before he manages to leave the country, Boyle loses two people he is close to, Cathy, one of the Catholic nuns, who, along with several others is raped and killed

*Figure 2.5* Reagan
Courtesy of MGM

by a death squad, and John Cassady, who dies in a volley of gunfire from a government plane attacking insurgents. The latter's death, an instance of journalistic courage under fire, seems to provide an epiphany for Boyle, who seems to draw inspiration at the moment when he clasps the hands of the dying John Cassady. Certainly, at a minimum, Boyle seems to shed much of his persistent cynicism at that point. However, to his credit, Stone never makes Boyle a full convert. Moreover, the dialogue tells only the part of history that Stone wants to provide. While some of Boyle's remarks during conversations and statements by the character representing the (subsequently) murdered Archbishop Romero (in a sermon) are vehicles for presenting the film's version of the war and its political background, much of the political impetus of *Salvador* is provided by the camera work. The spatial contrasts and their relationship to perspectives on the reality of the violence are especially important. Often, the cinematic montage involves cuts between the scenes of the grim realities of violence in the city and countryside and scenes in San Salvador's Sheraton Hotel, where Boyle and Dr. Rock engage various characters involved in shaping the official frames within which the war is understood: Salvadoran military officers and politicians, and American diplomats, military, and journalists. For example, after Boyle and Cassady visit *El Playon* and that scene is followed by one in the tent where a human rights group is providing photos of the bodies for relatives, there is a cut to the Sheraton, where a swimming

*Figure 2.6* The Sheraton Hotel
Courtesy of MGM

pool dominates the frame, followed by tracking shots of hotel guests in vacation
wear, along with officials in suits and military uniforms.

Like most franchised environments—once you are in them, the singularities of
the locales within which they are inserted dissolve—the Sheraton Hotel is a space
of illusion. The realities of inequality, class status, and the processes of oppression
are in suspension, as the only interactions one can see are polite conversations
among a narrow segment of social and visiting constituencies and the consumption
of food and alcohol. The cinematic juxtaposition between the Sheraton as a space
of illusion and the outer dynamic of violence and repression reinforces the
verbalized illusions, as American diplomats, military personnel, and television
journalists interpolate a class war into a case of an outside communist conspiracy.
Interestingly, the development of the American franchise hotel chain was
conceived, at least in part, as an anti-communist statement. Conrad Hilton explicitly
remarked that extending his hotel chain to foreign turf was a Cold War statement
as well as a rational financial venture:

> Let me say right here that we operate hotels abroad for the same reason that
> we operate them in this country—to make money for our shareholders. . . .
> However, we feel that what we are saying about liberty, about communism,

about happiness, that we as a nation must exercise our great strength and power for good against evil. . . . We mean these hotels as a challenge . . . to the way of life prescribed by the communist world.[53]

The architecture of the El Salvador Sheraton, with its secure perimeter and long views, like the many Sheratons and Hiltons around the world, housed a presumably secure clientele that could peruse the outer landscape without being subject to its dangers: "The extended vista [is available] through the plate glass windows, offering visual control of an alien urban landscape, from an entirely secure site of observation."[54] However, as it turned out, the Sheraton was less than secure. In 1981, "the watering hole for El Salvador's security-conscious elite" was a murder scene, when "three top agrarian reform officials" were assassinated by masked gunmen.[55] Eight years later, a rebel insurgency temporarily took over the hotel, forcing U.S. soldiers to barricade themselves inside, as the guests were evacuated.

In Stone's film, the Sheraton figures in one of the most powerful and telling visual dynamics.[56] Reflecting the way *Salvador*'s moving images think, there is a piece of referential montage involving cigars.[57] During the first Sheraton Hotel scene, Boyle runs into the American colonel Bentley Hyde, whom he had known through his reporting assignments during the Vietnam War. After Hyde makes a few contemptuous remarks about "commie" sympathizers like Boyle, he lights a cigar and offers one to Boyle, which Boyle accepts, in part because he is trying to convince Hyde to get him on to a military mission in the countryside for a photographic shoot. The second cigar scene takes place in a seedy, seemingly locals-only, downtown restaurant/bar, where Boyle and friends are receiving menacing looks from local men. After Boyle states that the situation looks dangerous, his remark is registered by an elderly woman, who says (in Spanish), while the camera provides a straight-on close-up of her smoking a cigar, "Yes, we're living in a bad time." Given the difference in spatial context between her cigar and the one the colonel is smoking in the earlier scene (notably hers is short and stubby while his is long and phallic), the reference to the local reality of a "bad time" constitutes a critique of the colonel's Cold War, geopolitical model in which an outside conspiracy is blamed.

A politically relevant temporality as well as a spatiality emerges in that later cigar scene. The old woman's reference to "time" evokes a different history, one that has been suppressed by the Cold War, Western democracy–versus–East bloc communism imaginary. Harry Harootunian describes the Cold War-engendered forgetfulness of alternative histories that the cigar montage throws into relief:

> The massive polarization staged by the contest between the so-called free world and the totalitarian dictatorships—between democracy and Marxist-Leninist communism—narrowed the compass of competing alternatives, forcing them out of the field of contention or encouraging their assimilation into one pole or the other.[58]

*Figure 2.7* Colonel Hyde with cigar
Courtesy of MGM

The other significant referential montage involves two episodes of Boyle's clasping of hands. The first takes place after the nuns are raped and murdered by Salvadoran national guardsmen. When Boyle sees his friend Cathy's body, he takes off his ring and puts it on a finger of her lifeless, muddy hand. The second is the above-noted moment when Boyle clasps the hand of his dying fellow photojournalist, John Cassady. These connections between Boyle and exemplary characters, one selfless and the other courageous, seem to help him bring out the repressed politicized and humanitarian self that had been hitherto over-mastered by the survival-striving self. Boyle is ultimately a mobile subject. If one then recalls the trajectory of face shots of Boyle, it becomes evident that the shifty-eyed Boyle has been displaced more and more frequently by an ideologically resolute Boyle, whose face begins to register moral indignation and political purpose. As the film progresses, its center is occupied by what Deleuze calls affection images, which are close-ups that show a subject—in this case Boyle—taking account of itself while situated "between a perception which is troubling in certain respects and a hesitant action."[59]

After the deaths of his friends, there is a scene in which he is again with Colonel Hyde and the well-coiffed and -pressed State Department official Jack Morgan, with whom he had earlier conversed at the Sheraton. But this time, instead of

*Figure 2.8* Old woman with cigar
Courtesy of MGM

grinning and accepting Hyde's taunts and the Cold War rhetoric (also parroted by the yuppie Yale man–turned–State Department official Morgan), in order to get a favor, Boyle contests forcefully their Cold War political discourse. What is registered in his new face emerges in his utterances. Even though he wants Hyde to provide his lover, Maria (Elpedia Carrillo), with papers that will allow her to leave El Salvador with him, his new, more politicized persona is the one speaking:

> You've been lying about the number of advisers here, you've been getting "trainers" here on TDY . . . and you've lied about the switching of the so-called humanitarian assistance money into the Salvadoran military coffers— and you've lied by saying this war can be won militarily.

This is the point at which Boyle, the liar, has become Boyle the truth teller in both aural and visual registers. Along with the change in his facial expression is a change in the proportions of his discourse. Increasingly, a political commentary on the duplicitous U.S. role in El Salvador displaces his special pleading. However, the viewing audience is well prepared for the oppositional Boyle, because he is a subversive body from the beginning of the film.

If with Deleuze we recognize the "haecceity" of the cinematic body, a body not understood in terms of its substance or the functions it performs, but rather in terms of "the sum total of the material elements belonging to it under given relations of movement and rest, speed and slowness . . . [and] . . . the sum total of its affects and local movements, differential speeds . . . [and its] capacities to affect and be affected," we are alerted to Boyle as not a mere type but as a vehicle of change.[60] In particular, the change from Boyle the self-preoccupied liar to Boyle the politicized truth teller is registered in the discomfort he feels and the discomfort he creates in all of his relationships—with friends, wives, and lovers on the one hand and with bureaucratic, political, military, and journalist personnel on the other. As a disruptive and disrupted body throughout *Salvador*—disrupting all personal relationships and the illusions of the U.S. operatives enacting and reporting the events—Boyle's moving body conveys the meaning and stakes involved in the U.S. proxy war.

Vincent Amiel's observations about subversive cinematic bodies can contribute to our recognition of the moving Boyle effect. He refers to:

the cinematographic body [which] is no longer an object of film or knowledge; rather it is a model of knowledge via editing . . . [it is] simultaneously that which is filmed and that which (re)organizes the film in the mind/body of the spectator . . . [becoming the] source rather than the object of cinema.[61]

While in what Amiel calls "classic cinema" the moving bodies were simply vehicles for a story—in his terms, the tendency was to "abandon the body's density for the exclusive profit of its functionality," so that it was merely "at the service of narrative articulations"[62]—in much of contemporary cinema, and Stone's *Salvador* is an exemplar, "the idea is for the cinema to dis-organ-ize the body . . . by means of revealing its fragmented nature, by extracting from it the 'yoke of unity' and consciousness, by giving it back the complexity of its own determinations."[63] Thus, as the viewer witnesses the different Boyles, struggling within the same body, the complexity that emerges provides a radical contrast with the ideationally suborned bodies of the official American operatives and licensed members of the press, who perform as mere vehicles for the Cold War geopolitical imaginary and show no sensitivity or vulnerability to a Salvador convulsed with violence. Afflicted by what he sees, Boyle serves not to reproduce Cold War thinking but to provoke critical thought.

Effectively, the film's viewers experience a double affliction. By creating a complexity in Boyle's moving and grief-afflicted body, Stone's *Salvador* thinks. And by juxtaposing spaces through cuts between the anesthetizing space of a franchised environment, where people are comfortably consuming hospitality, and spaces of violence and repression where people are suffering, the viewers are confronted with a massive crime of indifference and complicity because they too are afflicted by what they have seen. While watching the protected foreign supporters of the aristocracy's violently protected privilege on-screen (the scenes at the San Salvador Sheraton Hotel), the viewers have the advantage of knowing what has been transpiring off-screen and how it gives the lie to the Cold War conceits driving U.S. policy.

## Conclusion: the fate of human rights in El Salvador and since

What can one understand about the present by heeding the United States–Salvador connection, a form of preemption-by-proxy, as it is critically rendered in Stone's film? It should be recalled that the victory of the right-wing reactionary forces over the insurgency in El Salvador was not won only through the battles in the countryside. What was preempted, with a combination of U.S. assistance and the United States' failure to press consistently for human rights, was the political vitality of the alliance between the urban Salvadoran intellectual and the working classes. And "vitality" is more than a metaphor. By the time the "political murders committed by the armed forces and the death squads [had] declined precipitously [in 1984]," it was not simply because of U.S. policy pressure (although there was some pressure) but because "so many targets had already been eliminated."[64] Paying no heed to distinctions between actual revolutionaries and political opposition, the armed forces and death squads murdered thousands in the cities. As a result, little political opposition was left. As Benjamin Schwarz points out, at a critical political juncture "the guerillas simply did not have enough allies left alive in San Salvador to organize a general strike."[65]

What is comparable between the U.S. support of a murderous regime in El Salvador in the 1980s and U.S. policy in the war on terror is the absence of an effective U.S. human rights policy. In the case of the former, obsessed with the Cold War paradigm, and fearing the "loss" of El Salvador, seen as one pawn in an East bloc political takeover of Central America and beyond, U.S. policy makers ignored human rights abuses, except to "make American aid to a homicidal regime more palatable" by falsely claiming that the Salvadoran government was making progress in human rights.[66] In the case of the latter, the war on terror, the United States has been recruiting allies as jailers and interrogators of "detainees"—for example in Uzbekistan, where "seven months before Sept. 11, 2001, the State Department issued a human rights report [that was] a litany of horror . . . tortures [such as] beating, often with blunt weapons, and asphyxiation with a gas mask." And "international human rights groups reported that torture in Uzbek jails included boiling of body parts, using electroshock on genitals and plucking off fingernails with pliers."[67]

Right after September 11, 2001, the United States established a base in Uzbekistan, to serve as a place from which to attack the Taliban in Afghanistan. Subsequently the United States used Uzbekistan as a surrogate jailer. However, as was the case in El Salvador in the 1980s, the behavior of their "ally," the Uzbekistan government, has been an embarrassment: "In the early spring of 2004, after a series of suicide bombings in Tashkent killed 47 people, many of them Uzbek police officers, the government cracked down against people on religious grounds, setting off international condemnation." And "three months later . . . the State

Department said it would cut $18 million in military and economic aid to Uzbekistan because of its failure to improve its human rights record."[68] However, just a month later, the chairman of the Joint Chiefs of Staff, General Richard B. Myers, visited Tashkent and announced that an additional $21 million in aid would be forthcoming from the Pentagon, allegedly to help Uzbekistan get rid of its biological weapon stockpile. Why provide such support? Apparently the violence-by-proxy that the Uzbeks supply trumps U.S. official concern with human rights: "General Myers said that the United States had 'benefitted greatly from our partnership and strategic relationship with Uzbekistan'" and that "'In my view, we shouldn't let any single issue drive a relationship with any single country. It doesn't seem to be good policy to me.'"[69]

Although Michael Moore's documentary *Fahrenheit 9/11* provides an important critique of aspects of the war on terror and the victimization of Iraqi civilians after the U.S. invasion, an Oliver Stone-type film history about the U.S. war on terror as a whole, which contains direct and violent intervention as well as proxy or outsourced violence, has yet to be made. What kind of history does a Stone film provide? Robert A. Rosenstone supplies an appropriate thumbnail sketch. The sequences in Stone's historical films, he writes, are:

> a cunning mixture of diverse visual elements—fact, near fact, displaced fact, invention . . . [and such a sequence] refers to the past, it prods the memory, but can we call it history? Surely not history as we usually use the word, not history that attempts to accurately reproduce a specific, documentable moment of the past. Yet we might see it as a generic historical moment, a moment that claims its truth by standing in for many such moments.[70]

The more difficult question that arises is whether cinema can be effective history, whether it can influence perspectives in the present by refiguring the past. Thanks to the archiving process by which films are preserved and are therefore available for ongoing viewing and critical commentary, that question remains open in each individual case. The treatment here of Stone's *Salvador* extends and reinflects for the present the kind of intervention that *Salvador*'s production and original showing intended. Here and now, as was the case with Stone's artistic rendering of the war in El Salvador, cinema-as-critique can turn attention toward war's victims. Once the world has achieved some distance from the violence associated with the current war on terror (which is not simply targeted on those whose violence provoked the disproportionate and badly aimed reactions that have produced an overwhelming degree of death and destruction and have ignored the legal and ethical bases of human rights), one would hope that the victims are the ones that will rise above the threshold of historical recognition. In chapter 3, such issues of an ethics of recognition are foregrounded.

# 3 Fogs of war

## Introduction: epistemologies of perception

In J. M. Coetzee's novel *The Master of Petersburg*, there is a conversation between a fictional Dostoevsky and the former landlady of his deceased stepson, Pavel, as Dostoevsky is about to read Pavel's diary:

LANDLADY: There is something I should warn you of, Fyodor Mikhailovich. Pavel made a certain cult of his father—of Alexander Isaev, I mean.
DOSTOEVSKY: How does one romanticize a person like that?
LANDLADY: By seeing him through a haze.[1]

The landlady's reference to Pavel's way of seeing has a significant intellectual history. Since the self-described "Copernican Revolution" in philosophy occasioned by Immanuel Kant's First Critique, it is widely recognized that the relationship of consciousness to its objects is productive rather than merely representational, that it is not the nature of the object that makes representation possible; rather, it is the nature of a structure and dynamics of apprehension that create the conditions of possibility for the emergence of an object of perception. Accordingly, post-Kantian developments in philosophy and psychology have offered a phenomenological view of perception. On this view, what is perceived is a function of a proleptic set of expectations, followed by an organization of consciousness that assimilates the world of objects and events in a way that coheres with those expectations.[2] When we are able to note a marked failure of perception—cases of misrecognition of persons or objects—one can attribute it to the fogging effects of a productive consciousness rather than to a haze that exists in the world, intervening between understanding or vision and object. Kant did not pursue his notion of the productivity of consciousness far enough to theorize the split that Lacan famously noted between the eye and the gaze, where what the subject is able to perceive is mediated by expectations based on what is prior to the eye, the "cultural screen" or "repertoire of representations by means of which our culture figures all those many varieties of 'difference,'" which mediate not only how we see the object world but also how we locate ourselves.[3] As Lacan puts it, "the gaze" performs like a phantom force, directing vision while remaining unobserved:

> In our relation to things, in so far as this relation is constituted by the way of vision, and ordered in the figures of representation, something slips, passes, is transmitted, from stage to stage, and is always to some degree eluded in it— that is what we call the gaze.[4]

In this Lacanian sense, misrecognition is not to be juxtaposed to correct perception. Rather, perception itself is predicated on misrecognition because it constitutes the subject's relation to "the real"; what is perceived is what is filtered through the gaze or "cultural screen" that is the condition of possibility for subjectivity. Heedless of the phenomenology of perception, and the extent to which everything that is visible is, as Lacan puts it, "a trap" (inasmuch as the culturally mediated action of achieving the visible locates us in a way that constitutes at once an invisible), war and security analysts, borrowing Clausewitz's rendering of "the fog of war," attribute the results and limits of perception to the lack of a clear view of the terrains of battle. In Clausewitz's terms, "War is the realm of uncertainty; three quarters of the factors on which action is based are wrapped in a fog of greater or lesser uncertainty."[5] Accordingly, neo-Clausewitzian war analysts impute the fog of war to external conditions rather than collectively engendered mentalities. For example, in a treatise on contemporary warfare, Admiral William A. Owens refers to a "view" of the battlefield that is "spotty" and proposes ways to overcome "the fog of war [that for example] continued to pervade military operations . . . as late as The Gulf War."[6] Seemingly without inhibition, he expresses his hope for the lethal potential of modern computer technology: "Having been a career military office for thirty-five years, I believe the computer revolution, if correctly applied, presents us with a unique opportunity to transform the U.S. military into a lethal, effective and efficient armed force."[7]

The influence of the admiral's treatise on the defense establishment is clouded in uncertainty. Nevertheless, since the Gulf War, the concern he expresses has been addressed with new technologies of military vision, among which is the Predator, treated in chapter 1. Recalling the episode discussed in that chapter, the killing of three non-combatants by a remote operator controlling a Predator Drone from a computer, we can be encouraged to think about the questions that are begged when an ocular metaphor dominates the conceptual frame of strategic thinking's quest for certainty. As a media report on the Predator's successor, the "Reaper" (aka the "hunter-killer," which is four times heavier, twice as fast, and a carrier of many more weapons), reads: "The Reaper is expected to be flown as the Predator is— by a two-member team of pilot and sensor operator who work at computer controls and video screens that display what the UAV [unmanned aerial vehicle] 'sees.'"[8]

If we heed the issue within the philosophical idiom with which this analysis begins, the lethal consequences of the strategic model of vision can be ascribed to the phenomenology of military seeing, the screens pertaining to national culture as well as to particular military cultures. As the example of the three dead non-combatants implies, the sense derived from seen objects is not merely a function of the degree of optical resolution; it derives from the projects and culturally induced expectations of the observer. The substitution of a targeted bin Laden for an innocent "tall man" and his companions was a function of culturally based, conceptual overdetermination rather than optical over- or underexposure. To place that conceptual determination in a more general frame, such episodes of ocular enmity are inflected by state-centered biopolitical commitments, by institutionalized and event-engendered extra-juridical policy decisions about protected versus expendable bodies. A pattern of official enmity, developed in the political arena and subsequently militarized, creates the predicates for the hostile ways of seeing immanent in defense and war policies and implemented at the points of lethal contact. Once we heed an approach to apprehension that treats a phenomenology of military seeing, the "fog of war" shifts its locus from the condition of the battlefield to the institutionalized perspectives and practices within which enmity is generated and reproduced.

The displacement of military rationality with critique requires reflection on the conditions of possibility for the emergence of the bodies that become targets of the "effective and efficient" lethality that the admiral (among others) seeks. Two recent films, Danis Tanovic's feature film *No Man's Land* (2001) and Errol Morris's documentary *The Fog of War* (2004), are realizations of such a critical displacement of the fog of war concept. In different ways and focusing on different wars, they provide challenges to the persistence of the neo-Clausewitzian approach to the fog of war. I turn first to Danis Tanovic's feature film *No Man's Land*, which begins with fog imagery and goes on to employ cinematic technology in the service of a critique of the enmities driving the war in Bosnia. Tanovic's feature film relocates the fog of war in the mentalities generating the enmities that have led to the war.

## Alternative "shocks and awes"

"Shock and awe" was the expression used by President George W. Bush's administration to describe the strategy involved in their massive air strikes at the outset of their March 2004 attack on Iraq. The rationale behind this war strategy, developed in an influential treatise published by the National Defense University Press, has as its aim "Rapid Dominance [which] rests in the ability to affect the will, perception, and understanding of the adversary through imposing sufficient Shock and Awe."[9] As is the case with Admiral Owens's treatise on the fog of war, the Ur-text for the *Shock and Awe* monograph is Clausewitz's *On War*. In contrast, Tanovic employs a critical rather than lethal approach to shock. His *No Man's Land* begins in a thick fog, as a patrol of Bosnians move across a field, temporarily shielded from their Serb antagonists.

As the fog lifts, another symbolic one descends. The commander halts his men in a grove of trees and says, "Guys, we'll wait here until the fog lifts." However, after all but two of the previously obscured soldiers are killed from the Serb position across the frontier, once they are visible, and one of the survivors makes it into the protection of a trench (the other survivor is dragged in as well and

*Figure 3.1* The Bosnian patrol
Courtesy of MGM

becomes conscious later in the film), much of the rest of the film treats a dialogue
between this survivor, Ciki (Branko Duric), and a Serb soldier sent out to look for
remnants of the Bosnian patrol, Nino (Rene Bitorajac), whom he encounters in the
trench. As the rhythms of their dialogue are shaped by the rhythms of conflicting
moments of coercion, as one versus the other holds a gun, it becomes evident that
the fog that remains is a function of the ethnic mythologies through which
antagonistic perceptions are screened.

Ultimately, the encounter between the antagonists, each of whose mundane and
vulnerable humanity is rendered in close-ups, belies the grounds of their mutual
hostility. For example, the Bosnian militiaman wears a T-shirt with clashing
insignia, a blood stain from a shoulder wound, and a large cartoon animal on the
front. The semiotics of the two antagonists' humanity (the Serb is in printed boxer
shorts), along with their comical conversations about who is to blame for the war,
serves as a microcosm for the absurdity of the wider conflict, which is rendered in
the ironies delivered by the shifting and layered film narrative as it exposes the
irrational enmities and hypocrisies of all parties to the conflict—antagonists, UN
peacekeepers, and journalists, among others. In Tanovic's treatment of war, the
fog therefore clears only materially; it remains dense as the pseudo-ethnic basis of
the antagonisms and in the conceits of the "humanitarian" forces.

In contrast with his characters, Tanovic's critical thematic is rendered cinematically rather than polemically. Because cinema's screen can show what the brain-as-screen cannot—all those contexts that perception tends to eliminate—Tanovic's film shows a world that the antagonists have cancelled in favor of a narrowed gaze. And what *No Man's Land* shows is shocking. The effect Tanovic achieves in the opening scene in a Bosnian landscape is reminiscent of Alfred Hitchcock's many cinematic landscape moments. Hitchcock's camera typically only begins by enacting a survey of a seemingly natural scene. Eventually, as the filming proceeds, it becomes evident that there is a perverse element in the landscape, for example in *North by Northwest* a biplane crop duster fogging the ground in an area where (as a bystander tells Roger Thornhill/Cary Grant) there are no crops to dust. A commentator on such Hitchcockian landscape scenes puts it astutely: "The film's movement invariably proceeds from landscape to stain, from overall shot to close-up, and this movement invariably prepares the spectator for the event."[10] Effectively, Hitchcock draws the audience's attention to the perversions sequestered within the seemingly benign and conventional scenes.

As he testifies, Tanovic seeks a similar effect. When the fog lifts during the opening sequence of *No Man's Land*, a beautiful, sunlit pastoral landscape is suddenly corrupted by death. There is a sudden cut from a panoramic shot of the landscape to a view through the telescopic site of a weapon, trained on the head of the patrol's commander. And after he is shot in the forehead, tank and machine gun fire dispatch all but two of the rest of the patrol. And subsequently, while filming the drama of the antagonism and shifting dominance of the Bosnian and Serb protagonists in the trench, Tanovic's camera pulls back to a panorama shot that makes the trench appear as a jagged and ugly scar in an otherwise aesthetically pleasing landscape. Describing the effect of the perversion visited on a seemingly unsullied and pacific landscape, Tanovic invokes the concept of the shock, noting that "seeing a black bullet hole in a building or a crater made by a shell in a field" encourages one to speculate about the production of shock in works of art. To illustrate the effects, he suggests, "Imagine if someone imposed a black-and-white photograph on a Van Gogh painting and you will understand what one feels when seeing this. The disharmony was a kind of visual shock." Tanovic adds that he strives for such an effect in the opening scenes of *No Man's Land*:

> This shock is something I have reproduced through my film. On one side, a long summer day—perfect nature, strong colors—and on the other human beings and their black madness. . . . Panoramic shots of landscape become unexpectedly mixed with nervous details of action.[11]

In chapter 4 I introduce a cinematic aesthetic based on a post-Kantian treatment of the sublime, and thus on the way representation loses its coherence because of events and contexts whose boundaries are too ambiguous to allow for easy conceptual domestication. Here I am emphasizing a cinematic aesthetics based on the "shock of the real." Beatriz Jaguaribe captures a shock-of-the-real cinematic aesthetics in her analysis of contemporary cinematic treatment of Brazil's favelas:

*Figure 3.2* Landscape with trench
Courtesy of MGM

The term "shock of the real" refers to specific representations in both written narratives and visual images that unleash an intense, dramatic discharge that destabilizes notions of reality itself. The "shock" element resides in the nature of the event that is portrayed and in the convincing usage of a "reality effect" that, nevertheless, disrupts normative patterns.[12]

Jaguaribe's approach presumes a phenomenology in which one's usual relationship with experience is filtered through already-formed expectations that must be shocked if they are to be disrupted. As one treatment of the aesthetics of shock asks, "if we always construct reality through the linguistic features and perpetual schemata of our everyday culture, how can we ever be capable of glimpsing what is truly other; how can we comprehend what underlies these filters?"[13] The aesthetics of shock on such a view is not unlike the aesthetic one can derive from Kant's analytics of the beautiful and sublime inasmuch as the subject's dynamic of apprehension is the constitutive condition of possibility for the disruption. For example, treating the shock value of the literature of the occult, Dorothea von Mücke notes that:

the conventions of psychological realism are undermined not merely at the level of the plot (by the strange concatenation of events and the final conclusion of the tale) but also in the omniscient narrator's manipulation of the reader's own approach to language and communication.[14]

In the case of visual texts as opposed to the discursive forms of literature, an aesthetics of shock stems from the way an image constitutes a perversion of normality. Kaja Silverman explicates the effects of such a perversion in an analysis of a photographic sequence beginning with "a woman wearing a Star of David moving in medium shot in front of a line of Jewish men being inspected by a Nazi soldier [in Auschwitz]." Silverman quotes the commentary accompanying the photographic sequence:

> A woman has arrived at Auschwitz; the camera captures her in movement. The photographer has his camera installed and as the woman passes by he clicks the shutter—in the same way he would cast a glance at her in the street, because she is beautiful.[15]

Treating the sequence's shock effect, Silverman writes, "At first, this text is shocking in its imputation to the Jewish woman and her Nazi photographer of viewing relations which we associate with 'normality,' and which seem unthinkable within a context like Auschwitz." Silverman goes on to treat the "specular relations" of the Nazi system of detection, within which inmates were subjected to "a hyperbolic visibility, stripping them of their clothes and possessions," and goes on to look at the issue from a critical point of view, which for her involves displacing the perceptual screen through which the Nazis constructed Jewishness in the camps: "The critical problem faced by the Auschwitz inmate is how to be 'photographed' differently—how to motivate the mobilizing of another screen."[16] While the main emphasis of Silverman's form of critique involves the mobilization of a "resistant look," her reference to "mobilizing a different screen" can be applied usefully to the critical displacement that Tanovic's *No Man's Land* enacts.

Walter Benjamin's remarks on the impact of Dadaistic poetry and art provide an additional context for the way that Tanovic achieves both his shock effect and his displacement of the perceptual screens governing the antagonisms in the Bosnian war. Benjamin figures the shock effect in the idiom of war weapons: "From an alluring appearance or persuasive structure of sound the work of art of the Dadaists became an instrument of ballistics. It hit the spectator like a bullet, it happened to him, thus acquiring a tactile quality."[17]

That effect, Benjamin asserts, is even more pronounced in the case of film, because "the painting invites the spectator to contemplation; before it the spectator can abandon himself to his associations, before the movie frame he cannot do so. No sooner has his eye grasped a scene than it is already changed." Thus, he concludes:

> The spectator's process of association in view of these images is indeed interrupted by their constant, sudden change. This constitutes the shock effect of the film, which, like all shocks, should be cushioned by heightened presence

of mind. By means of its technical structure, the film has taken the physical shock effect out of the wrappers in which Dadaism had, as it were, kept it inside the moral shock effect.[18]

Tanovic's shock-by-juxtaposition is thus enhanced by the very nature of critically used film form. His camera does not simply provide a linear narrative of an unfolding episode by following the movements of his two protagonists in the trench. Instead, he uses what Gilles Deleuze calls the "time image."[19] Instead of creating movement images to focus solely on the issues and tensions explicitly recognized by the antagonists, Tanovic's camera "creates time images that respond to the critical thinking of the orchestrated cinematic apparatus rather than the modes of consciousness of the film's actors."[20] He thereby substitutes the critically oriented cinematic screen for the (conflict-addled) brain-as-screen, which governs the perceptions of the actor-subjects.

## Tanovic's *No Man's Land*

Cartographically, the images and narrative in *No Man's Land* articulate a complex set of interactions among warscapes, ethnoscapes, and mediascapes. The actor-subjects within the warscape are unclear about where they are and what constitutes their responsibilities. At the outset of the film, before the fog clears, one of the members of a Bosnian patrol—a "relief squad" lost in a fog—expresses skepticism about the leadership of their commander: "Fuck me if he knows where we are!" While the remark has immediate reference to the confusion about where they are vis-à-vis the Serb lines, it also expresses the larger ambiguities about the relationship of the different ethnic communities to the evolving, post-Yugoslav territorial and ethnic antagonisms. As the Bosnian poet Semezdin Mehmedinovic points out, the Bosnian Serb leader Radovan Karadzic's insistence "that people of different nationalities couldn't live together," based on "creating a reality to fit his lies," produced a confusion between the former life-world of Bosnia and the newly imposed "reality." Reacting to that "reality," Mehmedinovic writes, "The truth was quite the opposite: peoples of different cultures had lived together for so long in Bosnia, and the ethnic mix was so deep, that any separation could only be accomplished through extreme violence and bloodshed."[21]

Mehmedinovic's figuration for what was required to instantiate the new reality is linguistic. He writes about the subjugation "to a disturbingly reductive vocabulary."[22] For Mehmedinovic, a resistance to the lies supporting Karadzic's new reality would require the kind of "word abundance"[23] that transcends nationality. He notes that the current imposed separations violate what Sarajevo and Bosnia-Herzegovina have been about historically—places where cultures were blended rather than separated, where, for example, rather than a single "national literature" "you could not say that the literature . . . was Bosnian or Croatian or Serbian."[24]

Tanovic uses visual rather than discursive tropes to convey the violence associated with the newly imposed, radically differentiated ethnic imaginaries. The Serb and Bosnian antagonists view each other through telescopic sights and binoculars. The first view of the lost Bosnian patrol is through the telescope of the rifle that shoots the commander in the forehead. Then, once the surviving Bosnians and the Serbs sent to eliminate possible survivors are in the trench, both sides peer at the trench through binoculars. While in terms of the immediate logistical problem the two sides are gathering data from a safe distance, in terms of Tanovic's critique of the war they are displaying the narrowed gaze of antagonists. Just as in Mehmedinovic's frame the war is promoted by a linguistic impoverishment, in Tanovic's it is encouraged by narrowed scopic regimes.

Briefly, the narrative dimension of the film is as follows: Two wounded soldiers, Ciki, a Bosnian (Branko Duric), and Nino, a Serb (Rene Bitorajac), end up together in a trench between their respective lines. The relationship is alternatively antagonistic and accommodating, and their plight is complicated by the existence of another Bosnian soldier in the trench, Cera (Filip Sovagovic), who is immobilized on top of a landmine. A French sergeant from UNPROFOR, the UN protective force, takes the lead in trying to help the three soldiers, despite the rescue being resisted by UNPROFOR's high command. UNPROFOR's commands—in both Bosnia and Zagreb (run by French and British commanders respectively)—finally decide to help, only because of media pressure, after a reporter from a British television network learns of the problem. But ultimately, the détente between Ciki and Nino breaks down. After Ciki and Nino are shot, the UN operatives in UNPROFOR cannot figure out how to disarm the mine. As a result, Cera is ultimately abandoned (after the rescuers deceive the media and pretend he has been saved and is being taken to a hospital).

However, to appreciate the force of Tanovic's approach to the war, we have to turn to images, which, among other things, allow us to recognize the way the landscape constitutes one of his protagonists. While his cuts back and forth to the Bosnian and Serb lines show antagonistic ways of seeing, accompanied by deadly opinions, his cuts to the landscape show a benign nature, which, as Nietzsche famously put it, has "no opinion." Here, Tanovic's use of landscape is reminiscent of the pioneering use of landscape by Roberto Rossellini in his war trilogy. Sandro Bernardi has captured that use in a treatment of Rossellini's *Paisa*, at a moment when two lovers, Carmela and Joe, "are sitting on the broken windowsill, on the boundary between two different worlds: inside and outside":

> The camera lens examines in close-up the faces of the two young people talking. It then looks at the distant murmuring sea in the half-light, far but also near. . . The bullet that comes from the sea does not only kill Joe but also reaches us, killing our expectations of a love scene.[25]

The opening scene in Tanovic's *No Man's Land* is almost precisely homologous. Before the fog lifts, we see close-ups of a group of men enjoying comradely intimacy—joking, sharing cigarettes, and engaging in mock disparagements. When the shots are fired from the midst of the landscape, killing all but two in the patrol, *our* expectations of enjoying a continuing comradeliness are killed. Thereafter, in a telling scene that speaks to the shallowness of the violent ethnic imaginaries, the

Serb, Nino, has been forced at gunpoint by the surviving Bosnian, Ciki, to stand outside the trench and wave a shirt (as a white flag) to discourage the Serbian side from bombarding them. First we get a mid-range shot of Nino, naked except for his shoes and boxer shorts. Then the camera pulls back to behind the Bosnian lines, where, seeing Nino through their binoculars from their side, two Bosnians wonder whether he is a Bosnian or a Serb. One of them says, "What the hell is he?" and the other replies, "It's not written on his boxers!" In a subsequent scene, when the bombardment begins, because Nino had been identified as a Serb, both Ciki and Nino, in a rare moment of cooperation, stand outside the trench, waving white flags while facing their respective lines. Effectively, Tanovic's images articulate the difference between the arbitrary ethnic ascriptions driving the war and thus alienating the men from each other and the men themselves, stripped to their bare humanity so that their differences cannot be discerned.

After their brief moment of cooperation, Ciki becomes once again aware of the persistence of the Bosnian–Serbian antagonism and says, "Next time we see each other, it will be through a gun's sight." Here, as elsewhere, Tanovic identifies guns as more than killing instruments. For example, as noted, the rhythms of coercion in the trench are a function of one versus the other holding a gun, but what is coerced, aside from either Ciki or Nino having the other do his bidding, is "truth."

*Figure 3.3* Ciki and Nino
Courtesy of MGM

Only at gunpoint is either willing to say that his side is responsible for the war. For Tanovic, the gun-as-trope reflects the vagaries of the forcefully imposed truths during the war. The truths that Tanovic explores comport precisely with the ones that Foucault addressed throughout his investigation, the "connections between mechanisms of coercion and contents of knowledge."[26]

Tanovic does not restrict his parody of the war to the space of the separate lines. Once it becomes clear that the wounded men in the trench, Ciki, Nino, and Cera (who is immobilized on top of a mine because his body has been booby-trapped by Nino's field commander), are victims of remote forces, Tanovic's cuts to the UNPROFOR headquarters in Bosnia and Zagreb extend the warscape internationally. Moreover, this extended warscape contains other levels of insensitivity to the life-world for which the international community is supposed to be supplying protection. For example, when the Bosnia UNPROFOR group is first engaged, Tanovic cuts to a remote conversation between a UN peacekeeping outpost and some of its field operators. As the conversation proceeds in the jargon of coded military communication (between "Arizona 2" and "Tango"), the UN presence is also rendered as a perverse stain. Cuts to a serene landscape are shown as staccato UN exchanges are heard: "Affirmative, over"; "Negative, over"; "Over and out." Apart from the shock effect of the juxtaposition of an aesthetically rendered landscape and the sounds of military bureaucracy, the talk itself is rendered disjunctively. After the conventional coded conversation on the UN's wireless system, the camera returns to the UN outpost, which is operating under an injunction to stay out of hostilities, and one of the UN officers says, "Why the fuck are we here?," thus reflecting the same ambiguities about ethnic territorial imaginaries as the opposing Bosnians and Serbs.

Ultimately, the conflict is rendered perverse on an international scale. Tanovic indicts the UN with a juxtaposition of shots between the violence on the battlefield and the UN command office in Zagreb, where a commander sits in a book-lined library, playing chess with a secretary with whom he is obviously intimate, while he says he can do nothing about the problem in the trench without a vote of the UN General Assembly. Thereafter, Tanovic's narrative and images expand the indictment, treating the relays between the warscape and mediascape in two ways. In terms of the primary dramatic narrative, he has a British TV journalist intervene to force the hand of an UNPROFOR command that would otherwise ignore the plight of the wounded men in the trench. However, much more powerful than the fictional narrative, which shows a media more interested in capturing its audience with scoops than with the human costs of the war, are Tanovic's cuts to documentary footage of bodies strewn around the city- and landscapes and buildings burning, interspersed with media footage of political leaders—for example Mitterrand's pledging of "humanitarian aid," and the United States' 6th fleet being deployed, while the United States and others are participating in a weapons embargo that leaves the Bosnians unable to protect themselves from Serbian firepower. The deaths of the men in the trench are shown, by dint of the cinematically rendered details of their stories, to be a microcosm of the war's larger tragedy, a result of the Bosnians' futile attempts to attract effective assistance.

Nevertheless, the film's impact is doubtless based in part on the way feature films can portray people's shared humanity in the face of historical events of violence that summon bizarre pretexts without historical justification. Additionally, its effects are likely a function of the way Tanovic follows a trail blazed by Rossellini and others in the cinema of neo-realism tradition. With its interspersed documentary footage, *No Man's Land* breaches the boundaries between cinematic time and historical time, between the spaces of fiction and those of the life-world, and between feature films and actual documentaries. The Errol Morris McNamara cinematic biography to which I now turn has similar boundary-breaking effects while, at the same time, summoning the fog imagery featured in *No Man's Land*.

## McNamara at war: autobiography and history

> What I find so interesting in philosophy is how it chooses to divide things up: it groups under one concept things you would have thought were different, or it separates things you would have thought belonged together. As for film, it also divides things up, proposing distinct groups of visual and sonorous images. And distinct modes of grouping visual and sonorous images can and do compete with one another.
>
> Gilles Deleuze[27]

Watching Morris's *The Fog of War*, a film that (à la Deleuze) thinks by dint of the divisions and groupings of its visual and sonorous images, has to remind anyone who has been attentive to the media history of the Vietnam War of how persistent America's Vietnam experience remains as a marker in the ongoing autobiographies of those who played a part in shaping it and in the related, continually revised, national self-understandings of the United States as well. Ward Just's post-Vietnam novel *American Blues* articulates the radical entanglement between history and autobiography that the continuing Vietnam-related media events reflect. A writer, the novel's narrator and main character, finds that his return to Vietnam, where he had been posted during the war, fails to produce a resolution that will allow him to complete his history of the war and allow him to achieve a sense of personal resolution as well. As one commentator on the novel puts it, "What the narrator confronts in postwar Vietnam is not historical clarification but new categories of mystery."[28] And, implying that the "mystery" can be attributed to his nation's pervasive conceptual fog that surrounds the Vietnam experience, Just's narrator adds, "I had grown comfortable inside the American illusion and could not comprehend the Vietnamese, so it was hopeless weighing and measuring today against yesterday."[29]

In stark contrast with Just and his narrator, Robert McNamara has committed himself to clarity about the Vietnam experience and to a definitive post-Vietnam pedagogy about the future of war. After seeking to reflect on and illuminate retrospectively his policy-making role during the Vietnam War,[30] he turned from autobiography to dialogue, seeking the kind of enlightenment that he thinks can be derived from treating history in general, and the American–Vietnamese experience in particular, as an "argument without end."[31] Stating that he wanted to "learn from history" and, in particular, to identify the "missed opportunities" to terminate the conflict before it achieved a monstrous death toll, he puts his methodological faith in documents as a corrective to faulty recollections. "The record is clear," he insists, and he proceeds to seek participation by his former enemies, General Giap among others, in a dialogue aimed at identifying "misunderstandings."[32] Although the former Vietnamese leaders turned out to be resistant to McNamara's shared misunderstanding model, his return to Vietnam seemed to satisfy his enlightenment faith nevertheless. With or without full cooperation from his Vietnamese counterparts, he produces "lessons," which he hopes will make the twenty-first century less violent than the twentieth.

Like Norman Schwarzkopf, who returned to Vietnam five years earlier to reflect on *his* personal Vietnam War role as well as to try to affect Vietnam's place within the American collective imagination, McNamara aims much of his effort at the past rather than the future. In Schwarzkopf's case, the return, broadcast in June 1993 as an episode in the CBS television series *CBS Reports with Dan Rather*, was "designed [as I have noted elsewhere] to restore 'the soldier hero' to an honored place in the American political culture."[33] The dialogue between Schwarzkopf and Rather and the cuts to testimony of soldiers who had served under Schwarzkopf in Vietnam (and have also returned seeking resolution by communicating with their former "enemies") focus on the sacrifices they made while serving their country in a war about which they retain doubts as to its official justification.

At a minimum, the Schwarzkopf return, like McNamara's, is more than a lament about the tragedy of warring violence and a commitment to diminish it in the future; it is also a history-rectifying enterprise, working at both autobiographical and national levels.[34] What distinguishes the Rather-assisted Schwarzkopf return from McNamara's is the cooperation of Schwarzkopf's interlocutor, Rather, with the Schwarzkopf perspective and the unambiguous cooperation of their Vietnamese interviewees. Those selected, ranging from business administration students to public officials, seemed eager to participate in a definitive resolution of the former enmities; they testified that they bear no grudges and are eager to bury the past and move on to a successful, entrepreneurial future.

While McNamara's return failed to produce the level of resolution-through-dialogue for which he had hoped, it doubtless seemed to him that the documentary format, in which he produces long monologues in response to queries from someone with whom he has no history, gives him free rein to elaborate his purchase on the "eleven lessons from the life of Robert McNamara" that organize the flow of the documentary and thus allows him to impose the kind of resolution he seeks on his and America's Vietnam experience. Doubtless, he expected effectively to lift the "fog of war" with lucid and progressive thinking. But such documentaries merely give the interviewee the illusion of personal control over meaning making. Reviewer Roger Ebert refers to the documentary's presentation of McNamara's lessons as "his thoughts . . . as extrapolated by Morris."[35] However, extrapolation is hardly the appropriate analytic. McNamara's articulated "thoughts" do not exhaust the narrative space of the documentary. Morris's camera work—the ways in which he frames the speaking McNamara, and the cuts and juxtapositions of his editing, as McNamara's words are interspersed with historical, archival footage and taped conversations (along with contrapuntal cast of Philip Glass's musical score)—renders a conflicting, dysnarrative challenge to McNamara's accounts. Ultimately, as I will argue, attention to the form of Morris's documentary reveals alternative loci of meaning making, McNamara's verbalized accounts on the one hand and Morris's assemblage of voices, scenes, and sounds on the other. Rather than lifting the fog of war, Morris's documentary offers conflicting thoughts about what it is that constitutes the fog. The documentary can be seen as a drama that, not unlike feature films on war, renders a context that threatens the sense making of its protagonist.

As I have suggested, documentaries should not be radically distinguished from feature films. Michael Renov, affirming the ambiguity of the distinction, points out that documentary's use of:

> high or low camera angles (. . . effects conventionalized in fiction film and television), close-ups which trade emotional resonance for spatial integrity, the use of telephoto or wide-angle lenses which squeeze or distort space, the use of editing to make time contract, expand or become rhythmic . . . [are all effects that] . . . documentary shares [with] . . . its fictional counterpart.[36]

Given the blurred boundaries between documentaries and feature films, we can observe that many of the effects achieved by Tanovic are reproduced in Morris's McNamara documentary. For example, as in the case of Tanovic's feature film, Morris's camera work creates shocking and disjunctive contexts for the meaning making that McNamara sought to control during the interviews. Like *No Man's Land*, Morris's documentary begins with perverse intrusions on an aesthetically pleasing scene, in this case a seascape. A serene ocean setting is the background for sailors scrambling on a battleship as weapons are loaded into firing positions. And as the weapons- and fighting-despoiled land- and seascapes are shown, the camera cuts to historical footage in which McNamara is shown at a press briefing. *His* weapon in this instance is a pointer, aimed at a map as he addresses the media with an air of supreme confidence. He manifests the same confidence at the beginning of his interview with Morris, as he states that he remembers exactly where the conversation had left off.

As was the case while he addressed the media during the Vietnam War, McNamara seems assured that his words and gestures will make their way through the medium without reinflection or recontextualization. By including both moments, Morris effects a referential montage (where one scene reproduces the significance of another). Such effects align Morris's argumentation-through-documentary with a tradition of documentary filmmaking pioneered by Dziga Vertov, arguably the first to realize the potential of assembling a wide variety of materials and genres through editing in order to turn what may appear to be mere information into political argumentation. As one commentary puts it, "Vertov aspired not to 'inform dispassionately' but, rather, to 'influence the mind in a

*Figure 3.4* Seascape with weapons
Courtesy of Sony Pictures

certain direction.'"[37] Accordingly, in Morris's film, right after McNamara expresses
his sense of control over the interview and proceeds to state his major theme—that
rationality is not sufficient, that leaders can make mistakes that kill people—the
assemblage of shots and sounds imply a different set of forces at work. As the
documentary's historical footage is shown in rapid cuts and juxtapositions, Philip
Glass's contrapuntal musical score contains clashing musical voices that match the
rapidity of the montage. Here, as elsewhere in the documentary, the music doubles
the disharmony between McNamara's and the film's meaning making.

The Glass score has two reinforcing effects on the disjuncture between
McNamara's meaning making and the documentary's. First, the contrapuntal music
conveys alternative, conflicting voices that contrast with McNamara's confident
monologue. Second, the speeded tempo reinforces the rapid, kaleidoscopic
montage, which, along with the music's dark tonalities, suggests that the speed of
events is part of a dangerous dynamic well beyond the control of the rationality
and proportionality that are the primary tropes of McNamara's account. And at
certain moments, for example when the casualties of the fire bombing from the air
are shown, the music shifts from the rhythmic, repetitive tempo to a slowed-down,
threnodic tempo and mood. Glass's use of counterpoint, as opposed to melodic or
lyrical harmonies, effectively reinforces Morris's disruption of the rationalistic talk

that emanates from the defense establishment's habitual discourse. Counterpoint introduces ironies that are conceptually disruptive, in contrast with pleasant melodies that reinforce habitual patterns of thought. As Glass notes, his music is influenced by Samuel Beckett, whose writing delivers exemplary shocks to habitual forms of intelligibility. Accordingly, his music "denies habitual patterns of expectation."[38] Moreover, his score for Morris's documentary displays the quickening emotional tempo he found in Beckett's plays, providing an emotional counterpoint to the cool and methodical tone in McNamara's monologues.

Nevertheless, the most powerful disruptions to McNamara's meaning making in the documentary are visual. Two aspects of Morris's documentary filming wrest control over meaning making and reinflect the interpretations one can derive from McNamara's accounts. The first, most obvious, and more familiar meaning-making effect of the documentary is achieved through the editing process. While documentary evidence belies some of McNamara's accounts, especially his self-positioning as one reluctant to endorse military action during the Cuban Missile Crisis and during the military escalation in Vietnam during Lyndon Johnson's presidency, my focus here is on form, on *how* the cuts to archival footage and taped conversations disturb or alter the contexts that McNamara uses to frame his claims, rather than on their veracity.

Two brief examples of the most significant challenges to McNamara's perspective on his role should suffice. First, under the rubric of lesson number 2: "Rationality will not save us," McNamara asserts the limits of rationality, noting that the world was saved from an all-out nuclear war by luck because all the relevant decision makers were rational. But here his discourse is wholly geopolitical. What was at risk, he says in explicating this lesson (and it is repeated in other segments), is the existence of "nations," by which he means sovereign states. Juxtaposed to his remarks, however, are scenes of populations. The viewer is shown a combination of fast-forwarded panning and tracking shots and slow-motion shots of pedestrians in dense urban venues, a blur of moving crowds with different tempos. Among other things, the juxtaposition is one between geopolitical time—the historical time of nation-states—and the times of the life-world, articulated through moving bodies rather than the geopolitical collectives that McNamara calls "nations." At such moments, McNamara's reasons of state, his macro-level, geopolitical focus, effectively evacuate vulnerable civilians from his scenario, while, in juxtaposition, Morris's editing brings them back, foregrounding the human lives rather than the states that were at risk.

Apart from the way in which McNamara's concern for the survival of nation-states trumps his sympathy with war's human victims is his blindness to the process by which the vaunted "nations" to which he refers came in to existence. However, a brief analysis of the history of "nation-building" makes evident that this concept, so precious to generations of historians and social theorists, is a euphemism inasmuch as the process of nation-building usually involved nation-killing. Accordingly, heeding actual history as opposed to those legendary histories that imagine nations as being formed on the basis of a social contract, Michel Foucault points out that state-initiated legalities or jurisdictions cannot be attributed to a history of an emerging social consensus. Rather, the laws and jurisdictions have followed in the wake of battles.[39] Foucault's historical field of reference is the European continent, but a similar and compelling case has been made for the United States, which took shape as the kind of "nation" to which McNamara refers as a result of "the rule of the gun." Richard Slotkin correctly locates America's national consolidation in its Indian wars rather than in the deliberations leading to its foundational charters.[40] And his analysis should be extended to the violence through which Euro Americans displaced the Californios (the people once occupying California as part of a large Mexican empire). The Mexican Americans, who lived in the far west during the period in which Anglo conquerors took over California, Texas, and the rest of Spanish America, were "those who had been Mexican [and] suddenly found themselves inside the United States [as] foreigners on their own land."[41]

The second challenge to McNamara's account is in the segment treating lesson number 4: "Proportionality should be a guideline in war." There, McNamara evinces an awareness of the slaughter of civilian populations, admitting, in the case of the fire bombing of civilian populations in Japan for example, that he was "part of the mechanism that in a sense recommended it." Here, McNamara's evasive circumlocution clashes with a remark about how his life has been shaped by a commitment to responsibility, which was engendered by the courses in ethics he took at Berkeley. While here, as elsewhere, McNamara's discourse is primarily logistical rather than ethical, Morris's editing situates the mechanisms that deliver violence from a perceptual and technologically mediated distance: meetings of the Joint Chiefs, military planning sessions with maps and charts, teletyped messages, numbers rather than bombs raining down on landscapes, and scenes of industrial production and the fitting out of weapons, alongside scenes of the devastation caused by the bombing: cities destroyed, and heaps of burned and maimed bodies in burned-out landscapes.

The juxtapositions make McNamara's career of logistical distance bizarre and insensitive to the human costs to which his war planning contributed *disproportionately* (as Morris's images point out, for they show many scenes of McNamara in planning session at many levels of executive and military decision making). And they make his vocabulary and grammar, especially when he frequently resorts to the passive voice in this segment, distancing as well. In short, much of the editing process of the documentary changes what McNamara renders as a necessary evil (McNamara's lesson number 9 is: "To do good, you have to do evil") to an evil, followed by its legitimation as necessity.

While in *The Fog of War* the editing carries much of the burden of the documentary's interpretation of the consequences of McNamara's (former and current) perspectives, there is another, more subtle aspect of the camera work that wrests control from McNamara's responses and monologues. Although the interrotron (Morris's filming device) allows McNamara to make eye contact with his interlocutor and thus to look directly at the viewers, he is rarely in the center of the frame. Effectively, the decentering of McNamara is a large part of what I have termed the dysnarrative flow of the documentary. Morris's camera offers us

*Figure 3.5* Rationalized bombing
Courtesy of Sony Pictures

a body that is recalcitrant to the story it is telling. A McNamara that wants to fill the entire space of the narrative fails to command and fill the frame. Often he is shown off to one side and cut off so that one sees him from just below the neck to only part of his head. There are but two moments in which Morris allows McNamara to slide into the middle of the frame. One is the point at which McNamara admits he is "sorry that in the process of accomplishing things that I have made errors." The other is a place in which he notes that, if the United States had lost the war, he and Curtis LeMay, the lieutenant colonel who managed the bombing runs, could have been tried for war crimes. Thus the McNamara who evades responsibility is located out of the center of the frame while the McNamara admitting responsibility is moved to the center. Subtlety and effectively, Morris's camera values candor.

The dysnarrative effect of Morris's continual repositioning of the McNamara body comports with the critical effect of some feature films in which bodies are positioned to resist narrative complicity. To repeat the insight of Vincent Amiel (to which I refer in chapter 2), whereas in classic cinema the tendency was "to utilize the body as a simple vector of the narrative, abandoning its density for the exclusive benefit of its functionality," the more critically oriented, contemporary directors offer a body that is not an "instrument in the service of narrative

*Figure 3.6* The decentered McNamara
Courtesy of Sony Pictures

articulation."[42] Lest there be any doubt about the semiotic effect of the way he distributes McNamara's body around the frame, cutting more at some moments (especially when McNamara is being the least self-disclosing) and less at others, but rarely allowing him a centered and full-bodied exposure, Morris's epilogue seals the effect. At the end of the film, as McNamara is called to account, Morris asks him if he feels "responsible," even "guilty," about his contribution to the enormous loss of life in Vietnam. While McNamara, now seated behind the wheel of a Ford, refuses to answer the question, he is more radically cut than at any previous moment. First, only part of his head and one eye is in the frame; then his whole face is available, but only in the car's rear-view mirror. For McNamara, as he states toward the end of the interview, the "fog of war" is merely war's complexity, the large number of variables one must consider and manage. Morris's filming suggests, however, that the fog is elsewhere; it exists, among other places, in the lens through which McNamara saw and continues to see the world—emphasized in the last shots of McNamara's face (the only ones taken from an oblique angle) in which the most centered element is one lens of his glasses.

Ultimately, the overriding conclusion about his tenure as Secretary of Defense that McNamara wants to emphasize derives from the contrast he sees between what he calls the success of the Kennedy administration's actions during the Cuban

Missile Crisis and the Johnson administration's failure to terminate the Vietnam War before huge casualties occurred. He ascribes the success of the former to "empathy," the ability, in his words, "to get inside the other person's skin," and the failure of the second to lack of empathy. It is clear from his writings as well as from his remarks in Morris's documentary that empathy for McNamara is not an ethical concept. It is, rather, a perception of one's enemy's motives and intentions. The conceptual armament with which McNamara treats the "other" is of a piece with his general tendency to regard the world through a strategic lens. From his perspective, insofar as he has accumulated debts during his career, they are to the people he served in government, not the alterity that was the target of his government's war policy.

However, there is another way to approach one's debts, an alternative to McNamara's perspective on responsibility and to the persistence of the militarized lens through which the United States sees its current "enemies." A Canadian professor of literature, Claude Mark Hurlbert, teaches Iraqi literature in order to overcome the alienation of his students from a people who are represented as, alternatively, fanatic and enigmatic by the militaries and the media of Western powers. Hurlbert draws upon the work of Bill Readings to locate the question of our obligation to "explore the nature of our incalculable obligations to others," which Readings renders as a "network of obligations" that emerges when we can appreciate "singularities," the "unique aggregates of historically specific characteristics existing within webs or relations to other singularities."[43] Hurlbert's and Readings's attention to one's debts to otherness contrasts markedly with McNamara's "empathy," which is a management tool rather than an ethical disposition. The fogging effect of the policy discourses within which McNamara constructed the enemy-other continues to allow him to remain comfortably at home with himself. In contrast, an ethical regard, as Emmanuel Levinas has famously enjoined, allows the other to remain a respected stranger, "who disturbs the being at home with oneself."[44] What is revealed when Morris's documentary lifts the fog of McNamara's strategic thinking is the absence of a self-reflective sense of responsibility to those who turned out to be the victims of the policies that he helped to put in place. A lyrical passage from novelist Arundhati Roy's *The God of Small Things* provides a good summary of the effect of the McNamara documentary. Morris's *The Fog of War* serves to "nudge [McNamara's] hidden morality from its resting place and make it bubble to the surface and float for a while. In clear view. For everyone to see."[45]

## Conclusion: history's victims

In place of a sense of sympathy with his victims, Robert S. McNamara—under the rubric of lesson number 4—suggests that killing should involve a sense of proportion. He admits that perhaps the killing of over a million civilians engineered by Lieutenant Colonel Curtis LeMay (as commander of U.S. bombing units that, for example, burned to death over 100,000 civilians in one night), assisted by McNamara in his role as the "Statistical Control Officer" in charge of "operational planning," was "not proportional." Morris's editing bypasses such circumlocutions, showing documentary footage of the devastation of populated cities and providing on-screen data on what population percentages of deaths in comparable U.S. cities would have ensued.

Adam Gopnik, in an injunction about the responsibilities pertaining to academic scholarship, has an effective response to the self-serving apologies for past violence that enjoin "a sense of proportion":

> Whatever academic scholarship may insist, surely a sense of proportion is the last thing we want from history—perspective certainly, not proportion. Anything, after all, can be seen in proportion, shown to be no worse a crime than some other thing. Time and distance can't help but give us a sense of proportion: it was long ago and far away and so what? What great historians give us instead, is a renewed sense of sorrow and anger and pity for history's victims.[46]

One feature film, Alain Resnais's *Hiroshima Mon Amour*, locates the atom bombing of Hiroshima from the point of view of the human tragedy in an effectively complex way. It is sensitive, disturbing, and ambiguous. Resisting the Argos Company's request that he do a short documentary (because several had already been done), Resnais collaborated with Marguerite Duras on a screenplay that yields no simple interpretation.

It contains documentary footage of the effects of the atomic bombing of the city of Hiroshima and its people in a time-shattering, non-chronological drama that interweaves a one-day love story in one city (Never) with the war story as it unfolds in Hiroshima, after the bombing. The film's characters, two lovers, contrast dramatically with McNamara in that they confess to an epistemic uncertainty. At the end of the film they "acknowledge [an] inability to comprehend either personal or historical tragedy."[47] The film's innovative form and both figural and temporal complexities (with connected and disconnected flashback moments) render it a critical text that continues to provoke ethico-political thinking about war's victims. Despite its deformation of chronology, the film manages to give its "viewers the sensation that what they are going to . . . see is not an author's creation but an element in the real world."[48] If we heed Henri Bergson's famous distinction between voluntary and involuntary memory, the film's aesthetic can be located in the latter. For Bergson, the past is perpetually available and alterable because of the way it can surface, changing its significance as it insinuates itself within the present. In the case of Resnais's film, one sees the past in the present specifically but is encouraged to appreciate, in general, how the past always "is" rather than "was," as it inflects the way perceptions in the present are structured.[49]

While *Hiroshima Mon Amour* began as a documentary project but ended up as a feature film, I want to conclude by examining the documentary I summarize briefly in the Introduction, Linda Hattendorf's *The Cats of Mirikitani*. Hattendorf's *Cats* began as a documentary of a homeless street artist but ended up as a complex and critical treatment of war's victims. Like Resnais's *Hiroshima Mon Amour*,

*Figure 3.7* Jimmy Mirikitani
Courtesy of Createspace

*Cats* re-presents the past from the point of view of the present while at the same time providing sympathy for the Japanese victims of World War II. As a documentary, *Cats* begins with an approach quite similar to Morris's in *The Fog of War*. Hattendorf is off-screen, behind her camera, and intrudes only as an occasional voice, asking questions of her subject. The initial venue for *Cats* is lower Manhattan, where Hattendorf plans simply to do a documentary about a homeless street artist, Jimmy Mirikitani. She follows him to his position on 6th Avenue and zooms in on his colorful drawings of cats and tigers within an Asian-style landscape. When the film begins, it's winter, and a heavily bundled Mirikitani is drawing and responding to questions, first to Linda and then to a visiting Japanese American art professor who looks him up whenever he comes to Manhattan.

Hattendorf's camera occasionally tracks away from its focus on Mirikitani, showing, at one point, time-elapse shots of pedestrians with a speeded tempo that suggests a rapidly moving life-world taking place around Mirikitani. However, given the year in which the documentary is launched, 2006 (i.e. after the 9/11 attack on the World Trade Center), Hattendorf's occasional long depth-of-focus shots, with the Twin Towers in the background, render New York as a warscape rather than merely the venue of a street artist. Not long after such shots, edited in early in the film, we begin to see historical warscapes in Mirikitani's drawing. It turns

*Figure 3.8* Mirikitani's Hiroshima drawing
Courtesy of Createspace

out that he was born in Sacramento, California, but raised in Hiroshima. After returning to California as a young man, he was rounded up with most of the rest of the United States' Japanese Americans and sent to an internment camp in Tule Lake, California, where he was incarcerated for three and a half years and then incarcerated in two other places before coming back to New York. Meanwhile, almost all of his relatives in Hiroshima were killed in the atomic bombing in 1945, when the *Enola Gay* dropped the atomic bomb and, in Jimmy Mirikitani's words, "ashes, everything ashes."

As the documentary proceeds, two alterations take place. The first reveals how Mirikitani's personal memories, which connect with domestic and foreign Japanese collective memories, are inscribed in his drawings. As the process of documentary making reaches the spring of 2001, Mirikitani shows Linda his drawings of the Tule Lake detention camp with flora and fauna (a desert-scape with snakes and jackrabbits) and an ominous watch tower. Mirikitani states that when World War II started "take house, everything—God damn, born Sacramento, California. . . . This is history, you know . . . 120,000 of us out here illegally." He also shows drawings of Hiroshima—some with persimmons: "I eat them all the time as kid . . . I grew up in Hiroshima, beautiful." Others depict the bombing—for example one that he drew to commemorate the day of the bombing, August 6, 1945: "Real atomic bomb there . . . everything ashes . . . 260,000 killed . . . my mother's family was wiped out."

At this point, the second alteration in the documentary takes place, as Hattendorf begins to interweave historical and contemporary warscapes. The time is now post-9/11, and there are cuts back and forth between media footage of the smoking Twin Towers of the World Trade Center and Mirikitani's Hiroshima drawings. Moreover, the post-9/11 present has produced a threat to Mirikitani similar to the one that killed his mother's family; a toxic cloud descends on lower Manhattan, making his street venue unlivable. Hattendorf takes Mirikitani into her apartment to protect him from the toxicity, and together they watch the post-9/11 "war on terror" broadcast on her TV set. Out from behind her camera, which is now set up to witness her interactions with Mirikitani, Hattendorf has become an actor in the film. As they hear reports of the growing war and witness media footage of bombing runs—"Pentagon planning for large-scale air strikes against Afghanistan," says the TV news—Mirikitani says, "Can't make war—five seconds, ashes."

In addition to Mirikitani's voiced reference to the attack on Japanese civilians in Japan, Hattendorf's editing brings the war on terror back to the detention of the United States' Japanese citizens by cutting to a television news account of domestic profiling, with cuts between the television account and framing shots of Mirikitani. By way of summarizing the imperiled freedoms at risk in the war on terror, Hattendorf edits in a television voice saying "History tells us we have often reacted in time of fear by overreacting," while her camera zooms in on Mirikitani's Hiroshima picture, and he is heard saying "Same old story." Shortly thereafter, there is a cut of a newspaper headline: "Past recalled for Japanese Americans."

Ultimately, Hattendorf does not rest content with simply connecting the past and the present and thus showing the "same old story." She brings Mirikitani to a social service center, gets his social security number and citizen rights restored, gets him a welfare apartment, brings him to California for a visit to the Tule Lake detention camp (now a memorial), and reunites him with his sister in California, whom he had not seen in 60 years. I end this chapter with some remarks I wrote and delivered as a member of the peace prize jury at the award ceremony at the 2007 Tromsø International Film Festival—as I, along with Rashid Masharawi and Silje Ryvold, gave the award to Linda Hattendorf for her *The Cats of Mirikitani*:

> We, the jury for the peace film prize—Rashid Masharawi, a Palestinian filmmaker from Gaza (now living in Paris), Silje Ryvold, a Norwegian student at the University of Tromsø, and Michael J. Shapiro, an American political scientist at the University of Hawaii—were able, despite their diverse territorial identities, vocations, and perspectives, to reach a strong consensus. We are awarding the peace film award to Linda Hattendorf's extraordinary documentary *The Cats of Mirikitani*. Apart from the fact of the film's effectiveness both thematically and cinematically, the very process of filmmaking made an amazing difference in people's lives. A person was healed and made whole again, and his relationship with lost relatives was restored. Hattendorf's documentary project, which began as a result of some small sympathetic gestures, ended up as an extended generosity with universal implications. Specifically, that generosity made present and palpable the

details of a historical, structural as well as direct violence, associated with one of America's wars; it located that violence in the context of a contemporary American war, and it is an exemplary demonstration of the healing power of art. The film uses cinematic art to disseminate another form of art, one that speaks powerfully to a historical form of violence that rarely achieves the presence it deserves. While creating relays between one historical episode of warring violence with another, the humanity the film expresses has universal resonance. It is our hope that the awarding of the peace film prize to *The Cats of Mirikitani* will result in the film's wider dissemination, making its remarkable humanitarian sentiments contagious.

# 4  The sublime today

## Re-partitioning the global sensible

Well, holy shit! So you *are* human, Okwe.

Senior Juan (Sneaky) in the film Dirty Pretty Things

Let us say yes *to who or what turns up*, before any determination, before any antic-ipation, before any *identification*, whether or not it has to do with a foreigner, an immigrant, an invited guest, or an unexpected visitor, whether or not the new arrival is the citizen of another country, a human, animal, male or female.

Jacques Derrida, Of Hospitality

### Introduction: flows of bodies and body parts

Contemporary history is recalcitrant to the optimism that Immanuel Kant expressed about an international environment that would provide a welcome context for a growing "concord" among "men" and an increasing hospitality to those crossing borders from one state to another.[1] Since 2004 at least 62 people have died in the United States in administrative custody as "the immigration detention system balloons to meet demands for stricter enforcement of immigration laws."[2] The "balloon effect" is a pervasive part of contemporary immigration policy in the most developed capitalist countries. In the United States it is part of an immigration policy that concentrates on the flow of bodies rather than looking at the demands for them. Powerful interests run the demand side of immigration flows. As one analyst puts it, "it appears that development and wealth discrepancies are too great, the profits too large, the desire for undocumented labor and illegal drugs too strong . . . to be controlled given the level and style of border enforcement to date."[3] Not surprisingly, the administration of immigration control targets the vulnerable rather than the powerful. Horror stories abound as of late the Department of Homeland Security's "Operation Return to Sender" has intensified surveillance and the enforcement of immigration laws. Here's a "Father's Day" rundown of some of the horror stories:

There is the father from Honduras who was imprisoned and then deported after a routine traffic stop on Miami. He was forced to leave behind his wife, who was also detained by immigration officials, and his 5- and 7-year-old sons, who were placed in foster care. . . . There is the father from Argentina who moves his wife and children from house to house hoping to remain one step ahead of the immigration raids. And the Guatemalan, Mexican and Chinese fathers who have quietly sought sanctuary from deportation at churches across the United States. There's the Haitian father who left for work one morning, was picked up outside his apartment and was deported before he had a chance to say goodbye to his infant daughter and wife.[4]

As a result of their precarious situations, the vulnerable often rely on their most immediate resource, their bodies. Supplementing the inadequate border control policies, the detention and deportation policies are part of a vast system of global coercion that affects not only the flows of bodies but also the flows of body parts. An increasing demand for transplant surgery is the primary force engendering the latter flow. However, the two flows are intimately connected, as is dramatized in a feature film, *Dirty Pretty Things*, whose storyline is precisely about the complex connections between immigration policy and the flow of body parts.

## Stephen Frears's *Dirty Pretty Things*

The development of transplant surgery to extend lives that would otherwise be radically shortened is an ambiguous achievement inasmuch as it both enhances and threatens well-being. While the surgery extends life among those who can afford such expensive medical procedures, the lives of many of those from whom the organs are harvested are under severe duress. As one investigator of the global traffic in organs has discovered:

> The organs trade is extensive, lucrative, explicitly illegal in most countries [and] . . . transplant surgery as it is practiced today in many global contexts is a blend of altruism and commerce, of science and magic, of gifting, barter, and theft, of choice and coercion.[5]

One of the venues from which organs are often harvested is India, "a primary sight for a lively domestic and international trade in kidneys."[6] For example one researcher "encountered friends in Benares who were considering selling a kidney to raise money for a younger sister's dowry." As the researcher notes, "women flow in one direction and kidneys in another."[7] And more generally, as organ transplant technologies get widely dispersed, a "global scarcity of viable organs . . . has initiated a movement of sick bodies in one direction and of healthy organs . . . often in the reverse direction, creating a 'kula ring' of bodies and body parts."[8] The organ flow "follows the modern routes of capital: from South to North, from Third to First World, from poor to rich, from black and brown to white, and from female to male."[9]

While such flows were once regarded as culturally abhorrent, they become increasingly warranted by cultural authorities as the pressure of an expanding global economy affects the shifting boundary of the culture–economy interface.

From traditional cultural points of view, persons and certain kinds of objects are singular and thus non-exchangeable, while from a modern economic point of view persons and things are regarded as exchangeable. Although, historically, the tension between the two registers of value has resulted in inhibitions on economies of exchange, over time, especially in the modern era, economic interests have tended to overpower cultural inhibitions. As Jonathan Crary summarizes it, "modernization is a process by which capitalism uproots and makes mobile what is grounded, clears away that which impedes circulation and makes exchangeable that which is singular."[10] Moreover, the pressure toward mobilizing what was formerly grounded has differential effects. The global structures of vulnerability that create the flows are not only along the routes described above but also found among the immigrant populations *within* global cities such as London, which harbors an almost invisible Third World within the First. They are the ones who most often must compromise cultural commitments to survive.

Stephen Frears's film *Dirty Pretty Things* offers a close-up view of the kinds of vulnerable lives in London that are impacted by such flows. At the level of its narrative, it is a story of a Nigerian doctor and Turkish hotel worker who are both employed, without legal work permits, in a London hotel. Both of them are in danger of deportation and, because of their illegal statuses, both become subject to coercion by operatives within the black economy, which like the legal economy makes cynical use of undocumented workers. Okwe, the Nigerian doctor, and Senay, the Turkish hotel worker, acknowledge that they are largely invisible. Along with Juliette, a Jamaican prostitute who works in the hotel at night (and says at one point, "I don't exist"), they represent a "segment of British life, swelling in proportion yearly," that exists on the exploitable margins of the nation.[11] With images and a storyline that deliver compassion and critical insight, Frears's film counters the abjecting rhetoric of politicians who condemn the UK's exploitable "strangers." As Frears notes, "the government sort of whips up fears in the rest of England, as though these people have two heads or something, there's no attempt to explain the problem . . . it's just assumed that they're crooks or terrorists."[12] His film is one of a growing number that provide cinematic cityscapes and ethnoscapes within a far more hospitable imagery than has been available in the policy discourses of governments.[13]

To the extent that we are paying attention, Frears's title, *Dirty Pretty Things*, is likely to create a momentary arrest of our interpretive faculties, engendering, in Walter Benjamin's terms, a critique-enabling form of "distraction," and an experience that Immanuel Kant famously attributes to the feeling of the sublime: "the feeling of a momentary checking of the vital powers [which then leads to] a stronger outflow of them," and ultimately to an "earnest . . . exercise of the Imagination."[14] Kant's analytic of the sublime treats dimensions of judgment that exceed the interpretation-inducing effects of a momentary arrest. However, as my analysis develops, I argue that even Kant's notions of the mathematically and dynamically sublime provide additional inspirations for a political reading of the film. At a minimum, as a film that explores London's dynamic, constantly changing ethnoscape, it fulfills two aspects of the way Kant designated sublime objects;

unlike the beautiful object, it has indefinite contours, and, given the images it animates, it provides a "negative pleasure" because it "is ever being alternatively attracting and repelling."[15] Once we watch the film, we learn that the title is reflected in a statement by the film's cynical character, Senior Juan (Sergei Lopez), a London hotel manager who traffics in an illicit sale of organs, harvested from vulnerable immigrants and refugees and peddled to wealthy families who seek transplants. Speaking of the temporal boundary between a hotel at night that harbors illicit activities and a hotel during the day that is a place to attract guests, he remarks, "Strangers come to hotels to do dirty things; in the morning it's our job to make things pretty again."

However, the drama that surrounds the hotel's hidden-from-public-view activities renders the film's disjunctive and arresting title more complex and therefore encourages a turn toward the mobilized subjectivity to which Kant refers in his analytic of the sublime (as well as elsewhere in his treatment of reflective judgment). Viewers must make sense of a story that contains two complicated and intersecting levels of appeal. There is an aesthetic appeal delivered by scenes of London's rich and diverse city- and ethnoscape and an intellectual appeal delivered by a wider spatial reality, the geo-cultural trajectories that connect London with much of the rest of the world, which over historical time have made London a hybridized space of complex and fraught interrelationships. As one reviewer remarks, the film "contains great scenes of beauty and some disturbingly realist scenes of desperation."[16] Accordingly, the latter appeal requires the viewer to discern the levels of "precarious life" of the refugees–immigrants without legal credentials whose situations the film explores.[17] They are people who have either been attracted by opportunities or been forced out of political communities and, as Hannah Arendt famously observes, possess nothing but their "humanity." They have lost the qualities that position them for political and moral solicitude.[18] Senior Juan's "Holy shit . . ." remark about Okwe, an illegal refugee from Nigeria, who is wanted for a crime in Nigeria of which he has been falsely accused, resonates well with Arendt's observation. He is referring to Okwe's seeming capitulation, after much resistance, to a demand for an illegal service in exchange for (forged) legal papers. But at a more profound level the remark registers what Okwe shares with others expelled from political communities: he retains nothing but his bare humanity, a condition that *Dirty Pretty Things* addresses, not with pious moralizing but with well-composed film form.

When effectively composed, film can assist a discernment of the interrelation-ships between aesthetic and political registers because it can be assembled to provide critical reflection on the complex relations of the sensible, and the sayable.[19] The scenes display images and relationships that often undermine the verbalized self-understandings of the characters and the stories they think they are in, thus rendering judgments as to the facticity of events unstable. As Jacques Rancière has pointed out, much of the critical capacity of film arises from "*la contradiction que le visible y apporte à la signification narrative* [the contradic-tion that the visible brings to narrative signification]."[20] In addition, in *Dirty*, the cuts and juxtapositions that constitute much of the form of the film encourage the viewer to connect the above-noted two appeals; she/he must appreciate what is manifestly "pretty" (in the daily life of London) and, at the same time, understand that the city also teams with the precariousness of illicit arrival, which is the condition of possibility for what is "dirty" in the hotel at night. How this encouragement works is the focus of much of my analysis, but, before treating the film at length to evince the ethico-political implications it displays, I want to revisit the Kantian texts and their subsequent reinflection in contemporary post-Kantian approaches to the politics of aesthetics, in order to provide the philosophical frame for my analysis.

Because the film's title arrests interpretation and the film itself summons both aesthetic and the analytic judgments, we are pushed onto an intellectual terrain developed in Kant's *Critique of Judgment*, where he treats objects that cannot be subject to determinate judgments and thus illuminates, more generally, the complex problem of judgment in cases where reflection rather than derivation from concepts is involved. At the same time, because the obvious political resonances of the film involve the opposite of a cosmopolitan hospitality—the cynical exploitation of vulnerable strangers—we are also pushed onto the intellectual terrain of Kant's "Perpetual Peace," where he articulates an ethos of hospitality to those crossing national boundaries. Certainly in that essay Kant directly addresses what seems to be at stake from an ethico-political standpoint. But although the main dynamic of the film narrative, which treats vulnerable border-crossing strangers, would seem to privilege a reading of the Kant who explicitly addressed the global political terrains of moving bodies, I shall be insisting that a deeper political reading of the film is enabled if we privilege the Kant who addresses the perplexities of the sublime in his *Critique of Judgment*.

## Disjunctive intellectual communities and a disjunctive Immanuel Kant

Doubtless many international studies scholars are familiar with a collection of essays, *Kant: Political Writings*, especially "Perpetual Peace," which has continually attracted commentaries from that scholarly constituency. By contrast, rarely does Kant's Third Critique, *The Critique of Judgment*, make its way into the analyses of those interested in international or global politics. Yet among philosophers and political theorists, *Judgment* is continually mined for political insights.[21] At a minimum the textual disjuncture between these scholarly communities suggests that the collection's subtitle, *Political Writings*, is narrow and misleading inasmuch as it implies that Kant's major philosophical contribution—his three Critiques—provides no basis for political analysis. However, rather than pursuing the disjuncture among scholars, I want to point to one that functions *within* Kant's perspective. In some respects, the radical philosophical insights resident in Kant's Third Critique are at odds with the subjective necessity that he attributes to historical trends of consciousness in his excursion into global politics in his "Perpetual Peace," even though the Third Critique develops a political subtext that shapes much of "Perpetual Peace."

Certainly in contrast with his three Critiques, Kant's "Perpetual Peace" abounds in a familiar political vocabulary. The nation-state holds pride of place and is supplemented by frequent references to rights, as Kant expresses optimism about the future of global hospitality to border-crossers and to a general lessening of inter-nation antagonism. By contrast, to the extent that one finds familiar political terms in the Critiques, they appear to be metaphorical—for example what is arguably Kant's most important philosophical assertion, that the subject's faculties are legislative. However, the presence of familiar political terms does not necessarily make a text political, at least in the sense in which I want to presuppose a model of politics as dissensus among antagonistic constituencies rather than as simply an elaboration of state policy. Rancière's analysis of the politics of artistic texts makes the point well. "Art," he argues:

> is not political owing to the messages and feelings that it conveys on the state of [generally recognized] social and political issues. Nor is it political owing to the way it represents social structures, conflicts or identities. It is political by virtue of the very distance that it takes with respect to those functions.[22]

Thus for example Rancière sees Virginia Woolf's novels as more connected with democratic history than Émile Zola's, not because she wrote "good social novels" but because:

> her way of working on the contraction or distention of temporalities, on their contemporaneousness or their distance, or her way of situating events at a more minute level, all of this establishes a grid that makes it possible to think through the frames of political dissensuality more effectively than the "social epic's" various forms.[23]

To appreciate Rancière's point one has to understand his radical sense of what constitutes politics:

> Politics itself is not the exercise of power or struggle for power. Politics is first of all the configuration of a space as political, the framing of a specific sphere of experience, the setting of objects posed as "common" and of subjects to whom the capacity is recognized to designate these objects and discuss about them. Politics first is the conflict about the very existence of that sphere of experience, the reality of those common objects and the capacity of those subjects.[24]

To begin to assess the political implications of the Kantian legacy (which is among the inspirations for Rancière's version of the political), we must heed the ontological shift enacted in Kant's Critiques. Kant, as Gilles Deleuze points out, is "the great agent of substitution." His approach to "Critique replaces essence with sense."[25] Accordingly, Deleuze and Rancière, among other post-Kantians, focus their approaches to "the political" on the ways in which spheres of experience or sensibility are partitioned. Extending the radical political implications of Kant's *Judgment*, Rancière, among others influenced by Kant's Third Critique, trumps simplistic approaches to global ethics with a politics of aesthetics that derives from the ways in which the sensible world can be partitioned and re-partitioned. To begin to assess the metapolitical implications of a post-Kantian critical sensibility and resist the simplistic neo-liberal ethics that many derive from a singular focus on Kant's "Perpetual Peace," we must deal with a significant disagreement between the two Kant texts in question.

In "Perpetual Peace" Kant refers to nature as a "great artist" that guarantees "perpetual peace" because it "exhibits the purposive plan of producing concord among men."[26] Certainly Kant was not alone in seeing nature as a mimetic political text. For example, as I have noted elsewhere, Thomas Jefferson also saw nature as a source of political signs: "Far from enigmatic, nature seemed to warrant the design that Jefferson had in mind for his new democratic nation." Jefferson's "nature" is seductive as well as affirming. According to his romantic historical narrative, by the eighteenth century nature was beckoning the Euro Americans: "[W]e have an immensity of land courting the industry of the husbandmen."[27] Less than a decade after Jefferson had ascribed the results of his own productive imagination to the external summons of nature, Kant disqualified the possibility of such a summons.

In an earlier section of *Judgment*, Kant's analytic of the beautiful suggests a fit between nature and the mind, but this "marriage," as J.-F. Lyotard puts it, "this betrothal proper to the beautiful is broken by the sublime"; in Kant's elaboration of his analytic of the sublime, which is situated subsequent to his analytic of the beautiful, "[n]ature is no longer the sender of secret messages."[28] Effectively, Kant's critical treatment of aesthetic comprehension in his analytic of the sublime constitutes an annulment of the mind–nature marriage that Jefferson assumed. Moreover, the Kantian insight constitutes a pervasive discrediting of the Jeffersonian version of enlightenment, which prescribes "highly elaborated modes of attention, observation, and description, applied to natural objects," and gives too little heed to the productive imagination in which objects are presented.[29] As Kant puts it, "true sublimity must be sought only in the mind of the [subject] judging, not in the natural object."[30]

It should be noted however that the "sublimity" that Kant ascribed to the subject's mental topology involves a fraught mentality. In his analytic of the beautiful, Kant gives us a version of the mind that achieves a harmony among the diverse faculties of understanding and imagination. And because the beautiful is an object neither of cognition nor of desire, there is no one faculty that can govern apprehension. Given the unavailability of the object to a rule of either understanding or imagination—no one faculty legislates—the subject experiences what Kant calls a "free play" of the faculties, which produces a harmonious apprehension of experience by shifting the mind to the realm of the supersensuous, to a space in which transitions among the various faculties occur. This logic of form evinced by the judging subject in a confrontation with the beautiful (where the form of objects summons a reflection on the form-giving capacity of the interplay of faculties) creates the conditions of possibility not only for a harmonized subjective experience but also for the creation of a common sense, for a universal agreement or *sensus communis*. Accordingly, if one heeds only Kant's analytic of the beautiful, the resulting "metapolitics of aesthetics" militates in the direction of the kind of global harmony that Kant saw while reading the signs of history, leading to the optimism he expresses in his "Perpetual Peace."[31]

By contrast, in the analytic of the sublime the Kantian mind is in radical disarray. Unlike the case of the analytic of the beautiful, reason is called into play in the analytic of the sublime. But although the sublime is characterized by a free and spontaneous agreement of reason and imagination, "this new 'spontaneous' agreement occurs under very special conditions . . . pain, opposition, constraint, and discord."[32] In Kant's words, "the feeling of the Sublime is . . . a feeling of pain, arising from a want of accordance between the aesthetical estimation of magnitude formed by the Imagination and the estimation of the same formed by Reason."[33] However, the discordance to which Kant refers should be understood within the political subtext that shapes Kant's discussion in his analytic of the sublime. The two main dimensions of the sublime experience, which Kant calls the mathematically sublime and the dynamically sublime, shift the emphasis of the purposiveness that creates the sublime experience from the object to the subject. For example, when Kant notes, in his discussion of the mathematically sublime, that a sublime experience (for example a violent storm) is incomparably or "absolutely large" and thus outside of our ordinary conceptual determinations, he is insisting that the experience creates a "feeling of purposiveness quite independent of nature." We are turned not outward to apprehend the purposiveness of nature but inward to ourselves in "our attitude of thought."[34]

Similarly, in invoking the dynamically sublime, in which the subject recognizes the fearfulness of nature without fearing it, Kant is illustrating the way the sublime experience elevates the imagination:

> Insofar as it incites fear [nature] . . . calls up that power in us (which is not nature) [and] . . . nature is here called sublime merely because it elevates the Imagination to a presentation of those cases in which the mind can make felt the proper sublimity of its destination, in comparison with nature itself.[35]

Effectively, the subject recognizes its ability to transcend nature's purposiveness and thus experiences its freedom from the realm of determination. This mental attitude toward one's freedom, which is "proper to the vocation of mind," is also the basis of a political vocation, for it creates the conditions of possibility for a citizen subjectivity that functions against religious and political forms of domination. Here, therefore, in Kant's analytic of the sublime, is the political impetus (if not the optimism) that is articulated throughout his "Perpetual Peace." Kant's hope for a peace-regarding global citizenship is premised on the enlarged and free subject he constructs throughout his Third Critique.[36]

Nevertheless, despite Kant's assumption that the dynamic of subjectivity would overcome the discordance among the faculties provoked by the sublime experience and result in a subjective attunement or necessity that would bode well for a politics of freedom, the philosophical insights he developed have led in more critical directions. Rancière, for example, reinflects Kant's insights to address a politics among contemporary modes of subjectivity whose interrelationships differ from the simplistic elite–lower class partitioning that Kant recognized. Describing the Kantian discord occasioned by the sublime experience as a "meeting of agreement and disagreement," Rancière suggests that the dissensus occasioned by the sublime "allows the aesthetic experience to be politically significant—that is, to be more than a Kantian 'common sense' promising to bridge the gap between the refinement of the elite and the simplicity of the lower class."[37]

Rancière goes on to develop the implications of the sublime for a politics of aesthetics, which he sees as bearing on a variety of historical disagreements. Rather than accepting a model of harmony that "pins people down to their proper places," the aesthetic of disagreement he derives from Kant's sublime goes well beyond that between "those who work and those whose leisure is won on the back of workers."[38] Although this seemingly abrupt switch in idiom from the philosophic to the political might appear as an ad hoc, polemical extension without a warrant in Kant's text, it is evident that Kant himself mixes those idioms. Recognizing that the sublime imperils his attempt to derive the harmonious agreement or *sensus communis* toward which his Critique of Aesthetic Judgment is aimed, Kant admits that, while "the necessity of a universal agreement that is thought in a judgment of taste is a subjective necessity",[39] and while encounters with the

> numberless beautiful things in nature [allow us to presume] . . . and even
> expect, without being widely mistaken, the harmony of everyone's judgment
> with our own . . . in respect of our judgment upon the sublime in nature, we
> cannot promise ourselves so easily the accordance of others.[40]

To finesse the seeming recalcitrance of the sublime to the "subjectivity necessity" that *Judgment* is designed to establish, Kant turns to a concept of culture and effectively plays into Rancière's hands by distinguishing the educated from the uneducated. Kant's "culture" turns out to consist in the sharing of a natural moral sensibility, which can unite those with a refined and those with a vulgar cultural sensibility. As Kant puts it:

> without the development of moral Ideas, that, which we prepared by our
> culture, call sublime, presents itself to the uneducated man as merely terrible
> . . . he will only see the misery, danger, and distress which surround the man
> who is exposed to it.[41]

For this reason, he adds, "the judgment upon the Sublime in nature needs culture (more than the judgment upon the beautiful)," an aspect of culture that "has its root in human nature."[42] The moral sensibility to which Kant resorts does indeed, as

Rancière's gloss on Kant suggests, "bridge the gap between the refinement of the elite and the simplicity of the lower class," because what Kant refers to as a "presupposition of a moral feeling" is something that affects even the "uneducated man"; it "is not merely produced by culture"—in an empirical sense (where the high and the low can be distinguished)—but it is "culture" in a formal sense, a shared sensibility (analyzed in his Second Critique) where, unlike the case of his Third Critique, there is a legislating faculty.

Thus although commentators note that Kant's sublime is distinguished by a lack of a dominant, legislating faculty (for example Deleuze states that within *The Critique of Judgment* no one faculty legislates and Lyotard states that "after the sublime we find ourselves after the will"[43]), they are correct only if we fail to heed the functioning of Kant's cultural supplement. When Kant turns to the natural moral sense in order to rescue the subjective necessity and thus the *sensus communis* that is imperiled by the sublime, he yokes the sublime to his Second Critique, *The Critique of Practical Reason*, in which the faculty of reason presides, implementing a mimetic mind–nature relationship. Here however the will is not subject to the laws of nature. Rather it is a *"nature that is subject to a will."*[44] The *"moral possibility of action"* according to Kant is based not on the object "but the law of the will."[45] Reason, which is the dominant faculty in this analytic, derives moral concepts through imitation; it "takes from sensible nature nothing more than what pure reason can think on its own." In short, although the mind–nature marriage may be annulled in the encounter with the sublime (as Lyotard puts it), with Kant's summoning of culture-as-moral-sensibility (from his Second Critique), a remarriage takes place as Kant retreats from the most radical implication of the sublime, its challenge to the idea of a naturally engendered common sense.

What are the implications of exposing Kant's conceptual retreat? If we want to heed the existing diversity of ethical/cultural/political sensibilities both throughout the globe and resident within large cities such as London, we must both appreciate the insights that derive from Kant's analytic of the sublime and resist his attempt to attenuate that analytic's radical implications. To assess those implications, we must recognize the significant departure that *Judgment* represents. Without going into elaborate detail on Kant's First Critique, it should be noted, at a minimum, that Kant overturned traditional philosophy's focus on the extent to which what appears can be reliably observed. Substituting a productive mode of consciousness for mere passive perception, and rejecting a search for the essence or thing in itself behind the appearance, Kant introduced a subject who is no longer subjected to the object. Kant's subject retains a receptive sensibility but also has an active understanding that legislates. It is a subject responsible for constituting the conditions in which things can appear as things.[46]

To summarize the model: In his initial formulation of the synthesis through which understanding is achieved, Kant located productive consciousness in three separate acts: apprehension, reproduction, and recognition. In his first narrative of comprehension, the various parts of experience extant in a world of multiple sensation undergo a spatio-temporal synthesis (where space and time are internal to consciousness) by the apprehension and reproduction of the *parts* before the third operation, recognition, takes place to complete the synthesis by connecting to the world of objects.[47] Ultimately, however, in *The Critique of Judgment*, Kant's staging of an encounter between the faculty of reason and the work of imagination renders unstable the perspective from which understanding can occur. Although he wanted to establish consistent and universal loci from which the "higher faculties" could achieve a harmonious accord, as the world of phenomena are synthesized, Kant's aesthetic explorations deepened his commitment to the subjective action and non-legislated free play involved in reflective judgment and comprehension. Although he failed to push his discovery very far toward its pluralistic implications, his *Judgment* creates the conceptual basis for a mobile geography of knowledge; the ultimate implication of Kant's last approach to comprehension is that there is no one central place from which a calculus for a synthesis can occur. Translated into implications for global politics, Kant's reluctant insight allows us to pluralize and contrast perspectives on global dynamics and thereby deprivilege that which has been historically attached to nation-state sovereignty models. But before approaching such a translation, we must delve more deeply into how *Judgment* carries the conceptual innovations that encourage such a translation.

Treating the striking difference that the Third Critique introduces, Deleuze notes that in *The Critique of Judgment* Kant poses a question that "was unformulated in the first critique: what counts as a part."[48] As he puts it, in *The Critique of Judgment* Kant realized:

> that the synthesis of the imagination, such as it arises in knowledge, rests on a basis of a different nature, namely that the synthesis of the imagination in all its aspects assumes an aesthetic comprehension, an aesthetic comprehension *both of the thing to be measured and the unit of measure* [my emphasis].[49]

Deleuze goes on to treat the ways in which the issue of aesthetic comprehension stands outside of Kant's desired synthesis and therefore registers the contingencies and fragilities associated with the understanding that the "synthesis" is meant to effect:

> You must be clear that aesthetic comprehension is not part of the synthesis, it's the basis [*sol*] that the synthesis rests on. I would say that it is not the ground [*fondement*] of the synthesis but that it is the foundation [*fondation*] of synthesis. At the same time that he discovers this basis, he discovers the extraordinary variability of this basis. He doesn't discover this basis without also seeing what this basis is. . . . Why? Because what the synthesis rests on is fundamentally fragile, because the aesthetic comprehension of the unit of measure, assumed by all effective measurement, can at each instant be overwhelmed, which is to say that between the synthesis and its basis there is the constant risk of the emergence of a sort of thrust coming up from underground [*sous-sol*], and this underground will break the synthesis.[50]

## Politics after Kant: implications for reading a filmic text

It is Kant's discovery of the fragility of his synthesis—his reluctant recognition that there is no single place from which to partition the sensible world—that is pregnant with political implications and sets up part of my reading of Frears's *Dirty Pretty Things*. The tendency among political theorists analyzing *Judgment* has been to search for what they call Kant's politics within the various analytics.[51] Rather than deriving political implications from Kant's most significant philosophical moment—his failure to instantiate subjective necessity in his analytic of the sublime—their focus has been on another of Kant's failures. Note for example Elisabeth Ellis's characterization: "Kant fails in *Judgment* to produce an internally coherent or empirically plausible theory of politics, or even the basis of a coherent or plausible construction of one."[52] In contrast, the political implications I want to derive from Kant's *Judgment* are based not on what Kant thought his politics was about (for example Ellis bases much of her reading on "Kant's own view of the status of investigation into the political world"[53]), but rather on what his analytic of the sublime opens up. The critical political implications I want to explore derive from his most significant failure. His inability to establish the subjective necessity he sought, when he evoked the encounter with the sublime, opens up the possibility of a plurality of loci of enunciation and thereby challenges the institutionalized perspectives that dominate those reigning political discourses that depend for their cogency on naturalizing or rendering necessary contingent modes of facticity.

To develop the pluralistic political implications of this latter Kantian failure, I want to begin by treating the way various genres manage to create the perspectives that determine the facticity that they presume, by turning to Deleuze's analysis of "points of reference" in his reading of the painter Francis Bacon's canvases. As I noted in chapter 2, observing the presence in some of Bacon's canvases of a figure or figures that have no narrative relationship to the central figure Deleuze refers to them as "attendants," who serve as "constant[s] or point[s] of reference." To repeat, an attendant is a "spectator," but not in the ordinary sense; it is the "kind of spectator" who "seems to subsist, distinct from the figure."[54] Reflecting his treatment of Kant's sublime, Deleuze sees the attendant as a provider of facticity of the scene, or, in his words, "the relation of the Figure to its isolating place," or "what takes place,"[55] for it "indicates a constant, a measure of cadence" and thereby serves to direct the (Kantian) fragile synthesis by being the basis of measurement for a scene that foregrounds the "thing to be measured."[56]

As I have noted elsewhere, the Deleuzian attendant function is robust enough to apply to other visual media. For example we can witness the operation of the attendant function in the most dramatic scene in Louis Malle's *Pretty Baby* (1978), a film whose plot involves the transition of a young girl, raised in a New Orleans bordello, from childhood to the vocation of a prostitute. In keeping with the bordello's tradition of an elaborate ceremony for the transition, the 12-year-old "virgin," Violet (Brooke Shields), is auctioned off in a setting that bears a startling resemblance to a slave auction. After being carried into the main sitting room on a large pallet, Violet stands on a small raised platform as the bidding progresses.

Prior to the start of the bidding, the camera explores the grinning faces of the potential buyers, but as the auction progresses the camera lingers for some time on the face of Professor (Antonio Fargas), an African-American piano player in the bordello, who until the moment of the bidding had seemed to share in the celebratory spirit of the occasion. In contrast, during the bidding there is a series of extended framing shots of his grave, contemplative expression.

The attendant effect of the framing shots inflects the facticity of the episode. Professor's witnessing of the scene constitutes the "taking place" of the event. The scene's facticity is rendered comparable to the historical episodes associated with the slave trade in which bodies are rendered as commodities to be sold to the highest bidder. Although he is now a free man, Professor's look is historically situated; it conveys the view of a former commodity among commodities, of one connected to a history of coercion, when humans were turned into exchangeable things in slave markets. In short, the basis for measuring the scene—for constituting its dominant facticity—is Professor's historical locus of experience as a "unit of measure."[57]

## Reading *Dirty Pretty Things*

The Deleuzian attendant function asserts itself in *Dirty* through the character Guo Yi (Benedict Wong), a forensic pathologist who becomes a friend, chess partner, and confidant of Okwe, whose story occupies the center of the film's drama. Briefly, the Nigerian doctor Okwe (Chiwetel Ejiofor), whom we first see soliciting passengers for his cab at Heathrow Airport in London, lives illegally, clandestinely sharing an apartment with Senay (Audrey Tautou), a Turkish refugee. Senay's precarious London life derives from her inability to work legally. She has refugee status but no work permit. Okwe, who is both illegal and unable to work as a doctor, drives a cab during the day, works as a desk clerk at a hotel at night, and chews a homeopathic herbal medicine to keep from falling asleep on the jobs.

The film's drama begins at the Baltic Hotel when the prostitute Juliette (Sophie Okonedo), who is one of the unofficial night personnel of the hotel, tells Okwe that there is a problem in one of the rooms. While attempting to fix an overflowing toilet, Okwe discovers that it is clogged by a human heart. Thereafter, he learns that the hotel has a clandestine organ harvesting and sales operation, under the direction of the manager, Sneaky. While struggling with the ethical issue his discovery raises for him, Okwe discusses the situation with Guo Yi, who articulates clearly what is the larger structural situation for Okwe. After asking him if he wants to face deportation, the likely consequence of his going to the police about the illegal organ harvesting, Guo states the most significant fact of Okwe's subject position in the UK: "Okwe, you don't have a position here; you have nothing; you are nothing." Although Guo's remark plays into the personal level of the film's dramatic narrative—until the end of the film Okwe is too disempowered to oppose the exploitation he sees around him—it registers a more general and pervasive political reality. It addresses the situation of the refugee who, in Giorgio Agamben's terms, is a "figure" that puts into crisis the political language attached to the modern

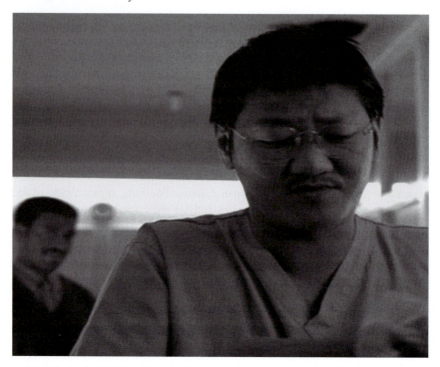

*Figure 4.1* Guo with Okwe in the background
Courtesy of Miramax

nation-state. The disruption created by the increasing flow of stateless people who constitute much of the infrastructure of large cities around the world is registered in the discourses of the political. As a result, Agamben insists, "We will have to abandon decidedly, without reserve, the fundamental concepts through which we have so far represented the subjects of the political (Man, the Citizen and its rights, but also the sovereign people, the worker, and so forth)."[58]

Agamben's suggestion helps us steer clear of the Kant who focuses on hospitality to the flow of stateless people in his "Perpetual Peace," because this Kant operates within a traditional geopolitical discourse. The borders of nation-states are at the center of his political imaginary; his "meta-geography participates in constructing the privilege of a state-oriented mode of both space and personhood."[59] Moreover, rather than recognizing the way that commerce disrupts a state-centric cartography and participates in the adversity of the refugee, Kant reinforces his meta-geography by treating commerce as a palliative to inter-state hostilities, seeing it as a force that encourages a recognition of mutual self-interest among nation-states.[60] In contrast, without resort to an explicit discourse on geography, *Dirty* nevertheless delivers a post-Kantian politics of aesthetics by shifting the political problematic from relations among states to relationships of dominance and submission and of coercion and strategies of escape in the city, and by displaying the ways in which networks and communication nodes loom much larger than national borders in the articulation of a politics of dissensus.

To frame the film's challenge to traditional geopolitical presumptions, we have to recognize the ways in which various genre-depictions of the modern city disrupt the traditional statist political discourse. For example, prompted by the Hanif Kureishi/Stephen Frears film *Sammy and Rosie Get Laid*, Gayatri Spivak points out that the city contains a variety of types who constitute a "challenge to the idea of the nation"—for example the "homeworker" among other "super exploited women in export processing zones."[61] London's participation in this mode of exploitation is displayed when *Dirty*'s Senay, having been chased by immigration inspections from her hotel job, works in a sewing sweatshop where she is sexually exploited by the shop foreman, who solicits sexual favors by threatening to report her to immigration inspectors. Referring, further, to the "negotiable nationality" of "economic migrants," Spivak points to the most significant utterance in *Sammy and Rosie*. The Pakistani immigrant Sammy says at one point, "We are not British. We're Londoners." Like Frears's later *Dirty*, his *Sammy and Rosie* explores an aspect of "the British social text," which in this case locates it in a dynamic of "global reterritorialization in the New World Order," as immigrants and postcolonials mingle within the varied London ethnoscape.[62] Similarly, *Dirty* connects the London text with a New World Order, which in the case of this film is the plight of the political refugee that is forced out of her/his political community and ends up residing in a place that offers neither economic nor political qualification. Nevertheless, through both its formal and narrative registers, *Dirty* supplies a redemptive politics while at the same time challenging the viewer to conjoin the aesthetic and ethico-political appeals to achieve a distance from (among other things) a politically obtuse "ethics of international relations" pursued by many neo-Kantian international studies practitioners.

The formal contribution of *Dirty*'s rendering of London is reminiscent of the way London emerges in the nineteenth-century novel. Mapping the London of the nineteenth-century novel, Franco Moretti points out that in most cases a partial and disarticulated London is presented—a half London, upper-class West End in Jane Austen's "silver fork" novels and separated East and West Ends in Sir Arthur Conan Doyle's Sherlock Holmes crime novels. However, Charles Dickens undertakes what Moretti refers to as the "great wager": to "unify the two halves of the city" so that "London becomes not only a larger city . . . but a more *complex* one, allowing for richer, more unpredictable interactions."[63] For example his *Our Mutual Friend* treats the "hostile forces" impinging on a character "caught between the fraudulent arrogance of the West End and the physical violence of the docks."[64]

Frears's *Dirty* also maps a complex London with diverse characters interacting across and within complex spatial differences. However, instead of a class map, figured on the basis of the middle- and upper-class West End versus the proletarian and impoverished East End, *Dirty*'s characters connect not only working-class fringes with some of Central London's tourist, financial, and bureaucratic venues but also London with distant points of departure, places that remain off-screen in the film. Certainly Dickens's novels also contain national spaces beyond England;

"a very large number of characters leave London at the end of Dickens' novels" for the same reasons offered in *Dirty*: "London cannot provide a plausible setting for a happy ending."[65] But for purposes of understanding *Dirty*'s rendering of a post-sovereignty, biopolitical model of global politics, the way a periphery is contained *within* London is more significant than the off-screen spaces toward which the film gestures.

London's situation as a nexus for both licit and illicit arrivals and departures is evident in the opening and closing scenes, which take place at Heathrow Airport, where at the outset Okwe is hustling taxi customers and at the end he and Senay are headed to Nigeria and New York respectively. The film's re-partitioning of a political world that operates within major cities is portrayed in two juxtaposed scenes, early in the film. The first takes place in a small minicab office in a section of London where non-white immigrants congregate (likely a South London section such as Brixton). Here, as in other places, architecture articulates the most significant spatial contrasts. The minicab dispatcher, whose color and accent locate him as a Caribbean immigrant, solicits Okwe's medical help by having him join him in a closed back room, where he drops his pants to reveal a case of venereal disease. Here, as is the case later, when his medical skill is solicited in the hotel, Okwe is a divided subject. He protests to the dispatcher, saying, "I'm a driver," but he is not in a position to contest the esoteric knowledge of his background that the dispatcher possesses.

After the back room encounter at the minicab office, the film cuts to another London, which is connected to the first one by Okwe's daily itinerary; a framing shot of the Baltic Hotel, where Okwe works at night, follows the encounter in the back room of the cab company. The Baltic Hotel, like most of what is shown of downtown London, is a place of whiteness, at least in terms of the clientele. Moreover, the hotel's name is reinforced by having a Slavic doorman, Ivan (Zlatco Buric), out front. This provides a double resonance of whiteness, because Slavic people from the Baltic regions are the largest ethnic group in Europe. And some speculate that "Baltic" derives from *baltas*, or *white* in Lithuanian. But what is out front is only one presentation of ethnicity and one aspect of the architecture of a hotel whose different spaces involve an ethnic and class partitioning. Following the shot of the hotel front is one of its basement, where the lockers for the non-white staff—maids and deskman—are. Subsequently, the less visible parts of the hotel—some of the rooms, the basement, the kitchen, and the parking garage—contrast with the lobby, where guests are seen entering and leaving.

That the hotel's partitions are a microcosm of a dimension of global political economy is made evident by the form of *Dirty*. In contrast with mentality-as-form within Kant's construction of subjectivity, film form displaces mentality with a cinematic apparatus, which in *Dirty* articulates the implications of the refugee's London experience. The composition of shots of the Baltic Hotel separates the relatively freely moving bodies of the guests from the suborned bodies of vulnerable refugees and immigrants, who are forced to either tolerate or collaborate in the hotel manager's (Sneaky's) organ donor business. If we heed Sergei Eisenstein's famous articulation between architecture and cinematic montage, we

*Figure 4.2* Okwe in the Baltic's basement
Courtesy of Miramax

can become sensitive to the role of the hotel, in which much of the action in the film takes place. Reading architectural treatises (for example Auguste Choisy's *Histoire d'architecture*) "with the eye of a filmmaker," Eisenstein was inspired by the way in which an architectural ensemble such as the Acropolis could be better composed through "a montage sequence" than with the one that our legs create by walking among the buildings.[66] As a result, as Yve-Alain Bois points out:

> architecture . . . is one of the underlying motifs in Eisenstein's films. . . . [He] had to find practical answers to the problem of how to film a building, how to transform it from a passive setting of the action, into a major agent of the plot.[67]

In *Dirty* the Baltic Hotel is at least as important a character as its manager, Sneaky.

After Sneaky, like the cab company dispatcher, becomes aware of Okwe's medical background, it is Guo who again articulates the relevant fact of Okwe's situation. When Okwe refers to his boss's demand, Guo asks, "Which one?" (of the bosses), to which Okwe replies, "They're all the same." Okwe's need to hide his identity is a resource for those who want to make demands on him. However, as the story unfolds, Okwe seizes the initiative to help vulnerable people (Guo has counseled him to stick to the people he is able to help instead of trying to fight corruption *tout court*) and ultimately to obtain the passports he and Senay need to escape their dilemma.

Hiding turns out to be an advantage. At one point in a conversation Okwe and Senay acknowledge that, given London's power relations within which they are seen to have little consequence, they are invisible. The hotel guests also manifest an invisibility, but of a different kind. As Friedrich Kracauer puts its, in his gloss on hotel lobbies, "The visitors in the hotel lobby, which allows the individual to disappear behind the peripheral equality of social masks, correspond to the exhausted terms that coerce difference out of the uniformity of the zero."[68] However, subsequently Okwe uses his ability to hide in plain sight to steal medicine to treat another African who sold a kidney and is dying from sepsis. The hospital is like London's other establishments. Architecturally, it is organized into spaces of privileged access for powerful practitioners or professionals and spaces for those who perform lower-paid services. However, servile help are allowed occasional admission to the spaces of privileged access, as long as they work rapidly and unobtrusively. Taking advantage of this structure, Okwe poses as a janitor and washes the floor of the room in the hospital where the pharmaceuticals are kept. As a foreign black man, he manages to fit into the hospital personnel's janitor imaginary. His ability to pose in order to get access to drugs and other hospital equipment sets up the dramatic final scene. When he learns that Senay, in desperation, has agreed to trade a kidney for a fake passport, he uses his relative invisibility to plan the film's major power reversal. Once the operating room (within a suite in the Baltic Hotel) and all the equipment are arranged, he drugs Sneaky, and with the assistance of Senay and Juliette, the hotel prostitute, removes Sneaky's kidney instead, takes the money when he delivers the organ, and finances his and Senay's departure with the fake passports they have gotten from Sneaky, who has presumed to have traded them in exchange for Senay's kidney.

The initiative that Okwe ultimately seizes has two powerful, politically relevant resonances. First, it belies his remark, "I'm a driver," to the minicab dispatcher, who asks for medical help early in the film, because it marks a moment in which Okwe's actions exceed any unitary and fixed identity attribution. Second, it challenges not only the cynical exploiters but also Arendt's observation that the refugee possesses only her/his bare humanity. As the film's dramatic conclusion approaches, and Okwe prepares to operate, we witness a complex micropolitical challenge to the macro, state-oriented policies within which the immigrant/refugee is politically disqualified. The action by Okwe and his collaborators constitutes an event of what Rancière calls subjectification. They become political subjects by "transforming identities defined in the natural order of the allocation of functions,"[69] because politics (as opposed to the policing of those who control "policy") occurs during those events that involve "a series of actions by a body and a capacity for enunciation not previously identifiable within a given field of experience [with the result that the action creates a] reconfiguration of the field of experience."[70]

Although they own no space, Okwe and friends operate effectively in time, taking advantage of those moments when the policing of space is lax to pull off the operation on Sneaky, the sale of the kidney, and their escape. Effectively they use tactics rather than strategies, for a "strategy," as Michel de Certeau has famously noted, is a practice enabled by those who control space. A strategy, he states:

> postulates a *place* that can be delimited as its *own* and serve as a base from which the relations of an *exteriority* composed of targets or threats (customers, competitors, enemies, the country surrounding the city, objectives of research, etc.) can be managed.[71]

In contrast, a "tactic" involves the political action of those whose potential field of action is more temporal than spatial because they lack institutionalized control over space:

> The space of the tactic is the space of the other; it must play on and with the terrain imposed on it and organized by the law of a foreign power . . . it takes advantage of opportunities and depends on them . . . it must vigilantly make use of the cracks and particular conjunctions open in the surveillance of the proprietary powers.[72]

Ultimately, the micropolitical dynamic that occupies *Dirty*'s dramatic turn of events has implications that exceed the challenges to the particular dirty business operating in the Baltic Hotel in the center of London. The film's politics of aesthetics, rendered through its composition of shots, articulates a re-partitioning of the field of political experience, as England's internal periphery engages in acts of political subjectification. And the spatio-temporal cartography that the film assembles poses a challenge to traditional notions of global political geography and thus to those ethical speculations recruited under the rubric of "the ethics of international affairs." To pursue the film's encouragement of an inquiry into the politics of aesthetics after the Kantian sublime, it is appropriate once again to summon one of Rancière's formulations of "the political": "Politics is a way of repartitioning the political from the non-political. This is why it generally occurs 'out of place,' in a place that is not supposed to be political."[73] This formulation turns our attention to the most significant implications of *Dirty*'s enactment of Rancière's recasting of the implications of the Kantian sublime for a radical ethical and political subjectivity. Above, I noted that the hotel room in which Okwe operated to remove Sneaky's kidney can be read as a microcosm of the global political economy. It should be noted in addition that, although it may seem out of place with respect to familiar architectural renderings of political space, it expresses well Rancière's insistence that politics occurs in episodes of a re-partitioning of the political from the non-political.

The hotel room, which was formerly a site of exploitation, a place in which a room intended to be a public accommodation was recast as part of the illicit black economy, was turned into a site of political subjectification. By reorienting that room along with the other spaces throughout the "Baltic" (as well as other London spaces) in order to mount a political challenge to the hotel's dirty business—and the political and economic exclusions that make that business possible—Okwe and friends re-partition the hotel, turning it from a place of business (whether welcoming touristic bodies or exploiting those of refugees/immigrants) into a space of political engagement. And given the global trajectories of the bodies that effect the hotel's re-partitioning, the film invites a rethinking of the geography of the political as a whole.

The dynamic of political subjectification that re-partitioned the Baltic Hotel constitutes a rethinking of the presupposed organization of political space. It is a political event that opposes the traditional inquiries, inspired by the "other Kant" (the Kant of "Perpetual Peace"), which pursue a concern with the ethics and politics of border control policy. The sensory bifurcation that *Dirty* creates, with its cuts back and forth between official and touristic London and London's vulnerable refugee population lodged within marginal spaces of enterprises, introduces us to "transcultural beings" whose participation within the host society involves "the transitory formation of peculiar spatial zones generated between opposing cultures."[74] In *Dirty* the Baltic Hotel is one of those zones. And the proliferation of such zones within cities constitutes a nodal cartography that opposes a micropolitics of cultural encounter to the traditional macropolitics within the geopolitical cartography that is featured in the mainstream discourses of international studies.

## Destabilizing humanitarianism

As I have suggested at the outset, the political insights one can draw from Kant's analytic of the sublime are not available when one poses the question of "Kant's politics." The critical issues that derive from Kant's failure to preserve his sought-after *sensus communis*, when he evoked the encounter with the sublime, emerge when a different question is posed: how to conceive of politics after the Kantian sublime. Two registers of a reoriented politics derive from the subject-in-disarray that emerges from the sublime encounter. The first register bears on the partitions *within* the subject and the second on the wider issue of the global partitioning of political subjects.

Treating the within-subject issue, Lyotard points out that, despite the dramatic insight deriving from Kant's analytic of the sublime, the breaking up of "the more or less presupposed unity of the (human) subject," a variety of approaches to "humanism" ignore that consequence. As he puts it:

> Humanism administers lessons to "us" (?) In a million ways, often mutually incompatible. Well founded (Apel) and non founded (Rorty), counterfactual (Habermas, Rawls) and pragmatic (Searle), psychological (Davidson) and ethico-political (the French neo-humanists). But always as if at least man were a certain value, which has no need to be interrogated.[75]

What is neglected when that value is not interrogated? According to Lyotard, it is Otherness. While here is a dimension of the inhuman that is a bad variety—

for example "repression and cruelty"—the good inhuman "is Otherness as such. It is the part in us that we do not control."[76] In the case of *Dirty*'s Okwe, we observe a subject in anguish, which in Lyotard's terms is "the anguish of a mind haunted by a familiar and unknown guest which is agitating it, sending it delirious but also making it think."[77] Ultimately, a part of the multiply partitioned Okwe, a potentially political part, asserted itself. It is not a part that reflects Kant's hope for universal moral sense, for Okwe does not share a common experience or occupy a universal locus of enunciation; rather it is a part that won a temporary victory over those parts of his subjectivity that had locked him into vulnerable modes of disqualification. What was released was that part of the Otherness in Okwe that could not be domesticated into a unity. He evoked the part of himself that held a potential for political subjectivity, which in Rancière's terms is constituted as "a capacity for staging . . . scenes of dissensus."[78]

The collaboration between Okwe and his friends, as they plotted to harvest and sell Sneaky's rather than Senay's kidney, evokes the second register of partitioning, the global partitioning of political subjects. While it is tempting to frame the drama of the film as a whole in an Arendtian way as a struggle between oppressors and those stateless refugees who are constituted as human subjects that, having been cast out of public political space, possess only their bare humanity, Rancière provides a more compelling interpretation, which generates a different mode of political discernment. Rather than seeing Okwe *et al.* as subjects outside of the political arena, we can see them as those who constitute the political by re-partitioning the spaces within which they act. They make themselves political subjects, while at the same time rendering a space that had been constituted otherwise as political; they enact a "dissensus" that implicates both subjectivity and space. Significantly, part of the political subjectification that Okwe and Senay enact is a function of the gap between the surveilling gaze and the look. While on desk clerk duty, it is Okwe who has available a bank of TV screens allowing him to surveille the activities in the hotel. Senay too is affording a discerning look. At one point, she is seen staring at the cameras that clock her arrival and work activities. The look back at the surveilling gaze ultimately avails because, at a dramatic moment in the film, Okwe's ability to look at the hotel's surveillance system saves Senay from apprehension by immigration officials. The "resistant look," which Kaja Silverman has theorized so well in her insistence that we distinguish between the surveilling gaze and the eyes of the surveilled, is very much a part of Okwe and Senay's political subjectification.[79] As a result of witnessing Okwe and Senay's effective resistance, we are encouraged to recognize that the political arena is not a fixed space; it emerges through actions which, among other things, have the effect of "putting two worlds into one and the same world."[80] And we are able to recognize the most profound spatial implication of *Dirty*. The scenes it shows reveal a world within a world, a world in which what was once the "periphery" has migrated into the former (colonial) center. The drama *Dirty* presents is one in which that formerly peripheral world is elevated into a political encounter.

## Conclusion: the "ethics of international affairs" versus a politics of aesthetics

As I put it earlier in this chapter, Kant's *inability to establish the subjective necessity he sought, when he evoked the encounter with the sublime, opens up the possibility of a plurality of loci of enunciation and thereby challenges the institutionalized perspectives that dominate those reigning political discourses that depend for their cogency on naturalizing or rendering necessary contingent modes of facticity.* The implications I derived from the Kantian sublime bear on ethical as well as political problematics. Simply put, the typical ethical sensibility tends to be elided with traditional morality and as a result is oriented toward the institutionalized codes that are enforced by reigning structures of power and authority. If with Rancière we understand politics as "the configuration of a space as political" and as "conflict about the very existence of that sphere of experience, the reality of those common objects and the capacity of those subjects [who exercise a capacity to designate objects of experience],"[81] we have to recognize that the ethical, like the political, is constituted as a series of events. The ethical does not make an appearance in moments of conformity to codes that regulate the interactions among already-formed subjects but instead asserts itself in struggles for legitimate co-presence in worlds that contain more than one world. As Deleuze has noted, in a remark that captures the identity movement that results in the political events in *Dirty*, "It's not on the periphery that the new nomads [those who escape capture within fixed identities] are being born (because there is no more periphery)."[82]

For critical responses to the oppressed, nomadic characters in *Dirty* it's instructive to consider two kinds of critical response, one vehicular and one philosophical. With respect to the former, there are the "critical vehicles" developed by a global nomad, Krzysztof Wodiczko, who, as he explains, has:

> emigrated and immigrated twice, from Poland to Canada in the 1970's, and from Canada to the United States in the 1980's [moreover he has worked from] a shifting base of operations, augmented by temporary residencies in Australia (1981) and France (1992–93).[83]

Two of his vehicles are performative instruments, the "alien staff" and the "mouthpiece," which Wodiczko refers to as part of a xenology. The alien staff is designed to give the alien a chance to "speak back to all those strangers or non strangers who would cast the stranger in some preconceived mold of an individual or collective identity." Wodiczko describes it as follows: "*The alien staff* is a piece of storytelling equipment and a legal and ethical communications instrument for immigrants. . . . It is equipped with a mini video monitor and a small loudspeaker."[84]

Because the screen has a small image, observers are induced to approach for a closer look, thereby diminishing "the usual distance between the stranger and the observer."[85] As I have noted elsewhere, "The staff gives the stranger a 'double presence'—one in life and one in media—that stimulates reflection on how persons are constructed in the imagination versus how they exist within their personal life-worlds."[86] Wodiczko's mouthpiece is also supplied to immigrant aliens. It too has a small monitor, and it covers the wearer's mouth like a gag, creating what Wodiczko calls a "speechless stranger."[87] It is yet another vehicle designed to provoke reflection on the violence of imposing meanings on strangers while depriving them of a voice. To locate Wodiczko's vehicles within the politics of aesthetics around which this chapter has been organized, we can note that Wodiczko re-partitions sensational experiences in public space, introducing sounds and visuals that make palpable the presence of aliens who are not usually seen or heard as legitimate participants in the social arena. Inasmuch as Wodiczko's vehicles are aesthetic operators, they are also ethical ones.

Elsewhere, and very much in accord with Wodiczko's "xenology," I suggested that one should construe ethics as event rather than conformity with codes. There, I identified with J.-F. Lyotard's displacement of the arbitration of dispute from subjective judgment to discursive encounter and noted that, rather than warranting a person's presence to the political on the basis of the traditional geopolitical discourses on global space, "we must consider encounters that cannot be effectively encoded within those discourses."[88] Here I want to add that we are instructed by *Dirty Pretty Things'* enactment of the implications of Kant's analytic of the sublime—and the sensibility enacted in Wodiczko's performative vehicles—that acts are always already underway to reconfigure the spaces of the political and to demand expansion of the scope of ethical recognition.

The philosophical response is developed by Jacques Derrida in remarks on the question of the foreigner in a conversation with Anne Dufourmantelle, in which, as Dufourmantelle puts it, Derrida draws out "the contours of an illicit geography of proximity."[89] Derrida's responses comport well with Frears's images. While Frears provides close-up views of the predicament of the oppressed foreigner, Derrida poses questions "from the place of the foreigner," noting that in so doing we can recognize the extent to which "the foreigner shakes up the threatening dogmatism of the paternal *logos*."[90] Where Wodiczko's vehicles are aimed at closing the distance between individual inhabitants and foreigners, Derrida's philosophical discourse is aimed at thinking through a welcoming ethos, a *Sittlichkeit* in the form of an absolute hospitality, "graciously offered beyond debt and economy."[91] Derrida's recognition of the tension between ethics and economy harks back to one of Hegel's earliest philosophical treatises, which focuses precisely on that tension. Hegel points out that from the point of view of the ethical life, *Sittlichkeit*, the commercial life can be seen as both necessary and destructive. As a result, he adds, the relationship between the two should be regarded as tragic.[92]

It is evident from Derrida's examples, primarily from ancient Greek culture, that the *Sittlichkeit* he values featured individual householders who had the domestic sovereignty that enabled them to "say yes *to who or what turns up*."[93] Today, "hospitality" for foreigners, be they immigrants, refugees, or asylum-seekers, has been displaced from households to bureaucratic policing institutions, whose lack of hospitality is a state-policy-generated unwelcoming normativity. As a result, to think about the lack of an ethical regard is to recognize that the regard is not an ethically oriented perception; it's a governmentally evoked and institutionalized screen, which radically separates citizen subjects from border crossers.

Among other things, the specific focus of *Dirty* on refugees turns out to be especially propitious for an ethical and political perspective. If we recognize that the tensions between persons as human and persons as citizens are not easily resolved within a state-centric political imaginary, especially when reasons of state and the subjectivities they warrant produce institutions that overcode generosity to otherness, narrowing the gaze on legitimate versus illegitimate consociates, we can appreciate what one discerning analyst points out about the effect of the refugee on attempts to resolve the citizen–newcomer tension: "Refugees disturb this resolution to the extent that they represent a conceptual, empirical, and psychical breach in the relationship between 'humans' and 'citizens.'"[94] And, significantly, refugees militate against those "normative" approaches to international studies, which are increasingly in focus, in which conflicts are turned into mere policy issues (for example the one about how to ensure human rights in a state-centric world).[95] Against the assumption of the possibilities for developing a normative consensus on an "ethics of international affairs," Rancière insists that the ethical and the aesthetic must be conjoined in order to show that ethics involves continuous dispute about what is the case in a world that contains competing worlds, for aesthetics, as Rancière conceives it, involves the partitioning of the sensible world.

For this insight, he deserves the last words in this chapter:

> Ethics is indeed on our agendas. Some people see it as a return to the founding spirit of the community, sustaining positive laws and political agency. I take a fairly different view of this new reign of ethics. It means to me the erasure of all legal distinctions and the closure of all political intervals of dissensus.[96]

# 5 Aesthetics of disintegration

## Allegiance and intimacy in the former "Eastern bloc"

Intimacy is not solely a private matter; it may be protected, manipulated, or besieged by the state, framed by art, embellished by memory, or estranged by critique.

Svetlana Boym[1]

. . . a reality that dominates our time: that of the migrant self—a self whose condition is not merely defined by practices of shifting habitats in relation to seasonal labor . . . but a self whose dilemma is representative of postmodern times. Going from place to place, shifting borders, displacing identity are phenomena of our time.

Trinh T. Minh-ha[2]

### Introduction: the politics of literary geography

In his *Atlas of the European Novel*, Franco Moretti analyzes the participation of the literary geography of the nineteenth-century novel in the dynamic of nation-state consolidation. Sir Walter Scott's historical novels are exemplary in this respect because their mobile geography, inscribed by the movements and interactions of characters, effaces anthropological, ontological, and axiological borders. The role of film in the twentieth century was similar. Although feature films occasionally challenged the myths that sustained the coherence of the modern nation-state throughout that century, for the most part their role was not unlike that of much of nineteenth-century literature; they aided and abetted the cultural articulation of the nation-building and sustaining projects of states. However, increasingly as the twenty-first century progresses, literature and film are playing a more critical role. Resisting the codes of national affiliation, they have been registering and affirming post-national forms of both malaise and commitment.

In this chapter, I treat various centrifugal economies—emotional, moral, libidinal, and monetary—that are attenuating the social bond and identity coherence in some of the states in the former Eastern bloc. With readings of Milan Kundera's novel *Ignorance* and Vyacheslav Kristofovich's film *Friend of the Deceased*, I examine the characters—exiles in Kundera's novel, and managers of a black economy, along with others who seek survival at a minimum and intimacy if possible, in a city whose social bond has disintegrated, in Kristofovich's film. In both texts, the actions of the characters are symptomatic of the breakdown both of the national allegiances that allowed states to effectively govern their cultures and economies and of the social bonds that sustained affection, mutual respect, and commitments to just exchanges. I end with an analysis of the politics of aesthetics and a broader mapping of the kinds of characters whose situations and political allegiances function on the pale of the terrains that have hitherto privileged the traditional citizen-subject and reliable consociate.

Turning first to the novel: Moretti's analysis of the nineteenth-century novel features two aspects of literary geography. The first is a matter of mere size. He notes how Jane Austen's sentimental novels reflect a "small England," which is smaller than what is now known as the United Kingdom. The space of Austen's story coincides with a "national marriage market." Featuring "scandals, slanders, seducers, elopements—disgrace," the novels' actions are spatially induced because, as Moretti writes, "the marriage market (like every other market) has produced its own brand of swindlers: shady relatives, social climbers, speculators, seducers, déclassé aristocrats."[3] "Reflect" is the appropriate textual imagery to treat the space–narrative relationship because, as Moretti rightly insists, "Space is not 'outside' of narrative . . . but an internal force that shapes it from within . . . in modern European novels, *what* happens depends a lot on *where* it happens."[4] The second spatial concept that Moretti employs is "distance," which derives its sense from the rationales for the movements of characters. But distance is not a mere geographical issue. It has emotional depth and therefore takes on its meaning from the sensibilities projected on it. Thus, for example, Darcy in *Pride and Prejudice* provokes a smile in Elizabeth when he shows up at Longbourn, because he has come fairly far to see her.

When Moretti turns to the historical novel, "the most successful form of the century," he discerns forces pulling in the opposite direction from those operating on the sentimental novel. The historical novel features a story that is "running away from the national capital."[5] Offering what Moretti refers to as "a veritable phenomenology of the border,"[6] the European historical novel is one in which the narrative is generated by "external frontiers."[7] However, there are also internal borders, which in the case of Sir Walter Scott's novels are anthropological. Moretti refers to those internal, anthropological borders as the "on/off switch of the historical novel."[8] They are needed to "represent internal unevenness" in a narrative whose main impetus is to erase those internal borders in behalf of a dynamic of national consolidation.[9] We can thus appreciate the difference in literary tropes as a difference summoned by the alternative geographies of the sentimental versus the historical novel. Austen's core and Scott's borders represent different dynamics, the emotional and financial fortunes of aristocratic families in the former and nation-building in the latter. As Moretti concludes, "the novel didn't simply find the nation as an obvious, pre-formed fictional space. It had to wrest it from other geographical matrices that were just as capable of generating narrative,"[10] for example supra-national spaces such as those treated in *contes philosophiques*.[11]

Since the period treated in Moretti's analysis, in which the novel played into the centripetal forces involved in national consolidation, novels have begun to reflect diverse centrifugal forces that pull against the earlier, centralizing dynamic. Certainly, as M. M. Bakhtin demonstrates, the novel has always privileged centrifugal forces. If one heeds voices rather than borders, we witness, in Bakhtin's terms, many contending voices that pull against the verbal-ideological center of the nation.[12] Moreover, in the case of the United Kingdom, the erasure of internal borders has been subject to continuous contention. Thus, for example, in Roddy Doyle's contemporary novel, which features a member of the Irish revolution that led to Ireland's independence, the main character, Henry, expresses profound ambivalence toward the national independence and consolidation that he is helping to effect. One of his co-revolutionaries, Jack, is an architect (both actual and symbolic) who is very much committed to consolidating the identity/difference that will distinguish the new Ireland. He states that he will only be able to design houses "fit for people . . . when the last Englishman was on the boat or in a box" and adds that "we'll have no use for granite. . . . It's the stone of the empire builder." In response, Henry reminds him that the granite comes from Irish soil, Wicklow. Jack then exclaims that Wicklow is an area of "traitors and Protestants who've made our country's history such a misery." On reflection, Henry, who keeps an ironic distance from the war and who, accordingly, maps Ireland differently from those committed to singular national allegiances, thinks:

> It struck me even then, although I didn't think much about it at the time, that his Ireland was a very small place. Vast chunks of it didn't fit his bill; he had grudges stored up against the inhabitants of most of the counties. His republic was going to be a few blameless pockets, connected to the capital by vast bridges of his own design.[13]

Doyle's novel is one among many that complicate the political geography to which they are addressed by exposing centrifugal and contending emotional and ideational forces. However centralizing the literary geography of the nineteenth-century historical novel might have been, the literary geography of novels since then has been articulated with a variety of geopolitical dynamics that challenge simple "nation-building" scenarios. They often deploy geographies that map the disintegrating forces—political, cultural, and economic—that afflict national societies. Not surprisingly, given the fraught post-revolution dynamics in Ireland, Doyle's Henry character becomes an exile in a sequel and goes on to help map aspects of a complicated U.S. political geography in the early twentieth century, which involves relationships among political, artistic, and criminal subcultures, all pulling in different directions.[14]

Nevertheless, despite its over-emphasis on the dynamics of consolidation, Moretti's approach to the novel, which focuses on the spaces that are created by following the action of characters throughout the narrative, is adaptable to many aspects of the geopolitical present. In what follows, I treat one of Milan Kundera's global mappings of the spaces that extend from the former Czechoslovakia to various European countries where Czech exiles reside. The novel provides a perspective on the fate of the geopolitical allegiances and structures of intimacy that followed the post-Cold War breakup of the Eastern bloc and the consequent advent of Czech independence. While Sir Walter Scott, among others, was writing and thinking during a period of European national consolidation, many contemporary novelists are dealing with characters whose interactions map the geographies of national deconstruction in a post-Cold War world. In this respect Milan Kundera's novel *Ignorance* is exemplary.

## Kundera's *Ignorance*

*Ignorance* begins with an alienating remark delivered to Irena, a Czech ex-patriot living in Paris, by her friend Sylvie: "What are you still doing here?" When Irena asks in response, "Where should I be?," Sylvie's rejoinder is "Home." It is 1991, and Sylvie has the expectation that Irena, despite having lived in Paris for 20 years, still thinks of Czechoslovakia as home and will want to return to participate as a citizen in the new independence, after the dissolution of the former Soviet bloc.[15] The intermittently contentious dialogue continues briefly until Irena breaks off into a book- and film-influenced fantasy about emotional returns. Irena's silent meditation about emotional returns triggers Kundera's break from his characters to a richly annotated, philosophical discussion of nostalgia, with references to a range of fictional and actual émigrés who either returned or resisted returning (for example Odysseus, who returned to Ithaca, and Schoenberg, who did not return to Austria, respectively). Apart from the specifics of the particular fictional and historical characters he treats is the kind of global cartography Kundera constructs. The novel provides a mapping not only of the post-Soviet geopolitical world but also of the inter-articulation of geopolitics and passion. To assess the thinking that the mapping enacts, we are in need of a philosophical perspective that can address the overlay of passion on political territoriality that frames Kundera's narrative.

Many of Kundera's philosophico-literary excursions in his novels are Nietzsche-inspired, most famously his *The Unbearable Lightness of Being*, which shares Nietzsche's sentiment that the possibility of an eternal return renders Being heavy. The thought of an eternal return gives "to acts and events the moral import they would lack in a godless universe wherein every act or event occurred only once."[16] Ever since that novel, Kundera has pondered the problem of moral and emotional weight as he has connected Nietzsche's version of a mythological return with the problem of the émigré's actual or potential return. Because for Kundera emotional and moral registers are intimately connected, it is not surprising that toward the end of his meditation on nostalgia in *Ignorance* he refers to the way Homer sets out a "moral hierarchy of emotions," which provides the basis for Odysseus's abandonment of Calypso, whose "tears" are represented as less worthy than "Penelope's pain."[17] From Kundera's Nietzschean perspective, moral hierarchies are oppressive. Hence we are able to understand the demoralized Odysseus, who suffers from the terrible bargain he has made by giving up an intense passion for the weaker emotion of nostalgia and the self-applied pressure from his expected responsibilities as a husband and patriarch. He has become the forlorn Odysseus (the Ulysses) so well described in Tennyson's famous poem (1842), the Ulysses who laments, "Match'd with an aged wife, I mete and dole Unequal laws unto a savage race, That hoard, and sleep, and feed, and know not me."

Most significantly for what Kundera sees Odysseus's travail lending to his story of contemporary émigrés and returnees, Odysseus discovers that while "for twenty years he thought about nothing but his return . . . the very essence of his life, its center, its treasure, lay outside Ithaca," and, further, while he had enjoyed a receptive audience while in exile (for example "the dazzled Phaeacians" who listened to his adventures "for four long books"), in Ithaca "he was one of their own, so it never occurred to anyone to say, 'tell us.'"[18] Similarly, when Irena returns to Prague, her old acquaintances evince little interest in her 20 years of life outside Prague. It was one thing for her former friends to ignore the French wine she brought and instead persist in drinking beer but quite another to ignore her words: "They can drink beer if they insist, that doesn't faze her; what matters to her is choosing the topic of conversation herself and being heard."[19] Inasmuch as the identity of an individual, like the collective identity of a nation, requires recognition, the inattentiveness of her Prague acquaintances to Irena's Paris life deprives her of confidence in the identity narrative she has adopted.

If we examine the other side of the self–other relationship to identity, we confront the perspectives of Irena's interlocutors in Prague who manifest a disinterest in Irena's other life, an unwillingness to extend sympathy across national boundaries. When we consider the identity issue at stake in Irena's encounter with these former acquaintances, we have to appreciate the politics of the history–memory disjuncture that Kundera is addressing through the fates of his characters. "History," as Pierre Nora points out, is produced by the way "our hopelessly forgetful modern societies, propelled by change, organize their past."[20] In the process of that organizing, memory tends to be eradicated: "Memory and history, far from being synonymous appear now to be in fundamental opposition." While memory is "a perpetually active phenomenon" reflective of the sense making of people coping with their life-worlds, "history is the reconstruction, always problematic and incomplete, of what is no longer."[21] Nora's distinction is effectively enacted in Kundera's narrative of the experience of *Ignorance*'s émigrés. While others try to impose a geopolitical allegiance on them, predicated on the way these former compatriots want to organize history, the émigrés try to maintain an intimacy with their memories, their lived temporalities. To the extent that the novel lends its characters an ethico-political outcome, it is the achievement of a refusal to give in to the identities, resident in an imposed history, which are thrown at them by their non-listening families, friends, and acquaintances. Hence, applying Nora's distinction to the historical moment of Kundera's novel, "history" imposes allegiance, while "memory, the "perpetually active phenomenon" that ties people to an "eternal present," is the condition of possibility for intimacy.[22] To put it another way (in the language of Deleuze and Guattari), "history" involves the imposition of officially inscribed molar codes, the collective identity spaces tied to the macropolitical world of states, while memory is what contains the molecular level, the multiple layers of individual micropolitical potential for becoming, experiencing, and associating.[23]

To be allied to the codes associated with "history," which are the geopolitically oriented temporalities that Irena's friends and husband impose on her, Irena must ignore her "life." As Deleuze puts it, "the sensuous signs of memory are signs of life."[24] Thus when Irena sees Josef in Prague, a man whom she recalls from a brief romantic liaison, her memory of a sensuous past is activated and, crucially, she is encouraged to think. As Deleuze notes, for Proust "truth depends on an encounter with something that forces us to think." And here that thinking helps Irena to distance herself from the expectations of others and allow intimacy (with herself as well as with another) to trump geopolitical allegiance. Intimacy challenges what Lauren Berlant refers to as "the normative practices, fantasies, institutions and ideologies that organize people's worlds."[25]

Irena's experience of a return is similar to that of the man she encounters romantically in Prague. Josef is an émigré living in Denmark, whose wife, subsequently deceased, had urged him to visit his old homeland once the Soviets had departed ("Not going would be unnatural of you, unjustifiable, even foul," she said[26]). When Josef visits his former friend N in Prague, whom he had not seen for 20 years, N and his wife ask nothing about his Danish life:

> There was a long silence and Josef expected questions: If Denmark really is your home, what's your life like there? And with whom? Tell about it! Tell us! Describe your house! Who's your wife? Are you happy? Tell us! Tell us! But neither N nor his wife asked any such question.[27]

Before following Irena and Josef, who meet and have an affair during their brief return, we need to appreciate Kundera's approach to the politics of the identity struggle they undergo. Kundera's attachment to Nietzschean philosophy, which he deployed in his *The Unbearable Lightness of Being*, notwithstanding, I want to pursue the position that his *Ignorance* is best given philosophical and political weight with reference to David Hume's rather than Friedrich Nietzsche's philosophical inquiries into the passions. While his *The Unbearable Lightness of Being* thinks in a Nietzschean way, Kundera's *Ignorance* thinks in Humean way. The overlay of passions on the novel's literary geography complicates mappings that focus exclusively on national allegiances and summons the Humean argument that passions direct ideas. To capture the kind of network that Kundera's novel proposes, we can extrapolate from an insight that Gilles Deleuze derives from his reading of Hume on human nature (which I note briefly in the Introduction). In contrast with much of the political theory canon (often drawn, for example, from the writings of John Locke) in which the social bond within the socio-political order is ascribed to a contract between ruler and the ruled, Hume's philosophy offers "a radical change in the practical way the problem of society is posed."[28] Given the Humean insistence that it is "affective circumstances" that guide people's ideas (because the "principles of passion" control ideational inclinations), association within the social domain becomes a matter of modes of partiality.[29] Accordingly, the problem of the social is to be understood not through the concept of the contract, which implies that the main political problem is one of translating egotism into sociality, but in terms of partialities, which makes the problem one of how to stretch the passions into commitments that extend beyond them, how, as Deleuze puts it, "to pass from a 'limited sympathy' to an 'extended generosity,'"[30] for, as Hume insists, "the qualities of the mind are *selfishness* and *limited generosity*."[31] To the extent that the extended generosity that justice represents is to develop, "it takes its rise from human conventions" that are necessitated by the "*confin'd generosity of men, along with the scanty provision nature has made for his wants*."[32]

The extrapolation I want to apply to Kundera's narrative locates the problem in a global rather than merely social space. In this expanded spatial context, the issue becomes one of a person's moderating her/his partialities in relationships not with the consociates of a national society but with potential consociates within alternative national spaces. Hume did contemplate the problem of extending sympathy across national boundaries, noting that "we sympathize more with persons contiguous to us, than with persons remote from us. . . . With our countrymen, than with strangers."[33] However, to appreciate Kundera's overlay of sensibilities on the dynamic mapping that exiles have created, we have to recognize a complication that Hume's notion of "selfishness" fails adequately to register. The self-consciousness required to be selfish—to be in touch with one's passions—is difficult to achieve in a world in which others impose regulative ideals with respect to what those passions are supposed to be. The disruption to Irena's hard-won sense of self as a French citizen with a French "structure of feeling" is a result not of the newly won Czech independence, which would not by itself have summoned an ambivalence, but of having to deal not only with a French friend who pressures her to reassume a former feeling and its attendant national commitment but also with pressure from a husband of Swedish origin who, ironically, has no such feeling for his "native" country. Her husband, Gustaf, a committed cosmopolitan, argues that, although he has no nostalgia for *his* country of birth, she should have some for hers. Similarly, Josef must deal with his wife's expectation about how he should feel and behave and, subsequently, the censorious feelings of his brother and sister-in-law, who had remained during the Soviet occupation. Certainly there are those who possess what Pico Ayer calls "a global soul"[34] or who, like Salman Rushdie, detest the "narrowly defined cultural frontiers" implied in the very idea of a "homeland."[35] But however passionate cosmopolitans may be about their attachments to multicultural urban settings and their commitment to resist narrow geopolitical allegiance, the emotionally charged cartography they define looms less large, in terms of both space and affective intensity, than the one defined by exiles.

Kundera ascribes that intensity, as it impinges on the kind of émigrés who are dramatized in his novel, to particular historic episodes that "have taken . . . a voracious grip on every single person's life."[36] Specifically, in the case of the persons like his characters Irena and Josef, the events of the 1950s and 1960s created the pressures they experience. Irena's situation is described more elaborately than Josef's. On the one hand, a Czech émigré in France is made to feel unwelcome, because a refugee from communism is not treated as an object of sympathy by a people for whom the great evils came from fascism. And the Irenas of the world have immediately worn out their welcome from the places they left, for, as Kundera puts it, "Loyal to the tradition of the French Revolution, the Communist countries hurled anathema at emigration, deemed it to be the most odious treason."[37] As even Mercator, who is best remembered for the technical and mathematical aspects of modern cartography, recognized, it is "a small step from locative sentimentality to territorial bigotry."[38] Accordingly, Irena, who is in the process of trying to get her emotional bearings, finds herself caught between two censorious political cultures. At the same time, she is pushed toward trying to renew her Czech existence by her husband, Gustaf, who has his firm open up a Prague office. Gustaf experiences none of the pressures experienced by his Czech émigré wife. He hurls anathema rather than receiving it. He "wholeheartedly detests" his Swedish town. Moreover, it is accepted that he "refuses to set foot" in his place of origin; "in his case it's taken for granted. Because everyone applauds him as *a nice, very cosmopolitan Scandinavian who's already forgotten all about the place he comes from.*"[39]

In one of the novel's most politically pregnant moments, Irena responds to Gustaf's offer to be her "link to your lost country," with the remark, "Please do understand that I don't need you to be my link with anything at all."[40] She is here trying to construct a coherent identity in time, in a way that she can call her own. Like all such moments, the effort takes on its implications within the spatio-temporal imaginary that dominates her historical moment. At the most abstract temporal level, her problem at this juncture is much like the one St. Augustine pondered when he sought an answer to the ontological challenge to selfhood, or one's presence to oneself through the passage of time. Augustine's response to the problem of the unity of one's existence in time is well known. After asking about how to reconcile the nonpresence of the past and the future ("how can these two kinds of time, the past and the future, be, when the past is no longer and the future as yet does not be?"[41]), he conceptually enlarges the soul. Life, he says, is "distended into memory" in order to incorporate one's past, and the future is drawn into the self as well, in this case through expectation, such that the future "which does not yet be . . . will have become present."[42]

To complicate Irena's identity-in-time problem and carry it beyond its Augustinian problematic we must consider more fully the spatio-temporal aspects of Irena's moment of identity crisis. If, inspired by J. G. A. Pocock's treatment of Machiavelli's "moment," we recognize that a moment is a crisis in the forces shaping territorial allegiance, Irena's struggle to extract herself from the expectations of a mother, a husband, friends, and acquaintances becomes intelligible.[43] To back up briefly: Kundera's novel begins in a dramatic political moment, the liberation of Czech society from Soviet hegemony. Thereafter, this larger, macropolitical moment is articulated through the micropolitical crises of allegiance it engenders, which are mapped first by following Irena through her visit to and return from her old "homeland" and then to the round trip from Denmark to Prague of the other exile, Josef.

To capture the conceptual contributions that the novel lends to Irena and Josef's shared historical moment, we can contrast it with the one central to Pocock's monumental study of the birth of civic republicanism in his treatment of Machiavelli's moment. While Pocock's focus is on the development of a mode of civic allegiance, Kundera's is about the disintegration of allegiance. Painstakingly, Pocock shows how "early modern thought," which is concerned with the requirements of civic allegiance and the activism it produces, became possible only after people were able to displace or at least complement the entrenched religious model of eternal time with a sense of historical time and could therefore think of themselves as citizens of a republic. As Pocock puts it:

> The republic was not timeless, because it did not reflect by simple corres-pondence the eternal order of nature; it was differently organized, and a mind which accepted republic and citizenship as prime realities might be committed to implicitly separating the political from the natural order.[44]

"To affirm the republic," he adds, "was to break up the timeless continuity of the hierarchic universe into particular moments."[45] In short, the historical becoming of republican subjects required that they first become specific historical subjects, existing in a spatial finitude rather than an eternal cosmos.

The post-Machiavellian world to which Pocock's analysis is addressed has been one in which first the city-state and subsequently the nation-state had become consolidated as the imaginaries attracting allegiance. First the one and then the other had operated as the territorial boundaries and horizons of political activity and engagement. By contrast, Kundera's fictional characters reflect a dynamic of disintegration, one in which former nation-state allegiances are being attenuated and a new ethos of engagement must be thought to array against the norms governing citizen political engagement. Inasmuch as the grip of state capture on political thinking has been tenacious, both as a mode of active state-directed cultural governance and as a feature of the codes insinuated in the discourses of the political, resistance and self-possession require a becoming conscious along what Deleuze and Guattari famously call "lines of flight" from the capturing mechanisms of state-directed consciousness.

If we heed the Humean frame within which I suggest that Kundera's novel is operating, the escape mechanism must involve a form of sympathy or partiality that ultimately becomes an extended generosity. For this to happen, the subject, which in Hume's treatment is an achievement following a process of the growth of the mind, must be able to escape its "homegrown habitual circuits."[46] In Deleuze's terms, "the [Humean] subject is constituted with the help of principles inside the given, but it is constituted as an entity that goes beyond the given."[47] In Kundera's *Ignorance*, where "the given" is constituted as the geopolitically driven expectations hounding the main characters, their ability to go beyond that "given" results from an interlude of passionate romance. To access the effect of that interlude, we need to become more acquainted with the novel's other main exile, Josef, whose return to Prague coincides with Irena's. Josef's exile has been in Denmark, which, in terms of the kind of patriotism it has historically encouraged, makes it similar to Czechoslovakia. Kundera contrasts the patriotism in such small countries to the kind that operates in large nations: "Their patriotism is different: they are buoyed by their glory, their importance, their universal mission." In contrast:

> The Czechs loved their country not because it was glorious but because it was unknown; not because it was big but because it was small and in constant danger. Their patriotism was an enormous compassion for their country. The Danes are like that too. Not by chance did Josef choose a small country for his emigration.[48]

As it turns out, love of country for both characters pales in comparison with their drives toward self-possession. To the extent that the love of country is at all enabling, it is because it arouses the kind of passion that can be deployed on persons. Kundera points out that Czech patriotism is articulated not as a feeling of reflected glory but as a mode of compassion whose articulation we can follow in the mental dynamics of his characters. In Irena's case, having her passions liberated in her relationship with Josef helps her recognize that her past intimacies were detoured through dependencies and were reflected in the self-denying emotion of gratitude: "What she wants now is love without gratitude."[49] In Josef's case, the affair turns his attention back toward what has always loomed larger in his emotional imaginary than any attachment to his homeland, his years of intimacy with his wife. At one point, on the road to Prague, as "the landscape slips away around him, the landscape of his small country whose people are willing to die for it . . . he knows that there exists something even smaller, with an even stronger appeal to his compassionate love":

> he sees two easy chairs turned to face each other, the lamp and the flower bowl on the window ledge, and the slender fir tree that looks like an arm she'd [his deceased wife] raised from afar to show him the way back home.[50]

Josef's epiphany while in Prague, in which he affirms what had been most important about his past life—a shared intimacy that transcended the givens of geopolitical attachments—is paralleled by one experienced by Irena, who recognizes, also while visiting Prague, that she had for the most part lived a life "run by other people" and that, on reflection, her happiest years had been lived while single, when, as she puts it, "I was master of my own life."[51] In both cases, the émigrés rely on their imaginations to accept codes that are part of a self-possession rather than continuing to be guided by norms that are imposed. The importance of imaginative invention, which for Hume is constitutive of one becoming a subject, is also articulated in Kundera's account of Irena and Josef's lovemaking. Specifically, Irena, who had hitherto catered to her two husbands and mother rather than favor her passions, provokes a shared passion for herself and Josef with "dirty talk" in Czech. She wants, in that brief affair, "to experience everything she ever imagined and never experienced, voyeurism, exhibitionism, the indecent presence of other people, verbal enormities."[52] While her dirty talk becomes a powerful sign of self-possession for Irena, for Josef, who had lived in a language for 20 years that had made him feel clumsy, inarticulate, and not quite himself, the words are arousing because of the way they resonate with his long-suppressed memories. Irena and Josef's liaison does not awaken a nostalgia for their former homeland. Rather, it liberates them by allowing them to recognize what is most important to each. The outcome of their "diasporic intimacy" is well captured by Svetlana Boym, who characterizes it as an intimacy that "does not promise a comforting recovery of identity through shared nostalgia for the lost home and homeland." "In fact," she adds, "it is the opposite. It might be seen as the mutual enchantment of two immigrants from different parts of the world or as the sense of the fragile coziness of a foreign home."[53] At a minimum, it was an intimacy that was out of place. As a result, it encouraged a reflection on spaces of attachment by both parties.

What is the general import of Kundera's staging of the affair between two émigrés? As his narrative discharges passions that challenge the geopolitical matrix of national allegiances, a rarely heeded global cartography emerges. Kundera's map is vertical as well as horizontal; in addition to a set of geopolitical boundaries, which are the setting of the drama of movement, the map has emotional depth. To the extent that an ethos emerges from the kind of verticality that Kundera's map adds to the traditional nation-state cartography, that ethos is connected to the self-possession his characters achieve as they struggle to discover the passions that have been buried under imposed codes. To evoke once again the Humean insights that help to frame Kundera's plot, the sympathy or partialities that provoke the Irena–Josef liaison fulfill the model of sociality that Hume constructs. The partiality becomes an extended generosity. In this case, it is a generosity toward oneself, as the characters learn to resist normative pressures and accept the lives they have been living. Given that, as Kundera notes, "everyone is wrong about the future," and there is thus no stable basis for attachment, one must in the last analysis trust one's own passions. At the same time, however, by dint of the juxtapositions Kundera creates—for example the *ressentiment* expressed by Josef's brother and sister-in-law toward those who have not accepted the constraints under which those who remained have lived—Kundera gestures toward an ethos of generosity toward otherness as well. Thus although Kundera's story may suggest that generosity begins at home, it also implies that an effective interpersonal and trans-territorial generosity requires that one transcend the givens of geopolitical allegiance and become generous to oneself. It is an ethos that becomes especially apparent when the struggle to attain it is enacted by exiles.

Although, as is typical of the novel form, much of the emphasis in Kundera's narrative is on individual fates, the narrative contains a parallel, if understated, discourse on the impact of global capital. Irena's husband Gustaf's attempt to try to impose a Czech life on Irena is a result of his belonging to a global corporation. It becomes evident that the world, as a pattern of passions and partialities, is transected by capital endeavors and flows. At one point Kundera explicitly treats the tensions between patriotic feelings of allegiance and the impact of capital on shaping the spaces of allegiance in a conversation between Josef and his friend N. Josef says:

> The Soviet empire collapsed because it could no longer hold down the nations that wanted their independence. But those nations—they're less independent than ever now. They can't choose their own economy or their own foreign policy or even their own advertising slogans.

N rejoins:

> National independence has been an illusion for a long time. . . . But if a country is not independent and doesn't even want to be, will anyone still be willing to die for it? ... I'll put it another way: does anyone still love this country?[54]

This minor theme—the tensions between intimacy and allegiance in the face of the shaping forces of the global economy—loom much larger in Vyacheslav Kristofovich's film *Friend of the Deceased*, which is situated in Kiev, a place in which a chaotic piracy version of capitalism is compromising the sympathies, passions, and senses of justice and fairness that constitute the social bond. Based on Andrey Kurkov's novel *A Matter of Death and Life*, the film provides a mapping of much of the economy–intimacy tensions in a key sector of the post-Soviet world.

### *Friend of the Deceased*

Kristofovich's film, like Kurkov's novel, addresses a stark reality affecting life and death in the former Soviet Union. At roughly the time at which the novel and subsequently the film appeared, life expectancy for men in the former Eastern bloc had fallen from 62 to 58, a statistic influenced in large measure by a rapid rise in the suicide rate. According to an investigation undertaken by the United Nations Development Program, the fall in life expectancy was a "demographic collapse" resulting from "the transition to market economies in many post-communist societies of the former Soviet Union and other former eastern bloc countries in Europe."[55] In the case of the Kiev represented by Kurkov and Kristofovich, lives are radically unstable, as the economy is run by pirates. And as people experience the economic squeeze and lack of work opportunities, rising animosities provide work for a plentiful array of contract killers.

The film, like the novel, treats a city in economic chaos and emotional crisis, at a time when "the normative relays between personal and collective ethics [had become] frayed and exposed."[56] Kiev, the venue of the story, is the capital city in a post-communist Ukraine where the Russian mafia dominates the economy. As a result, black market transactions constitute the major forms of exchange. At the center of the film narrative is a deteriorated marriage. The husband, Anatoli (Andre Lazarev), is an intellectual with a linguistics degree. As the film opens he is an unemployed translator in a place that has little use for his talents. In contrast his wife, Katia (Angelike Nevolina), has become a successful advertising executive with little emotional largess for a depressed, apartment-bound Anatoli. She is having an affair with a coworker, and the temporal rhythms and spatial uses of their apartment life keep her and Anatoli as separated as their small space allows.

*Figure 5.1* Anatoli in Kiev
Courtesy of Sony Pictures

The opening shots, as the credits are run, seem ordinary. We get a view of Kiev's skyline, showing aspects of Russian architecture through the window of Anatoli and Katia's apartment. However, if we heed what is distinctive about the diverse spheres that constitute the modern life-world, the relays between domestic and social or public space that the shots create, as we look alternately through the window and into the apartment interior, are telling. To place the significance of what the camera is showing (and thus how the film is thinking), we can invoke Hannah Arendt's insights about the distinctiveness of modern life where she addresses "the emergence of the social realm." Whereas historically, from the time of the ancient city-state, "the distinction between a private and public sphere of life corresponds to the household and the political realm," the "social realm, which is neither private nor public, strictly speaking, is a relatively new phenomenon whose origin coincided with the emergence of the modern age and which found its political form in the nation-state."[57] Crucially, that state form increasingly involves "a nation-wide administration of housekeeping." So to analyze the new relationships, it is "no longer political science [to which one must turn] but 'national economy' or 'social economy' or *Volkswirtschaft*, all of which indicate a kind of 'collective housekeeping.'"[58]

As the film progresses, what is shown is a dual fracture; both the marriage and the social contracts have been sundered. And both fractures are owed in large measure to the state's loss of control of a chaotic economy. Effectively, the film articulates the temporal rhythms of domestic and social affect with the rhythms of historical shifts in political economy. Anatoli's college education has gone for naught, largely because his government (we learn as he speaks on the phone) has been unable to pay for the services he has rendered thus far and has nothing else to offer. At the same time his attempt to earn in the private sector yields very little as well. Throughout the film, shots of phone calls play an important role. In the early apartment scene, Anatoli's futile attempt to connect with a work opportunity on the phone is interrupted as Katia takes a call from her lover/colleague. Significantly, the phone's receiver is taped down. Voices from the outside enter the apartment as a whole rather than in the ear of the listener. The lack of intimacy between the couple is thus paralleled by the lack of intimacy in the technologically mediated connections between the interior of the apartment and the outer society. Further, in the second apartment scene, Katia has acquired a cell phone, which allows her to exit from a shared experience of the exterior. When it rings while she is in the bathroom, she has Anatoli hand it to her (later explaining that it belongs to a colleague). When Anatoli moves to hand Katia the phone, he murmurs that it is "a portable," which is in contrast with his radically unportable, taped-down phone.

Their economic lives are thus symbolized by their phones. Katia is upwardly mobile in the economy (she is seen/heard on her cell phone arranging a transaction that involves billions in rubles), while Anatoli's economic existence is on hold. Moreover, Anatoli and Katia occupy very different kinds of socio-economic roles in relation to desire. As a rising executive in an advertising firm, Katia's vocation is one of stimulating a desire for things. Because she helps produce the social codes that provoke desire for consumption, her vocation is well attuned to an under-standing of modern market economies. Understanding consumption had become more important than understanding production. By the mid-twentieth century, "economists increasingly understood that in their new science, it was not that useful things were desired but that desired things were useful."[59] In contrast, Anatoli's vocation as a translator is one of bridging interpersonal socio-linguistic difference, of bringing people who are culturally separated into an accord. That Katia is successfully employed while Anatoli cannot find work says much about the impact of anarchic decentralized capitalism in the former Eastern bloc.

Within their domestic sphere, Anatoli and Katia's spatial and temporal estrangement parallels the gulf in their financial existences. For example in one of the early apartment scenes, Anatoli gets in bed and feigns sleep rather than greeting Katia. In another scene, when Anatoli forgetfully barges in while Katia is using the bathroom, she covers up. Once the spatio-temporally fractured domestic space is first displayed, Katia leaves for work and is met by the shiny red car of her well-off lover. Then the underemployed Anatoli walks out, descending through the apartment building's dark stairway. Arendt's description of the shift of "housekeep-ing" from a domestically controlled to a publicly controlled phenomenon comports well with the cinematic imagery of spaces through which the characters move in Kristofovich's scenes. For example, Anatoli leaves his apartment to venture into the city throughout the film, each time moving from a dark interior to a bright outdoors:

> The emergence of society—the rise of housekeeping, its activities, problems, and organizational devices—from the shadowy interior of the household into the light of the public sphere, has not only blurred the old border line between private and political, it has also changed almost beyond recognition the meaning of the two terms and their significance for the life of the individual and the citizen.[60]

It is the (already-mentioned) immovable telephone that is the instrument mediating and blurring the inside–outside line. Except for a couple of face-to-face visits at the apartment, it is the medium through which society penetrates private space. The ambiguities and instabilities of the social organization of the modern age, to which Arendt refers, are further exacerbated in the Kurkov and Kristofovich modeling of Kiev. The book version of the story addresses that instability explicitly, as Anatoli says after one conversation, "repeating the words to myself I wondered what they meant. The words doubled their meanings, even deconstructed themselves."[61] In the film version, having witnessed the destroyed marriage contract, the viewer is invited into public scenes that bear witness to a destroyed social contract that has baffled people's words and widened the gulf between what is said and what is seen. Anatoli's first stop, after he leaves the apartment, is the office of an entrepreneur for whom he is providing English lessons and translation services. Anatoli translates the interaction between the entrepreneur and a South Asian salesman who is, as the receptionist puts it, "proposing oranges." Through Anatoli's mediation, they reach an agreement, but, while the entrepreneur is smiling genially at the salesman during the negotiation, many of his words, which Anatoli does not translate, are hostile, for example "if they're damaged, I'll smash his head in." The accord reached is simply an economic agreement. Their cultural estrangement remains in place.

Civility and friendliness seem to have been almost completely evacuated from Kiev's social domain, and Kristofovich's cinematic story is largely about that evacuation. As he puts it:

> The story we tell in this film concerns the majority of cultured people living in the territory that used to be known as the Soviet Union. In the absence of liberty, these people helped one another. Human warmth was very present. But freedom suddenly appeared and, with it, coldness and solitude. And we realize that not everyone was ready to embrace this new freedom.[62]

Certainly the entrepreneur is a poor candidate for warmth and friendship because, as Jacques Derrida notes in his treatment of the politics of friendship, "the mean, the malevolent, the ill-intentioned" cannot be "good friends," because their focus is on possessing things.[63] And in a remark that captures the temper of the post-Soviet times, Dima, Anatoli's old (and refound) acquaintance, says, in response to a question about whether an associate is a friend, "no such thing nowadays, just business relationships." However, not all the economically well-positioned characters in the film are merely predatory entrepreneurs. The lonely kitchen table where Anatoli sits and either stares out the window or takes phone calls is one of two kinds of tables central to the story. The one in domestic space has counterparts in social space. It is in the café that Anatoli frequents to enjoy coffee and drinks in a public setting. The woman who runs the café is friendly and generous toward Anatoli. In several scenes she extends him credit when he's short or offers him a gratis strong drink or two when he seems depressed. In contrast with the illicit transactions that penetrate Anatoli's domestic life through the phone, while he sits at his kitchen table, is his regular table at the coffee shop, where he frequently enjoys the benefits of an amiable generosity that is face to face rather than mediated by an instrument that provides only voices.

From the film's first scene of Anatoli's experience of friendly interaction in the café, we see Anatoli heading out toward Contract Square, where he spies his old acquaintance, the above-mentioned Dima, through the window of what turns out to be a black market outlet. Dima waves him into the store, where their conversation is interrupted by Dima's various transactions; a well-dressed couple come in for a bottle of vodka, which is apparently unavailable on the legal market, and over the phone Dima promises to set aside German powdered milk and Pampers for a young father. When Dima and Anatoli, who have agreed to meet for drinks later that afternoon, get together again, Dima learns about Anatoli's fractured domestic life and offers to connect him with a contract killer (who turns out to be the purchaser of the milk and Pampers), allegedly to have his wife's lover killed. When Anatoli protests that he has no money to pay the high fee for such a service, Dima offers to loan him the money and remarks, "Families are sacred."

Dima's remark about the sacredness of the family is one among instances in which the discourse of traditional morality rings hollow in the spaces of the fractured social bond. For example, desperate for money at one point, Anatoli agrees to testify in court to an affair he never had for a high fee, to be paid by a husband who wants out of a marriage. Before agreeing, Anatoli worries about "bearing false witness." Adultery, a pervasive part of the domestic relations treated in the film, is not confined to interiors. As the relays between domestic and social space are effected in cuts between apartments and public spaces—courts, coffee shops, and sales outlets—it becomes evident that the breakdown in marriages is paralleled and inflected by the breakdown of senses of civic responsibility. In a discussion that effectively connects conjugal deceit and good citizenship Laura Kipnes writes:

> Yes of course adulterers behave badly; deception rules this land [and] charges [are] typically leveled against the adulterer . . . failure to demonstrate the requisite degree of civilized repression . . . "selfishness" (failure to work for the collective good). . . . [If] adultery summons the shaming language of bad citizenship, this also indicates the extent to which marriage is meant to function as a boot camp for citizenship instruction. A training ground for resignation

to the *a priori*. Anything short of a full salute to existing conditions will be named bad ethics.[64]

In the case of Kristofovich's Kiev, "bad ethics" abounds in both domestic and social spheres. At the outset of the film, Humean sympathy (at a minimum) and the kind of "extended generosity" necessary for social and beyond-social solidarity seem to be rarely in evidence. The plot that unfolds issues from Dima's black market shop, which, ironically, is situated at "Contract Square." In contrast, the café is on "Fraternal Street," a contrast that speaks to the difference between amoral transaction and social intimacy. Dima's business turns out to be a place for *criminal* contracts. It is both a store that stocks illegally obtained goods and a communication node for illicit services. Briefly, Dima calls Kostia, a contract killer, and gives him Anatoli's phone number. When the scene then shifts back to Anatoli's apartment, the taped-down phone on the kitchen table rings. When Anatoli answers, Kostia gives him instructions: provide a picture of the victim, details of a place he hangs out and times that he frequents it, put them in an envelope, and drop them in a post box in a building at. . . . The demoralized Anatoli then arranges his own death by putting a picture of himself, the address of the coffee shop/bar he frequents, and a time of day he plans to be there in the envelope.

About to lose his wife (Anatoli has told Dima that she has been planning to leave him for the past year), unable to use his education, and without intimate friends, Anatoli wants out of a life that holds no promise. And as one who regards money as a dirty necessity, Anatoli is unable to seek redemption in strategies for financial improvement. In the book version, Anatoli, having had some money returned to him by Dima, is tempted to wash his hands:

> My thoughts turned to the dollars given back to me by Dima. As I put them on the table, I felt suddenly that I must wash my hands. . . . Washing one's hands after handling money—dollars at that!—savored of the puke-making, moral reading prescribed in a distant past in the pages of the *Literary Gazette*.[65]

Here Anatoli is experiencing a "monetary vertigo" resulting from a historical moment in which values are in flux and money earned is no longer connected with traditional values of work and reciprocity. It is the kind of historical moment well analyzed in André Gide's novel *The Counterfeiters*, which treats a different historical moment of such instability, the period in which France has abandoned the gold standard, and, more generally, there is a crisis of meaning that has destabilized the guarantees connecting words and things. It was a moment similar to that in the Kurkov/Kristofovich story, in which meaning instability is accompanied by monetary instability and both are "accompanied by a more general anxiety about the way in which social life was being appropriated by economic life, a collapse of certain profound ideological mediations between economic life and life proper."[66]

In contrast with Anatoli, Katia appears to be comfortable in a predatory economic environment. The red car in which her colleague/lover drives her around, while Anatoli is always on foot, plays a similar role to the difference between

Anatoli's taped-down phone and her "portable." In one apartment scene, at a moment in which the spatial estrangement between the married couple is momentarily overcome, Anatoli's bodily comportment and the image of the red car intervene to reassert an estrangement. As Katia sits across from Anatoli at the small table and evokes a shared memory of a friend's father, now deceased, she mentions that the father had always liked Anatoli, and that the son/friend wants Anatoli to have his books. Throughout this part of the conversation, Anatoli looks out the window instead of at Katia. When he finally faces her, he asks whether her "colleague" drives a red car. At that point, Katia wordlessly leaves her seat.

In a later scene, we finally see the lover and his red car come for Katia. Like Katia, he is stylishly dressed and well coiffed. Their bodily comportment suggests that they are a familiar couple, but no gestures of affectionate intimacy are apparent, as we watch the scene from Anatoli's perspective (as he hides behind a tree). At this point Anatoli has had a significant change in his outlook. He has met a prostitute, who works under the name of Vika but uses her given name, Lena, while with Anatoli, whom she treats as an intimate lover rather than a client: "You would have to pay Vika but not Lena," she says. While Katia is in a relationship that appears to be based on a shared desire for consumption of clothes, travel, and public entertainment (early on they go to the theater together) rather than an affectionate bond, Anatoli and Lena's emerging relationship is shown as physical and playful. Lena's clothes barely cover her when she is dressed—only part of the time when she is in the apartment. Katia shows almost no skin; she wears tights and tops that come up high on her neck.

The new relationship between Anatoli and Lena, which is intimate and affectionate (in contrast with the estrangement between Anatoli and his wife), changes Anatoli's view of life. Events at this point have conspired to delay his death. After the café closes early on the day of the planned contract killing, Anatoli goes to Dima to try to call off the contract but is told that these things cannot be called off. Wanting now to live, Anatoli tears up the page on his desk calendar (July 26) that was to be his last and burns it. He then answers an ad for a "bodyguard," another contract killer named Ivan, a Soviet army veteran whom he retains to kill Kostia, the one he hired to have himself killed. By the end of the film, Ivan has killed Kostia, but the now remorseful Anatoli brings the money for the hit (returned from Dima) plus what was in Kostia's wallet to his widow, Marina, identifying himself as a "friend of the deceased." At the end of the film, during a third visit to Marina, affection between the two is developing; Anatoli is wearing the deceased Kostia's house slippers, and when he goes to check on Marina's crying infant, while Marina is occupied in the kitchen, the baby smiles and calls him Papa.

However, a simple narrative account of the film's ironies does not capture how it thinks about intimate versus predatory associations and the social and global contexts within which they transpire. Much of what is thought within the film narrative involves moving images that portray complex layerings of experience and time. As Deleuze has pointed out in his remarks about the films of Orson Welles, a single depth-of-field shot can be a time image.[67] Hence, the several depth-of-field shots in *Friend*, in which Kiev's traditional Russian skyline is shot from within Anatoli's apartment, provide a juxtaposition of the venue of current and changing relationships against a background that is historical, having been the space of a variety of past relationships and associations. The city, as a historical space, is marked in other ways as well. For example the metro stop at Contract Square is on the old tram line that once ran from (Tsar) Alexander Square. That metro stop is now Independence Square.

In addition to the ways in which the cityscape and its interiors are lent temporality are the layers of time immanent in the images and discursive modalities of the characters. For example, while the adults in the film are subject to economic pressures and life-and-death struggles, childhood is presented as times of innocence. Moreover, that generational time is deployed in alternative historical modalities. There are three "little girl" scenes in *Friend*. The first occurs at the point at which Anatoli and Ivan are returning to Kiev from Ivan's town on a tram. A little blind girl walks through their car, begging and speaking in a religious idiom, saying something to the effect that God will bless those who are kind and generous. The second scene takes place in the café, as Anatoli and Ivan await the fateful encounter with Kostia. From their vantage point one can see into another room of the café where a little girl is dancing in a modern and provocative way to the rhythms of a contemporary ballad. The third little girl episode takes place by self-ascription. Late in the film, Lena shows up at Anatoli's apartment, battered and bruised. She has been beaten by her Russian pimp to "shut her up" as he sells her to a Turkish pimp who is trying to establish himself in Kiev. Lena, reflecting on how she had been misled by her pimp's promise to marry her and take her on a long honeymoon, refers to herself as "a stupid little girl."

## Conclusion: identity/difference, intimacy/estrangement

Anatoli and Dima's relationship is played out in conversations. Dima's remark, after Anatoli asks whether Kostia had been his friend, that *today* there are no such things, only business relationships, expresses two aspects of time. Among other things, Dima cannot be a friend because, as his activity makes clear, he is among those who, in Jacques Derrida's terms, "prefer things (*pragmata*) to friends. They stock friends among things, they class friends at best among possessions, among good things."[68] But more compelling are the temporalities implicit in Dima's remark. In addition to noting the passage of historical time, with his reference to "today" as opposed to formerly, the friendship relation to which he refers also contains a temporal structure. As Derrida has put it, the essence of friendship is its endurance: "Primary friendship does not work without time . . . it never presents itself outside of time: there is no friend without time . . . and no confidence which does not measure up to some *chronology*, to the trial of a sensible duration of time."[69]

Apart from the relationship between Anatoli and Dima, the paired associations throughout the film are articulated with images. In this respect photographs play a key role. Before he uses a professional photographer to take a picture for him to leave for Kostia, Anatoli is seen looking at old pictures of himself and Katia looking like an affectionate couple in better times. Anatoli uses scissors to cut a picture of himself away from one of the photos in which he and Katia are together, a gesture that epitomizes their current estrangement. But in terms of the trajectory of resolution in the film, three other photos and the relationships they express are telling. First, while the camera lingers in Ivan's hovel in the suburbs, as Ivan finishes dressing in front of a mirror, we see a photo of him in his military uniform stuck at the top of the mirror. When considered along with the ones that Anatoli had saved of his former life, we see an identity. Both their former roles and the associations that went with them are past; the student Anatoli, who shared an intimacy with his student-wife, and the soldier Ivan, who was once part of a military unit, are now both loners. Nevertheless, despite the shared obsolescence of their former lives, their only bond is strictly contractual. They sit separately on the tram into town and in the café, once they arrive, ostensibly to mask their association. However, aside from the strategic dimension of their positioning, their physical separations in both places, like the way in which Anatoli had shared his apartment with Katia, reflect estrangement. In contrast, when Kostia comes looking for Anatoli in the café, he sits at Anatoli's table. After the contract killing, Anatoli looks in Kostia's wallet and finds pictures of him and his son. This discovery seemingly moves him to visit Kostia's widow and infant, where he rapidly takes over Kostia's identity space, wearing his slippers in the apartment and beginning a relationship with his widow. And, finally, after Anatoli's intimate friend Lena is beaten by her pimp, he uses a picture of the pimp she gives him to set up a revenge contract killing, employing Ivan once again.

To return to the Humean model of association I evoked to treat Kundera's *Ignorance*: a series of encounters provoked Anatoli's feelings of sympathy— toward Lena, toward Marina, and toward the man he warned about a contract killing that had been arranged for him. The sympathy had become extended generosity, not only to others but, ultimately, to himself. He had decided he had a life worth living. In the case of *Friend*, the new intimacies that develop are paradoxical. Capitalist modernity, which has reached Kiev, is a time in which capital has displaced the interpersonal relations that were once evident in barter economies. As J.-J. Goux puts it, "the capitalist relation is an unprecedented rift between intersubjective relations and what functions henceforth as economic relations."[70] At the same time, in a situation in which the economy of Kiev is pirated rather than governmentalized, characters on the margins of the social order are able to achieve intimacy by, among other things, resisting nostalgia for their lost pasts (at one point Marina says, referring to the deceased Kostia, "The dead should be allowed to remain so"). Achieving intimacy for Anatoli and Lena and Anatoli and Marina, as was the case for Irena and Josef, requires resistance to the regulative ideals imposed on family members as well as on citizen-subjects. Intimacy, as opposed to traditional modes of allegiance, reflects, at an individual level, the micropolitics of survival and, at a collective level, the frailties of the capture mechanisms of the modern state.

# 6 Perpetual war?

The soldier, that corpse in a trenchcoat, to his military autism.

Semezdin Mehmedinovic[1]

## Introduction: saying and seeing

In chapter 1, in which I follow the trajectories of a war photo back to the "home front," much of my analysis is focused on the forces involved in recruiting the bodies that end up in zones of danger. In this chapter, with analyses of two films, Michael Cimino's *The Deer Hunter* and Terrence Malick's *The Thin Red Line* (hereafter *TRL*), my emphasis is on the bodies themselves. Cimino's film thinks primarily about the limits to what the men are able to say, while Malick's film thinks primarily about the limits of their vision. Although both films contain war footage, a very limited amount in *The Deer Hunter* and a considerable amount in *TLR*, neither of them is typical of the war film genre. Both evoke complex political and philosophical questions about life and death as they connect wars with the life-worlds from which American soldiers have entered them. Accordingly, both films achieve what Deleuze ascribes to cinema in his remark "[cinema] does not just present images, it surrounds them with a world."[2] Although neither film delivers an unambiguous position on war, on good versus evil, or on the responsibility for the death and suffering associated with war, they both employ storylines, images, and the juxtapositions that film form can deliver to think about both. Now, as at the time in which they were released—Cimino's during an intense cinematic reflection on the Vietnam War, as increasingly critical films contested the traditional heroic versions of war cinema, and Malick's during a cinematic revival in which films appeared to be aimed at resuscitating World War II as the "good war"—both films retain a powerful impetus to think about warring violence while providing appropriate vehicles for extending the reflections and analyses with which this investigation began.

## Prelude to *The Deer Hunter*: Mr. "Fuck it"

By the fall of 2007, after more than one million Iraqi deaths and the deaths of nearly 4,000 U.S. troops, the life experiences of many of the American G.I.s seemed to imitate those of the key characters in Michael Cimino's film *The Deer Hunter*. In the film, Mike (Robert De Niro) and Nick (Christopher Walken), two close friends from the mythic Russian Orthodox community of Clairton, Pennsylvania, have escaped a cruel imprisonment in Vietnam. Mike loses track of Nick and returns home, while Nick, obviously suffering from "post-traumatic stress disorder" (*avant la lettre*), is left behind, subsequently to become obsessively involved in the same Russian roulette games that his former captors had imposed on him and his friends. Mike, ill at ease after returning home, ultimately returns to Vietnam to bring Nick "home" but ends up bringing Nick's body home, because Nick, after spurning Mike's invitation to return with him, has shot himself.

With an uncanny resemblance to Mike's experience, American G.I.s in Iraq have begun testifying about the pain of returning home without their close friends. For example: "Heartache can be heard in the quiet voice of Specialist Gerald Barranco-Oro, who at 22 is on his second tour of Iraq and will leave for home without two close friends who were killed on May 19."[3] Barranco-Oro goes on to describe an unconsummated plan for the return home to attend the wedding of his friend, Pfc. Matthew Bean, who was shot by a sniper, and says "You would never, never think one of your friends won't be there with you—never," and adds that now going home cannot be the same: "We'll still go see the families and stuff, but it's going to be different."[4] There are strong homologies between the experiences of Gerald Barranco-Oro and Mike in Cimino's *The Deer Hunter*, but in the film the wedding precedes the process of loss and mourning. My treatment of *The Deer Hunter* begins with a reflection on one of its exemplary scenes.

In a seemingly enigmatic moment at their friends Steve and Angela's wedding, Mike and Nick spot a Green Beret, on leave from the Vietnam War, standing at the bar. Because they, along with the groom, Steve, are soon headed to the war front, they are excited about seeing someone who can tell them what it's like "over there." However, the Green Beret proves to be remarkably inarticulate. In response to their queries, his only utterance is "Fuck it"; he is unable to tell them (or the viewers) anything about the war. He reciprocates their animated gestures (for example glasses raised in toast) with an imperious stare. The scene is striking for its disjuncture between the visual and aural registers. The Green Beret's uniform is immaculate, his posture is upright and confidence-inspiring, and his gaze has the kind of depth one associates with comfortable self-control over one's past and present. Because of his commanding presence, his interlocutors persist with their queries until, finally weary of the fruitless interrogation, Mike and Nick begin calling the bi-syllabic Green Beret "Fuck it."

In the context of the film narrative, the scene turns out to have a double resonance. First, it becomes clear in the second part of the film that *nothing* could have prepared the men from the small industrial Pennsylvania town for their Vietnam experience. Second, the film as a whole features young men who are remarkably inarticulate; they inhabit a subculture within which the exchange of verbal signs is minimal. The film's tableaux of minimal verbal sign exchange could stand alone as telling glimpses of a life-world. However, in the context of the film narrative, it is implied that the linguistic poverty of the film's primary characters, who never elaborately

*Figure 6.1* "Fuck it" at the wedding
Courtesy of Universal Studios

discuss their fates, renders them susceptible to an unreflective transition from working bodies (they are all employed in a steel mill) to warring bodies (they end up at the war front in Vietnam). In this sense, the film poses a question that traditional war films tend to ignore: why do people adopt and enact enmities that have little to do with, or are even disjunctive with, their personal experiences? Peter Weir's *Gallipoli* (1981) is also an exception. Like *The Deer Hunter*, the film begins with male bonding scenes and emphasizes unreflectively adopted enmities, especially in a scene in which young ranch hands in Western Australia are reading a newspaper aloud to each other about Gallipoli, a venue of contested terrain in World War I. Although they cannot even pronounce the name of their destination, the men inspire each other to join the army and head to the Turkish front in order, they aver, to show the world what Australian manhood is about.

As the film narrative of *The Deer Hunter* carries its characters to a war zone and then home again, we can discern an aspect of a war's impact (the Vietnam War in this case) that is unaddressed in *Gallipoli*. Cimino's film also implicitly raises the question of why those who are traumatized by the war, through a direct experience of violence and death, are unable to evince sufficient reflection, not only to recognize the danger that awaits them on the war front but also to come to terms with trauma and loss. As is often the case with critically oriented cinema, *The Deer*

*Hunter* gives us a perspective that its characters never achieve. Their failure to find words that would allow them better to cope with their experiences (exemplified in their inability to get information from the Green Beret) is located in a wider context for the viewer because, as I have continually noted, cinema gives the viewer a critical purchase not achieved by the actors. Critically formed film is not organized on the basis of subjective perception. Rather (to repeat Deleuze's remark), "because [of ]the mobility of its centers and the variability of its framings [it] . . . restores vast acentered and deframed zones," which are available to the viewer but not the characters.[5] In perhaps its most exemplary scene, *The Deer Hunter* mobilizes moving images to think about what the Green Beret's bi-syllabic responses are telling us, among other things.

The encounter with the Green Beret in the bar at the wedding inaugurates my reading of *The Deer Hunter* and helps to shift the emphasis from chapter 1's treatment of the ways in which an ecology of institutions produces the force field in which bodies are moved into zones of danger to an emphasis on the susceptibility of those bodies to accede to military recruitment and thence to suffer without indicting the policy initiatives and institutional structures responsible for their fates. Because the central focus of *The Deer Hunter* involves reading signs critically, it is instructive to revisit, at least briefly, Immanuel Kant's optimistic reading of signs, in the context of asking the question of what history was telling us about global antagonisms right after the French Revolution, a question he poses in both his "Perpetual Peace" and "The Contest of Faculties." In the former, Kant expresses optimism about the peace-fostering potential of publicity. He posits the pervasive global development of an "unwritten code of political and international right," so that "we can flatter ourselves that we are continually advancing towards a perpetual peace."[6] And in the latter, he suggests that there are exemplary events (here he has the French Revolution in mind) that serve as a "rough historical sign" that allows us to infer that there is an increasingly peaceful tendency. According to Kant, the publicity generated by such events is producing a level of enthusiasm which bodes well for the development of a "universal community."[7]

However, because of his consciousness-centered philosophy of meaning and experience, which is based on a narrative of mental faculties—the story begins with the process of interpreting raw experience, moves on to a productive understanding, and eventuates in a publicity that universalizes perspectives[8]—Kant neglects what Michel Foucault calls "the coercive structure of the signifier."[9] With a commitment to humanity's historically enlarging and increasingly shared consciousness, Kant provides no way to discern the variable power of signifying systems, which are especially coercive when they are deployed on people who possess a limited "stock of signs," an assemblage that, according to Roland Barthes, creates the conditions of possibility for decoding situations. Moreover, it should be noted that, in keeping with Barthes's and Foucault's models of discourse (and the spirit of Cimino's film), the language deficits are primarily a feature of discursive economies, especially of the available discursive assets that exist in various subcultures, rather than of particular individuals. At a minimum, Cimino's film provides grounds for contesting Kant's optimism (and inspires this chapter's title).

## *The Deer Hunter* with *The Thin Red Line*

Sometimes because of genre confusion and sometimes for simple hermeneutic reasons, much of the critical reaction to Cimino's film has been ill focused. With respect to the former: apparently it must be emphasized that *The Deer Hunter* is not a documentary. That its mountain scenes are not faithful to the Pennsylvania landscape or that the Russian roulette imposed on American and South Vietnamese prisoners by the Viet Cong "never actually happened in Vietnam" is irrelevant to an interpretation of their significance in the film.[10] With respect to the latter, the viewer is also misled if asked to judge the film's ideological position on the Vietnam War or its sensitivity to the relative suffering the war imposed on Americans versus Vietnamese.[11] While the war venue plays an important role in the film, the primary film narrative is not about Vietnamese or indeed not even very much about the Vietnam War. The political contribution of *The Deer Hunter*, I want to suggest, is to be sought in the ways in which it offers a politics of aesthetics, the ways in which it re-partitions the experience of war to yield insight into the self-motivating force of some of war's victims. It cannot yield significant insights as a cinematic treatise on the ethics of war. Unlike typical war films, *The Deer Hunter*'s effect is not to draw attention to the macropolitics of war strategy or policy and its justification but to disclose aspects of the micropolitics of individual and communal coping with danger and loss, and it does so more through the images it deploys than through any narrative thread. In short, the film belongs to what Jacques Rancière designates as the aesthetic regime of images. As he points out, both the ethical regime of images, in which images are questioned in terms of their purpose or the "ethos" affected by images, and the mimetic regime of images, in which art must represent or imitate, have been supplanted by the contemporary aesthetic regime of the arts. It is a regime that is realistic, not because of the ethos to which it can be attached or the veracity of imitation it achieves but because (as I note in chapter 2) it adopts "a fragmented or proximate mode of focalization, which imposes raw presence to the detriment of the rational sequences of the story."[12] Within such a regime, it is the details of "raw presence" rather than the film's "narrative drive" (which, as one commentator complains, is developed only late in the film) that deliver the film's significance.[13]

To adopt a basic interpretive standpoint at the outset, the film, as I have suggested, is primarily about linguistically challenged Americans who, lacking a discursive *savoir-faire* with themselves and others, are coerced by simplistic patriotic codes to risk their lives in a violent conflict that makes little sense to them. That said, the first major scene in a steel mill in the mythic, ethnically Ukrainian town of Clairton, Pennsylvania, sets the stage for a film whose major storyline pursues its theme of discursive impoverishment by focusing on the interpretation and exchange of signs. After an opening in which the camera pans the town's city streets and buildings, the scene shifts to the inside of a steel mill, where heavily costumed and visored men are surrounded by gigantic machines that spew smoke and fire. Barely visible to each other and unable to communicate verbally over the roar of the blast furnaces, they coordinate their work with simple hand signals,

*Figure 6.2* Factory interior
Courtesy of Universal Studios

until one signal overcodes all the others—the loud blast of the whistle that indicates the end of their work shift.

Before treating the next scene, which involves the animated male bonding and acting out of desire after being released from the bodily comportment demands of work, mostly in the form of exaggerated physical horseplay, it is instructive to consider aspects of Terrence Malick's feature film *TLR*, which shares *The Deer Hunter*'s anti-war impetus but effects a wholly different kind of narrative structure and, in terms of its non-narrative ways of seeing and saying, a wholly different mode of partitioning of the senses. Among other things, while the characters in *The Deer Hunter* engage in very limited and inhibited conversations—about war and anything else that is important—the characters in *TLR* almost literally talk each other to death. However, on the whole, the Malick film thinks primarily with images. Accordingly, the opening scene of Malick's film is heavily visual rather than discursive, although it is punctuated occasionally with a voice-over monologue by Witt (Jim Caviezel), the film's main character.

The film begins in the Solomon Islands, where we see a crocodile crawling in a dense, exuberant forest with bird sounds voiced over, with Witt's remark, "What's this war in the heart of nature? Why does nature vie with itself—the land contend with the sea? Is there an avenging power in nature? Not one power but two?" As the scene unfolds, we watch, with Witt, a seemingly idyllic life led by the islanders, while the soundtrack consists of church choir music, seemingly to spiritualize the scenes. The choir continues as Melanesian children are shown cracking kukui nuts, others of various genders and ages are seen moving about in their everyday peaceful lives, and in an underwater scene a group of swimming Melanesians appear as virtually weightless and unpressured. Witt's calm demeanor reflects what he sees until his and his army companion's postures shift suddenly, as an American warship enters within the island reef, prompting them to retreat from view. The set of images in which the battleship intrudes is shocking in the context of the preceding images and calls to mind Danis Tanovic's remarks about the opening scene in his *No Man's Land* (quoted in chapter 3), where he asks us to imagine "seeing a black bullet hole in a building or a crater made by a shell in a field . . . to imagine if someone imposed a black-and-white photograph on a Van Gogh painting," and adds:

> You will understand what one feels when seeing this. The disharmony was a kind of visual shock . . . shock is something I have reproduced through my film. On one side, a long summer day—perfect nature, strong colors—and on the other human beings and their black madness. . . . Panoramic shots of landscape become unexpectedly mixed with nervous details of action.[14]

As is the case with Tanovic's film, Malick's landscape is effectively a silent actor with a complicated semiotic burden. We are introduced to much more than simply the battle for Guadalcanal (the World War II battle featured in the film). As one analyst puts it, apart from serving to portray the military as an invader of a peaceful setting the landscape is configured throughout the film:

> As cartographic location [implied in a map scene aboard the ship], as strategic anomaly [implied in the enigmas of the Japanese presence], as paradise/hell [implied in the contrasts between idyllic island scenes and battlefields], as tourist location [mentioned in James Jones's novel version and implied in Malick's film], as topological identity [articulated in the naming of the hills], as logistical obstacle [implied in the difficulties of maintaining supply lines and finding a direction for the assault on the Japanese position], as dispassionate observer [where we see the action, seemingly along with the landscape], as repository of ancient cultures and natural wonders [implied in Malick's anthropological discourse].[15]

Landscape plays a more modest role in *The Deer Hunter* but, as is the case with Malick's *TRL*, it is one of the film's characters. In *TRL*, the landscape's exuberance and innocence play an anti-war role; it shows itself as a life-affirming world that succors the bodies inhabiting it, in contrast with the death-producing impetus of the antagonisms that abound in the world of war. And crucially, in contrast with the person–nature attunement manifested by the Melanesians with whom Witt connects while AWOL, the landscape for the men-at-war becomes real estate to be acquired at high cost to life and limb.

*Figure 6.3* Malick's landscape as warscape
Courtesy of 20th Century Fox

In general, the landscape scenes function very differently in the two films. In *The Deer Hunter*, the mountains are largely a space of reprieve, a space where elemental impulses can be exercised in a less complex environment, one free from the pressured temporal rhythms of everyday life in an industrial city. Away from the burdens of the working day, from fraught gender relations, and from culturally induced religious rituals, the men are more able to negotiate who they are and how they should behave. Although their usual male bonding/horseplay is still in evidence in the initial mountain scene during the film's first deer hunt, the agenda of the hunt in a space without their usual everyday props serves to focus them and provoke discussion about both what they share and what differentiates them. Nick's connection with the mountain and hunt is primarily aesthetic. As he says before they head out, he just likes to look at the trees. Mike in contrast is obsessed with the proprieties of a deer hunt. His penchant for a strong normative approach to life in general is articulated specifically in the coding he applies to the hunt—for example his insistence that a deer must be brought down with one shot. The rest of the men remain in character, falling back for the most part on their usual male bonding rituals, except in those moments when they must respond to Michael's instructive outbursts.

At one point, Michael's intense focus, which in the mountains is not buried in the multiple distractions of city life, provokes a crisis. Angry at the group's inability to take the hunt seriously, he first refuses to lend Stan his extra shoes, after Stan notices that he has forgotten his. Later he reacts to Stan's misplaced antics and inappropriate hunting weapon, a small pistol, by grabbing the pistol and threatening Stan with it, discharging an empty chamber while holding it to Stan's head. Ultimately, the initial mountain scene is more or less a still context for the various kinds of movement of the men. "Nature" functions here as a fixed canvas, while the bodies are what are animated.

In contrast, the landscape shots in *TRL* present a nature that is alive and resonating. In addition to the obvious movement of the crocodile in the opening scene are the more subtle movements of the vegetation. The trees and grasses are shown swaying in gentle breezes, while refracting light and shadow, much like the effect of a rotating kaleidoscope. The camera's framing of the landscape catches those moments in which nature is deployed as exuberant life, while the men-at-war are actively engaged in its extinction. In and of itself, Malick's nature is enigmatic; it issues no opinions about the ways in which human war is carried out in its precincts. It endures as a living facticity. However, if we recall Witt's queries about war in the heart of nature, we are able to discern a double resonance in the landscape scenes. A "war in the heart of nature" is both about the struggles within nature and about the human war going on in its setting. The within-nature agonism is noted when Colonel Tall (Nick Nolte), at the point at which he is in contention with Captain Staros (Elias Koteas) for his refusal to lead a direct and perilous assault on the entrenched Japanese, refers to nature's cruelty: "Look at this jungle. Look at those vines, the way they twine around the trees, swallowing everything. Nature is cruel, Staros." The human contention in the heart of nature, to which nature is not complicit, is noted with images. At one point, while the men are advancing upstream toward their Japanese antagonists, the camera isolates the water rapids, which are flowing in the opposite direction.

While the role of quiescent versus exuberant landscapes renders nature as very different kinds of protagonist in the two films, the men are also radically distinguished. In contrast with the characters in *The Deer Hunter*, Malick's characters are prolix. Once Witt rejoins his company and ends up in the brig for being AWOL, he is engaged in conversation by his sergeant, Top Welch (Sean Penn). Welch says, "You haven't learned a thing," and adds "Truth is, you can't take straight duty in my company," where "straight," we learn as the film progresses, is unambiguous forward movement, the delivery of death, and the acquisition of more and more "property" (as Top later calls what is earned in the company's advance). Finally, saying "You'll never be a real soldier," Top decides to do Witt the favor of transferring him to a medical unit as a stretcher-bearer rather than having him court-martialed. Witt responds with the remark, "I can take anything you can dish out. I'm twice the man that you are." While that remark could be construed as a macho challenge, it has a very different resonance if one heeds the opening scene, where a different kind of world is shown, along with Witt's earlier statement about the doubleness in nature. Accordingly, perhaps the most significant exchange between Witt and Top takes place when Top says, "In this world man himself is nothing," followed by "There ain't no other world but

*Figure 6.4* Witt in another world
Courtesy of 20th Century Fox

this one," to which Witt responds, "You're off there, Top; I've seen another world." As a result of the opening scene, the viewer has seen it with him. Thereafter, Malick's use of film form allows the viewer to see what many of the protagonists cannot—as his film thinks profoundly about life and, in an ontological sense, the relationship between Being and death. If Witt is twice the man that Top is, it is so by dint of his being able to entertain two worlds rather than one.

Thus Malick's film registers a different kind of ontological depth than Cimino's. As is clear from Malick's Heideggerian philosophical orientation, the problem of how we are in the world, and what "world" can mean, given human temporality, is central to the way his film thinks. As Malick explains in his translator's preface to Heidegger's *The Essence of Reasons*, "Where Heidegger talks about 'world' he will often appear to be talking about a pervasive view which we bring to things in the world." Malick hastens to add that for Heidegger the very expression "point of view" can be misleading, for, as he notes, "there is no more sense in speaking of an interpretation when, instead of an interpretation of the 'world' is meant to be that which can keep us from seeing, or force us to see, that which we have *is* one."[16] Not surprisingly, then, Malick's film focuses on the vagaries of seeing in relation to what the world is about. As a result, his film shares with Cimino's the relationship between sign and world, a relationship for which there is no better guide than Proust.

Reflecting on the sign–world relationship that emerges from Proust's *Le Temps retrouvé* Gilles Deleuze articulates the Proustian approach to the relationship succinctly:

> The worlds are unified by their formation of sign systems emitted by persons, objects, substances; we discover no truth, we learn nothing except by deciphering and interpreting. But the plurality of worlds is such that these signs are not of the same kind, do not have the same way of appearing, do not allow themselves to be deciphered in the same manner, do not have an identical relation with their meaning.[17]

However, to translate the relationship into the ways in which it is expressed within the two films, we have to heed the alternative cinematic grammars that Cimino and Malick employ. While ultimately both films generate ideas about the ways in which warring violence is enabled by failures to read worldly signs effectively, the grammar of subjectivity differs markedly in the two. And significantly, the ontology in Cimino's film features the problem of "home" rather than "world." The home focus is exemplified in one of Nick's remarks, just before the wedding. "It's all right here," he says, referring to the home habitus. Home plays a less central role in *TRL*; its presence is provided only in the flashbacks that help to situate the characters' issues with love and death. In both films, however, the images as well as the dialogue articulate the conditions of possibility for the characters' understanding of what they and the world are about.

In the case of Malick's *TRL*, the limits to understanding, as the different characters, Witt and Top, decipher signs in the worlds of war and in diverse life-worlds, are treated primarily with images. Bersani and Dutoit capture Malick's approach well, noting that "Malick's camera uses the closeup as a way of giving a face the particularities of its own point of view. It shows the imprint of the act of looking on the subject of the looking."[18] Specifically, Witt and Top manifest different ways of registering the world. Close-ups of Witt's face show a wide-eyed, wondering look, implying that Witt is open to a plurality of worlds, while the close-ups of Top often show a squinty-eyed look which, cinematically, articulates the narrowed gaze of a man insisting on a single world and, accordingly, an unambivalent approach to managing it. The characters, as Bersani and Dutoit appropriately note, "are individuated not as personalities but as perspectives on the world."[19]

Even the spaces of Malick's film are organized in terms of the problematic of perspective. The Witt–Top exchange early in the film takes place in the brig, where Witt has been confined because he was AWOL. After the opening scenes of the film, where one witnesses what Siegfried Kracauer famously calls the "human flow of life," we are suddenly in the visually claustrophobic environment of the brig. It is in this space, where one is of necessity short-sighted, that Witt says he has seen another world. Given where he is when he delivers the remark, he is then prompted to add, "Sometimes I think it's just my imagination," to which Top responds, "You'll see things I never will." After that exchange, we see Witt lighting matches, as if to produce better vision, followed by a flashback to an open-vista farm scene with Witt as a child.

In contrast with the visual idiom applied to inhibitions of understanding in *TRL*, Cimino's *The Deer Hunter* emphasizes the aural, beginning with the factory noise which compromises conversational exchange and then moving on to the inhibitions that contain conversations within unreflective, hackneyed sentiments. While in Malick's *TLR* the clash of perspectives inheres within the film, Cimino's cinematic grammar juxtaposes the perspectives of the characters with those of the viewer, while verbal exchange looms larger than non-verbal ways of seeing. Although Cimino also makes occasional use of the close-up (for example we are able to discern Mike's romantic interest in Nick's fiancée, Linda (Meryl Streep), because of close-ups that show how he looks at her during the wedding celebration, more typically the limits to perspective are shown when the camera draws back from characters. For example, in the early factory scene we see a moment when one of the workers slams his visor down before approaching the blast furnace. It is left to the viewer to decipher the signs that articulate aspects of perspective.

What we witness as viewers in *The Deer Hunter* is the group of worker-friends living in worlds of signs that most of them cannot (or are unmotivated to) decipher. Michael is the only one who endeavors to read signs and externalize the results, even though the exchanges in which he is involved are impeded by a radical restriction in modes of articulation. For example, when the friends Axel, Mike, Nick, Steve, and Stanley finally emerge from the noise of the steel factory and are able to hear each other, they speak solely in the form of clichés and typical men's sexual jokes and innuendos, for example Nick's joke: "Have you heard about the happy Roman? Glad-he-ate-her." As they exit the mill, still grabbing and jostling each other, the mood suddenly changes as Mike looks skyward and calls their attention to black spots in the air (doubtless caused by the sun hitting the heavy particulates in the polluted air). Using the code of the now-absent Native Americans, he refers to the spots as "sun dogs," which he notes are "an old Indian thing," a "good omen" for a deer hunt. Like Malick's Witt, Cimino's Michael is a reader of signs.

The arresting effect of Mike's code reading evinces two kinds of interpretive response. The first kind is within the film. Stan responds to Mike's pedagogy by saying that Mike makes no sense. Here and in another scene in which Mike insists that the only way to hunt a deer is to use one shot (to which Nick responds by calling Mike a "control freak"), Mike is established as not only the primary deer hunter but also the primary interpreter of experiences. In contrast with Witt, who is a bearer of a counter-experience, one who carries with him another world he has seen, which estranges him from the group (even though, as he puts it, he loves C Company), Michael is more effective as a leader of his coworker-friends (and ultimately of his fellow soldiers). Whether or not his codes are appropriate, at least he has some, which he applies resolutely, because, as he says to Nick, he "just doesn't like surprises." The second kind of interpretive response belongs to the viewer, who has just gotten a clue about the film's title, *The Deer Hunter*. A contemporary deer hunter is standing in for James Fenimore Cooper's American

*Deerslayer*. But the "old Indian thing[s]" are no longer on the scene. This is a different America, operating with different, largely imported, codes. Nevertheless, the viewer is invited to recognize that the men, who will be summoned to a violent venue outside the continent, are residing on a killing field produced by an earlier history of violence.

The break in the flow of the story, as male horseplay is interrupted by a discussion of enigmatic signs, should evoke another interpretive response in the viewer, one which, if the film is to be intelligible, must pervade the viewing experience of the entire story. While Cimino's story has one of the film's characters read signs and omens, the viewers are having a parallel experience; the cinematic deployment of signs continually demands attention. For example, one of the signs, to which the audience alone is privy, is a bad omen provided during the wedding of Steve and Angela. As they drink wine from cups with their arms intertwined, they are told that if they don't spill a drop they are guaranteed lifelong good fortune. While the wedding guests assume that the couple is successful as they drain their glasses, the viewer is shown, through a close-up shot, two tiny drops of red wine landing on the bride's gown.

The deployment of some of the other signs places heavier interpretive demands on the viewer. For example, when Michael returns to Clairton from Vietnam, while Nick is AWOL, Linda, seemingly giving up on the return of her fiancé, decides to make Michael her romantic partner. Just before she suggests that they go to bed together to (in her euphemistic expression) "at least comfort each other," a cross is visible around her neck. But before she delivers her proposition, with an unselfconscious and barely discernible gesture she shakes her head so that her hair hides the cross. To locate the gesture in the economy of signs within the Russian Orthodox subculture of Clairton, it is necessary to heed the gender differentiation that the film provides in its early scenes. After leaving work, the men assemble in a bar, run by their friend John. As before, their verbal exchanges are sparse, banal, and hackneyed. There, and subsequently, the lowest common denominator of their discursive poverty is exemplified by Axel, whose response to all queries, rhetorical or otherwise, is "Fuckin' A" (Axel says little else through the film). While assembled in the bar—effectively a hall of worship to their comradeship—their bartender/friend John presides. He pours and they drink. The beer and the romantic ballad, playing on the jukebox (to which they occasionally sing along), are the primary media that unite them, as they unwind together and begin an early, largely non-verbal, celebration of Steve's wedding that will take place that evening.

While the beer drinking proceeds, constituting one of the primary codes of manhood and comradeship, the scene cuts to the women, whose preparation for the wedding shows them consuming a different set of signs: the cultural and the religious. Steve's mother is shown seeking the Russian Orthodox priest's counsel about her fears about the sacrilegious depravity of the groom and his friends and the cultural insensitivity of the wedding couple's generation as a whole. And the younger women are shown observing the cultural forms as they dress for the wedding. To the extent that cultural and religious practices are sustained, it is primarily the job of the women. Like the men, they live in a world of signs that are

*Figure 6.5* The men in the bar
Courtesy of Universal Studios

pre-packaged and demand little reflection. And, like the men, they have secrets, requiring them to sedulously manage the signs they emit.

The sign management demands on the women are most evident in Angela, Steve's bride, and Linda, who is to become Nick's fiancée. As Angela dresses for the wedding, she turns sideways to see if her gown reveals her pregnancy, which is known to her mother but not the groom. In Linda's case, she applies makeup to hide a bruised face, which is a sign of family violence. Her drunken, abusive, bed-ridden father reciprocates for her care taking with blows. Michael's sign management, propelled by his immense self-alienation, is the most exemplary among the men. It is signaled early in the film during the factory scene, where he is shown slamming his visor over his face, masking the only canvas on which his thoughts and feelings might be rendered. Thereafter, his retreat from his self- and other-engagement takes the form of a dogmatic application of codes (for example his demand that a deer hunt must use one shot) and an extended displacement; the deer stands in for a dear. As I noted, it becomes clear from the camera shots that follow his eyes during the wedding celebration that he is attracted to Nick's fiancée, Linda, but there he muzzles his desire by turning to the alcohol-as-media that characterizes his experience among men; he suggests that he and Linda have a beer.

The deer hunt for Michael, who is the only one that takes it seriously, can be read as, among other things, a substitute for the pursuit of romantic attachments.[20] And during the hunt, while his friends goof around and exchange platitudes, Mike is involved in assiduous coding. For example, when the moment arrives in which Stanley, having forgotten his boots, asks to borrow Mike's, Mike refuses. After lamenting the constant lack of seriousness of Stanley on their hunts, he justifies his refusal with the remark: "This is this." In a response that reflects the impoverished level of meaning-exchanges among the men, Stanley says: "*This is this!* . . . What's that bullshit supposed to mean?" It's a remark that reinforces Stanley's earlier assertion about Mike (outside the mill, after the "sun dogs" are spotted), which suggests that only a symptomatic reading could make sense of Mike's utterances: "Sometimes only a doctor can understand you."

To return to the scene in which Linda suggests that she and Mike have sex, Mike's response to the proposition is of a piece with his earlier self-alienation, now deepened by his war experience: "I don't know. I feel a lot of distance—far away." Hitherto, all of his expressions of intimacy have been with men, expressed primarily through physical horseplay. The form of Mike's lack of cross-gender *savoir-faire* is not atypical among working-class men. As Mira Komarovsky discovered in her investigation of blue collar marriages, the sexes (her word) operate in separate worlds, and men are most comfortable deploying their intimacy on a "clique of buddies."[21] However, apart from a lack of romantic *savoir-faire*, Mike's response evokes a powerful theme in the narrative, the extent to which the young men are homeless. When Mike returns from Vietnam to Clairton, without his friend Nick (to whom he had made a promise to bring him back), home no longer seems like home. In the taxi on the way into town he spots a banner across the street that says "Welcome Home Michael," but he deliberately avoids the reunion. Was he ever at home? After the film's initial deer hunt, right after the wedding, Mike is able to enact his one-shot code and bring down a deer. But after the hunt, Mike is sitting among the men assembled in the bar, as John plays a melancholy Chopin sonata on the piano. The music of this "noted exile" evokes a somber mood among men who seem to be never at home.[22] They too are exiles from home, and the melancholic music reflects their state of melancholy. They confuse loss and lack; they are mourning a lost object—home—which they never possessed.[23] And their fundamental non-rapport with themselves (their inability to make sense of themselves) has rendered them vulnerable to hackneyed sense-making codes. The confusion over home remains fundamentally unresolved for Nick, while Mike finally achieves a measure of resolution. Once Nick's suicide removes him from Mike's confused conception of home (he goes on a final deer hunt without him) and Nick can no longer mediate Mike's relationship with Linda (he is finally able to have sex with her), he is able to stop enacting his deer–dear displacement. When he has the deer in his sights, he fires into the air instead of killing it and says, by way of release, "OK."

Inasmuch as "what melancholy obfuscates is that the object is lacking from the very beginning," it is clear that Nick is the exemplar of one who manifests the most severe melancholic symptoms. More precisely, Nick, in keeping with the tendency of "the melancholic to [engage in] an excessive, superfluous mourning for an object even before this object is lost,"[24] anticipates estrangement from his home, which he expresses in an early scene, as he and Mike dress for the wedding and contemplate their nearing departure for Vietnam. Reflecting on his attachment to Clairton as his home, he says, "I love this fuckin' place. . . . It's all right here," and he follows this remark with a plea to Mike: "If anything happens, don't leave me over there." But what is that "all" that is "right here"? Once Nick suffers the trauma of his temporary capture in Vietnam, his ability to connect verbally with home is finally sundered. Two adjacent scenes testify to Nick's linguistic incapacity to express his attachment. First, while in the trauma unit of the hospital in Saigon, he cannot come up with his parents' names for the doctor, and afterwards, when he looks at Linda's picture in his wallet and then begins to call her on the phone, he aborts the call and rushes off.

Ultimately, Mike returns to Vietnam, where Nick has stayed and become a player in a Russian roulette gambling enterprise, compulsively repeating his experience as a captive. Nick rejects Mike's offer to bring him home, spits in his face, and shoots himself in the head. As a result, Mike ends up bringing home his corpse. Why does Nick die? One commentator on the film has put it bluntly, but is more or less on the mark: "Nick is inarticulate. It's why he pulls the trigger."[25] There is certainly abundant evidence of Nick's discursive limitations. For example at the wedding, when Linda's eligibility to marry is signaled by her catching of the thrown bridal bouquet, Nick's attempt to bring what is on his mind into discourse is muddled. After asking Linda to marry him he says, "I don't know what the hell I mean."

However, Nick's discursive poverty is a general characteristic of the men as a whole, the most extreme case being Axel, whose "Fuckin' A" response to all queries is symptomatic of not only the friends' inarticulate interactions (for example, to greet friends, Mike simply says "Heyyyyy!") but also the community's inability to respond to tragedy. They defer to ritualized signs rather than discussing their fears or examining information from the global mediascape. For example the ballroom where the wedding is celebrated has signs of death—flag-draped pictures of young men who have died in Vietnam—but the only way the war is explicitly brought into discourse is in the form of a patriotic slogan on a banner that says "Serving God and Country Proudly."

Ultimately, Cimino's story, constructed with its cinematic cuts and juxtapositions, emphasizes the senseless brutality of the war and points out that the determination of who lives, who dies, and who gets maimed is more or less a deadly game of chance, of Russian roulette. (In the film, chance is inflected ethnically to accommodate his Russian American characters.) Meanwhile, the community relies on ritual practices—weddings and funerals—and ritualized utterances. The community's constant resort to platitudes rather than discussion is shown early in the film. Once the wedding celebration is in full swing and untoward acts are committed—for example Stanley's girlfriend is shown getting groped while dancing with the master of ceremonies—the response is always ritualized. The interpretation John offers to Stanley about the groping, when Stanley seeks affirmation that what he is seeing is wrong, is "It's a wedding!" And when platitudes will not avail, no words are used. Stanley simply gets up and slugs his girlfriend. Similarly, when Steve returns maimed from Vietnam and ends up in a Shriners hospital, unwilling to come home because, as he tells Mike, "I don't fit in," his wife, Angela, can't talk about it. When Mike insists that she tell him where Steve is, she silently writes a telephone number on a piece of paper.

Whatever home is for the people of Clairton, it's not a place for an elaborate exchange of meanings. "Home," as the cinematic signs tell us, is simply a Pennsylvania town, where in everyday life and in times of stress they resort to simple labels. For example, they drink Rolling Rock beer (the labels are clearly visible in the first bar scene), while "over there" has meaning also on the basis of simple labels; during the coerced Russian roulette game in Vietnam, the beer drunk by the Viet Cong is Miller. The minimal coding and the lack of self-reflection about "home" are ultimately underscored in the film's last scene, the post-funeral breakfast served in John's bar. As the mourners enter after attending Nick's funeral, John says, "Make yourselves at home," a remark that has ironic resonance inasmuch as we have been witnessing people who are fundamentally not at home and are unable to come to terms with what they feel or think. Because Nick's suicide makes no sense to them, and because they cannot find articulate ways to provide each other with solace, they finally resort to an empty patriotic gesture, a singing of *God Bless America*.

Whereas Malick implies, throughout the war portrayed in his *TRL*, that the men of C Company cannot escape the drive to do evil because they have not been able adequately to glimpse the good, throughout *The Deer Hunter* the men-turned-warriors cannot escape the insularity of their small town and the claustrophobic steel mill in which they work. While they are at war, they never seem to escape from their work venue. The opening scene in the mill, where the men are surrounded by flames, appears to be repeated when they get to Vietnam, where the opening scene also shows the men through a fiery haze created by the burning of a village. But the macho male bonding and community rituals that provide stability for their life around blast furnaces and in their after-work venues do not avail them in the firefights of their war experience, where senseless brutality traumatizes them, rendering them virtually speechless. There, even farther from home, only Mike's coding, with which he demands three bullets instead of one, allows him to defeat their captors with his loaded pistol but provides only a momentary sense. Just as his one-shot sense making during their deer hunt is shown to have its limitations once the hunt is over, his three-shot sense making, which provides a temporary rescue in Vietnam, does not avail the community, which is unable to make anything but ritualistic sense of what the war has done to its men.

Cimino's film has men going to war because that is what men are supposed to do, especially if their only discursive resort is a set of macho and patriotic codes. In Malick's film, men go to war and push ahead, acquiring exotic "property" because they cannot imagine a different, less antagonistic world. And men are still going to war. Since Immanuel Kant's hopeful reading of the signs of history in the eighteenth century, there has been no sign of a generalized accumulated wisdom

*Figure 6.6* Cimino's landscape as warscape
Courtesy of Universal Studios

which suggests that the publicity from momentous events will generate a "universal community." Nevertheless, despite their less-than-hopeful observations on war, both films encourage us to ask questions about conditions of possibility for perceiving alternative worlds and thereby transcending antagonistic national codes. In my conclusion, I explore possible redemptive moments and spaces.

## Conclusion: breaking the codes

In his gloss on the Kantian optimism that history would move in a more peaceful direction, Jacques Derrida essayed another reading of "the signs of the times"— two centuries later but with a cautious ambivalence:

> Hope, fear and trembling are commensurate with the signs that are coming to us from everywhere in Europe, where, precisely in the name of identity, be it cultural or not, the worst violences, those that we recognize all too well without yet having thought them through, the crimes of xenophobia, racism, anti Semitism, religious or nationalist fanaticism, are being unleashed, mixed up, mixed up with each other, but also there is nothing fortuitous in this, mixed in with the breath, with the respiration, with the very "spirit" of promise.[26]

Rather than posing the larger issue of a generalized, collective basis for a "'spirit' of promise,'" I want to evoke the perspectives of those people who have exceeded the experiential and discursive insularity of the community in *The Deer Hunter*, because they have an abundance of words, and are better equipped to resist violent animosities than the characters in *TRL*, because they have witnessed other worlds. With respect to the former, I want to call attention once again to Semezdin Mehmedinovic's writerly commitment to "word abundance" (noted in chapter 3), which was encouraged by his experience of "the boundary breaching literature in the former Yugoslavia." Observing the violent pseudo-ethnic nationalism in Bosnia-Herzegovina, Mehmedinovic challenges the basis of a policy of "racial" separation by, among other things, noting that "the literature written in Sarajevo or Bosnia-Herzegovina" cannot be clearly ethnically attributed to specific ethnic types. It is evident that in contrast with Mehmedinovic's rich literary vocabulary, which challenges ethnic boundaries, the violent ethno-nationalists of the former Yugoslavia pursue a discursively impoverished model of ethnicity.

With respect to both word abundance and an experience of other worlds, diasporic intellectual writer Salman Rushdie is exemplary. He articulates a similar attachment to boundary breaching in his novel *The Ground Beneath Her Feet*.[27] Operating within a musical frame, the novel challenges the enmities within the contemporary geopolitical world of nation-states by elaborating a metaphor of the shaking ground. It begins with the death of a world-renowned rock singer, Vina Apsara, who is swallowed up in a Mexican earthquake. Thereafter, the narration foregrounds the value of multiplicity of codes while disparaging Hindu nationalism in particular and national attachments in general. That multiplicity is realized musically, we are told, especially in the "earthquake songs" of Ormus Cama, which "are about the collapse of all walls, boundaries, restraints."[28] Rushdie, like one of the characters in his novel (Rai), is a permanent exile from his home country. He attributes his creativity as a writer to his resistance to the "reason" of any particular nation-state. His novel expresses the same East–West hybridity that Rushdie prizes:

> We are now partly of the West. Our identity is at once plural and partial. Sometimes we feel that we straddle two cultures; at other times, that we fall between two stools. But however ambiguous and shifting this ground may be, it is not an infertile territory for a writer to occupy.[29]

In accord with these sentiments, Rushdie's sentences in the novel contain American and British idioms, and Bombay argot, as well as various other idioms from diverse language formations. And the novel as a whole is constructed out of diverse cultural genres, as well as idioms, reflecting the inter-cultural semiosis (encounter of meaning systems[30]) through which fused musical forms emerge. As Rushdie puts it, his writing is influenced by both the Western "idea of the fable . . . which was originally a moral tale" and the Eastern "oral narration techniques . . . still alive in India."[31] Rushdie's writing is therefore stylistically homologous with the music of his Ormus Cama, who admits at one point that his lyrics—

"cockeyed words" and "vowel sounds"—are simultaneously his and someone else's.[32] Like Rushdie's prose, the world's musical hybridity is always already present in the pre-musical sounds of many national patrimonies. As the narration notes, Ormus's incorporation of so-called Western sounds in his music is not a betrayal of a pre-existing purity:

> The music he had in his head during the unsinging childhood years, was not of the West except in the sense that the West was from the beginning, impure old Bombay where West, East, North and South had always been scrambled, like codes, like eggs.[33]

Like Rushdie's novel, the Lebanese writer Hanan al-Shaykh's *Beirut Blues* evokes a musical idiom to contest the nationalistic codes of macho men.[34] Shaykh's novel contests the reasons of state and the macho codes that drive the enmities of the fighting men. Born in Lebanon and brought up in a "strict Shi'a family,"[35] Shaykh is also a diasporic intellectual, who was educated in Cairo and has lived subsequently in London. But apart from the contribution of her travels, which have moved her outside the frame of particular nationalistic imperatives, Shaykh achieves her distance from martial codes through her focus on the loci of enunciation of "strong women."[36] And, like Rushdie, she expresses the distance with a musical imagery. She appropriates the aesthetic of the blues singer Billie Holiday (to whom her narrator writes as part of the novel's epistolary structure). Moreover, her narrator is named Ashmahan, which is "also the name of a famous singer in the 1930's whose strength is inspiring."[37] Born a princess, the historical Ashmahan "fled from her country, Syria, to Egypt, leaving behind a husband, daughter and a principality of macho men."[38]

The strong women providing Shaykh's detachment from violent nationalism inspire her to recode the civil war and see it as a function of a conceptual claustrophobia, which she expresses in a passage reminiscent of Mehmedinovic's imagery (in this chapter's epigraph) of the unreflective warrior:

> Now I understand why when they are in tanks soldiers feel they can crush cars and trees in their path like brambles, because they're disconnected from every thing, their own souls and bodies included, and what's left is this instrument of steel rolling majestically forward.[39]

Yet another diasporic intellectual, the novelist Manuel Puig, who grew up in Argentina and spent much of his adult life in New York, was also influenced by the penetration of the world's mediascape into the macho male, nationalistic culture surrounding him. Unlike Rushdie, whose escape from local perspectives was inspired by the Western rock music he was able to receive from Radio Ceylon, Puig, who expressed suspicion of the numbing qualities of much of rock and roll, was more attuned to local music and instead used Hollywood film as a vehicle to detach him from local, macho codes.[40] As one biographical sketch puts it:

The movies played a liberating, almost transcendent role in Mr. Puig's own life. Born in Vallegas, Argentina, in 1932, he started his movie going career with "The Bride of Frankenstein." Through his childhood and adolescence, he went to the local theater five nights a week, using the same seat for 10 years.[41]

Beginning as a film script writer, Puig turned to novels, which he wrote in a cinematic style, and most significantly his novels staged encounters between the intensely ideational codes of political characters and the fantasies of characters whose imaginations are constructed from popular culture: pulpy romance novels, radio and television, the stories in the sensationalist press, and especially the world of film. Puig's movement into the world of imagination looms larger than his exile to New York, for even as a child and adolescent he was already outside of the local imaginary. Ultimately, the ideational transcendence of a Puig and the other diasporic intellectuals I have juxtaposed to the characters in *The Deer Hunter* cannot, for example, stop the tanks driven by those in thrall to a "military autism." But the contrast serves to highlight the importance of "word abundance," genre disruption, and the scrambling of codes as antidotes to the linguistic claustrophobia that often attends unreflective transitions from citizen-subjects to warring bodies. In particular, however, the significance of film in Puig's migration out of a local, or even a national, imaginary helps me to evoke once again the relationship of cinema to an anti-war politics of aesthetics.

As I have suggested throughout this investigation, the perception-transcending capacity of cinema is a crucial aspect of its critical impetus. If, rather than heeding the psychological attributes of characters, we attend to the ways in which their movements map the spatio-temporality of worlds and, further, if we heed the ways in which the camera affords perspectives other than those controlled by the characters, we are positioned to recognize the way a film thinks, particularly in ways that hint toward the possibility of imagining alternative worlds. To repeat Rancière's insistence about the politics–aesthetics relationship, "the aesthetic nature of politics" points us not to "a specific single world" but to "a conflictive world," to "a world of competing worlds."[42]

As a final illustration, which I think helps us effect a translation between such a politics of aesthetics and an opening to ethical concerns, I want to contrast a recent eruption of policy discourse with a feature film that treats the same issue. In October 2007, in response to the U.S. House Foreign Affairs Committee, as they prepared to vote on a measure that would declare the World War I killings of hundreds of thousands of Armenians in Turkey a "genocide," President Bush insisted that "its passage would do great harm to our relations with a key ally in NATO and in the global war on terror." And Bush's Defense Secretary, Robert Gates, complained that the action might hamper "access to air fields and to roads and so on in Turkey," pointing out that "95 percent of the newly purchased Mine Resistant Ambush Protected Vehicles are flying through Turkey to get to Iraq."[43]

In contrast with the war/geopolitics world within which the Bush administration opposed the House Committee's resolution is a world of grievance and injustice that is delivered with vivid emotional impact in Atom Egoyan's film *Ararat*, which first appeared at the Cannes Film Festival in 2002 and subsequently was awarded the prize as "best picture" by the Canadian Academy of Cinema and Television in 2003. In a complex plot that interweaves, in a non-linear narrative, a variety of life dramas and images of some of the historical victims as well as some contemporaries, the film's most poignant and effective images treat the life of the Armenian painter Arshile Gorky and his painting of himself as a young boy next to his mother, Shushan (who was one of the victims of "the Armenian genocide"). As the narration moves back and forth between contemporary Canadians and the historical episode of genocide, the film makes present both the human impact of the genocide and the contestation over a historical episode of violence that contemporary reasons of state continue to suppress. In effect, Egoyan's *Ararat* confronts nearly a century of discursive denials with what André Bazin famously calls "image facts," "fragment(s) of concrete reality," which provoke the viewer to connect them with other image facts and thereby achieve a narrative coherence.[44]

In the film, Egoyan's version of Arshile Gorky serves as a conceptual persona for history's war victims in general. As the victim toll continues to grow in a contemporary war, the powers that prosecute it seek to deny a warranted victim status to the victims of an earlier one. The Bush administration's argument effectively states that the concerns of strategic war policy must trump desires to recognize historical injustices. In effect a war against a contemporary (duplicitously invented) adversary entails, at the same time, a war against truth; the world of violent geopolitics seeks to occult a world of historical injustice, sequestered within it. A viewing of Egoyan's feature film provides an aesthetic and thereby an ethico-political challenge to a long history of this war on truth.

What is the ethico-political challenge that the analysis of cinema can offer? In reaction to those who question the value of the aesthetic judgments involved in cinema analysis, because they see artistic and fictional genres as radically isolated from ethical concerns, I want once again to evoke Immanuel Kant's *Critique of Judgment*. If we heed the political and ethical implications of both Kant's analytics of the beautiful and the sublime and the post-Kantian thinking manifested in critical approaches to aesthetics such as Jacques Rancière's, what is evident is not a diremption between aesthetic and ethical judgments but an articulation between the two. As I point out in chapter 4, that articulation was initiated with Kant's observation that the judgment of the beautiful object is distinguished because it is neither an object of cognition nor an object of desire. Given that such objects do not subject sensation to the rule of understanding and do not subject reason to the vagaries of sensation, the subject experiences what Kant calls the "free play" of the faculties.[45] The political and ethical sensibility implied in Kant's analytic of the beautiful derives from the Kantian subject's reflection on the form-giving capacity of the interplay of the faculties. As a result, an apprehension of "the beautiful" encourages critical reflection on the conditions of possibility for reconciling different modes of judgment.

Subsequent to his identification of this reflecting subject (and crucially for my point here), Kant himself reflects on the relationships among the diverse faculties and proceeds to connect the judgment on the beautiful with that on "the morally good." In his "general remarks," in his *Critique of Judgment*, in which he treats the implications of both his analytic of the beautiful and his analytic of the sublime, Kant concludes that the reflective judgments they engender create a space for a relationship with a moral sensibility.[46] In Kant's terms, they "prepare the subject for moral feeling."[47] Ironically, despite Kant's insistence that "the beautiful" is neither agreeable nor good, the kinds of judgments it summons create the conditions of possibility for ethical judgment. Without pursuing the many post-Kantian ways in which Kant's *Critique of Judgment* is critically elaborated and reinflected (the relevance of some of them are available in chapter 4), I want to note that, if we follow the implications of Kant's insights, one finds an articulation between aesthetic and ethical judgment.

Happily, contemporary technologies now render the ethico-political relevance of cinema pervasively present. Thanks to the contemporary phenomenology of film viewing, where films are available for viewing outside of theaters, the world of injustice can receive perpetual recognition because, to invoke Walter Benjamin's terms, its objects can be continually reactivated. The worlds of pain, suffering, and grievance remain readily available for reflection and renegotiation, even when those with actual experiential memories are no longer around to tell their stories. Among other things, Egoyan's restoration of the reality of the Armenian genocide, which garnered its initial recognition in film festival space, can find its way into other venues in which cinema contributes to a pedagogy on war and peace.

Finally, I want to end with a gesture toward one of the most important venues for such a pedagogy, the classroom. In the summer of 2007, I enjoyed the privilege of teaching a film-geopolitics class for graduate students in the International Studies Institute at the Pontifical Catholic University (PUC), Rio de Janeiro. After spending a few weeks viewing and discussing most of the films I treat in this book with the students, they showed Brazilian films which enhanced and extended our discussions of the cinema–geopolitics relationship and effectively extended my purview of some of the historical victims I had only had a vague appreciation of. As our course became a mini film festival, as well as an inter-cultural encounter, I learned that the critical capacity of the film festival can be had on a relatively low budget. I hope this book inspires many such pedagogical episodes, while, at the same time, helping to turn limited sympathy into extended generosity.

# Notes

## Introduction

1  The expression "cinematic heterotopia" appears in V. Burgin, *The Remembered Film* (London: Reaktion Books, 2004), 7–10. It is Burgin's adaption to film venues of Michel Foucault's concept of the heterotopia. For Foucault, the value of a heterotopia is the extent to which its separation from ordinary spaces affords one the possibility of reflection on the ordering effects of space. See his "Of Other Spaces," *Diacritics* 16 (1986): 22–27.

2  Quoted in M. T. Kaufman, "Film Studies," on the web at: http://rialtopictures.com/eyes_xtras/battle_times.html (obtained Nov. 3, 2006).

3  P. Matthews, "The Battle of Algiers: Bombs and Boomerangs," in the booklet accompanying the DVD version of *The Battle of Algiers* (Criterion, 2004).

4  Quotation from L. Proyect, "Looking Back at *The Battle of Algiers*," *MR Zine*, on the web at: http://mrzine.monthlyreview.org/proyect.html (obtained Dec. 8, 2006).

5  Quoted in S. Johnson, "The Battle of Algiers and Its Lessons," *CommonDreams.org News Center*, on the web at: http://www.commondreams.org/views03/0907-07.htm (obtained Nov. 2, 2006).

6  S. Eisenstein, "On Fascism, German Cinema and Real Life: Open Letter to the German Minister of Propaganda, Dr. Goebbels," in *Eisenstein Writings*, ed. R. Taylor, Vol. 1 (Bloomington: Indiana University Press, 1988), 280.

7  J. Rancière, *Film Fables*, trans. Emiliano Battista (New York: Berg, 2006), 28–29.

8  The expression is in T. Pynchon, *Mason & Dixon* (New York: Henry Holt, 1997), 395.

9  See G. Deleuze, *Pure Immanence*, trans. Anne Boyman (New York: Zone Books, 2005), 46.

10  D. Hume, *A Treatise of Human Nature*, 2nd ed. (Oxford: Oxford University Press, 1978), 494. In chapter 5 I repeat this Humean approach to the social domain to frame the implications of a Milan Kundera novel and a Vyacheslav Kristofovich film.

11  Deleuze develops his notions of the "image of thought" in several places. See for example G. Deleuze, *Proust and Signs*, trans. Richard Howard (Minneapolis: University of Minnesota Press, 2000), 115–23.

12  F. Kracauer, *Theory of Film: The Redemption of Physical Reality* (Princeton, NJ: Princeton University Press, 1960), 296, 292. (In this latter quotation, Kracauer is quoting John Dewey.)

13  W. Benjamin, "The Work of Art in the Age of Mechanical Reproduction," in *Illuminations*, trans. Harry Zohn (New York: Schocken, 1968), 228.

14  Rancière, *Film Fables*, 111.

15  See G. Deleuze, *Cinema 1: The Movement Image*, trans. Hugh Tomlinson and Barbara Habberjam (Minneapolis: University of Minnesota Press, 1986), 58, 86.

16  See Mann's correspondence with Theodor Adorno: *Theodor W. Adorno and Thomas Mann: Correspondence*, trans. N. Walker (Malden, MA: Polity, 2006).

17 T. Mann, *Joseph and His Brothers*, trans. John E. Woods (New York: Alfred A. Knopf, 2005), 541.
18 H. Bergson, *Matter and Memory*, trans. N. M. Paul and W. S. Palmer (New York: Zone Books, 1988), 25.
19 Deleuze, *Cinema 1*, 64.
20 Bergson, *Matter and Memory*, 161.
21 Deleuze, *Cinema 1*, 58.
22 M. B. Hansen, "Introduction," to Kracauer, *Theory of Film*, xi.
23 Rancière, *Film Fables*, 265.
24 Ibid.
25 T. Mann, *The Theme of the Joseph Novels*, Speech delivered at the Library of Congress (Washington, DC: Library of Congress, 1942), 6.
26 Ibid., 4.
27 Ibid., 11.
28 Ibid.
29 The quotations are from L. Bersani and U. Dutoit's introduction to their *Forms of Being: Cinema, Aesthetics, Subjectivity* (London: BFI, 2004), 6.
30 Ibid., 21–22.
31 The quotations are from D. Pye's reading of the film *Lusty Men* (1952), in "Movies and Point of View," *Movie* 36 (2000): 27.
32 See M. J. Shapiro, *Deforming American Political Thought: Ethnicity, Facticity, and Genre* (Lexington: University Press of Kentucky, 2006), 74–75.
33 Rancière, *Film Fables*, 24.
34 M. Scorsese, "The Man Who Set Film Free," *New York Times*, on the web at: http://www.nytimes.com/2007/08/12/movies/12scor.html (obtained Jan. 13, 2007).
35 The plot summary is on the web at: http://www.imdb.com/title/tt0295876/plotsummary (obtained Nov. 30, 2006).
36 I have "spatial expression" in quotes because I have been edified by its use in Daniel Morgan's interpretation of André Bazin on Jean Renoir's film *Le Crime de Monsieur Lange* (1936): D. Morgan, "Rethinking Bazin: Ontology and Realist Aesthetics," *Critical Inquiry* 32 (2006): 460.
37 The quotation is from T. Conley's *Cartographic Cinema* (Minneapolis: University of Minnesota Press, 2007), 2. In Conley's approach to film, the emphasis is on the ways in which the geography of a film confronts the viewer's own articulations of space.
38 G. Deleuze, *Cinema 2: The Time Image*, trans. Hugh Tomlinson and Robert Galeta (Minneapolis: University of Minnesota Press, 1989), 272.
39 Ibid.
40 Kracauer, *Theory of Film*, 306.

**1 The new violent cartography**

1 The quotation is from A. Feldman, "On the Actuarial Gaze: From 9/11 to Abu Ghraib," *Cultural Studies* 19 (2005): 205.
2 Caption from the *New York Times*, July 5, 2005, A-1.
3 E. Jünger, "War and Photography," *New German Critique* 59 (1993): 24–25.
4 The quotations are from Tomas Munita's e-mail correspondence with the author, July 6, 2005.
5 See Jünger, "War and Photography," 24–32.
6 I place "violent cartography" in quotation marks because the expression derives from my *Violent Cartographies: Mapping Cultures of War* (Minneapolis: University of Minnesota Press, 1997).
7 Ibid., ix.
8 M. Foucault, "The Order of Discourse," in *Language and Politics*, ed. M. J. Shapiro (New York: NYU Press, 1984), 127.

9 Shapiro, *Violent Cartographies*, xi.
10 E. Buscombe, *The Searchers* (London: BFI, 2000), 37.
11 A. Baricco, *City*, trans. Ann Goldstein (London: Penguin, 2002), 158–59.
12 See V. W. Wexman, "The Family on the Land: Race and Nationhood in Silent Westerns," in *The Birth of Whiteness*, ed. D. Bernardi (New Brunswick, NJ: Rutgers University Press, 1996), 131.
13 The quotation is from N. F. Cott, *Public Vows: A History of Marriage and the Nation* (Cambridge, MA: Harvard University Press, 2000), 10.
14 Ibid., 25.
15 When I refer to biopolitics, I am referring to those bodies regarded as politically eligible versus those that are either excluded or deemed worthy of killing without the presumption that the killing is homicide. See G. Agamben's distinction between politically eligible life that must be protected versus "bare life" in his *Homo Sacer: Sovereign Power and Bare Life*, trans. D. Heller-Roazen (Stanford, CA: Stanford University Press, 1998).
16 See R. Barthes, *Camera Lucida*, trans. R. Howard (New York: Hill & Wang, 1982), 27.
17 Ibid.
18 Ibid., 26.
19 G. Didi-Huberman, "The Art of Not Describing: Vermeer—The Detail and the Patch," *History of the Human Sciences* 2 (1989): 135.
20 Ibid., 149.
21 Ibid., 165.
22 Didi-Huberman, while inspired by Barthes's concept of the *punctum*, distinguishes the patch, not because the former is part of a photo and the latter part of a painting but because a *punctum*, unlike a patch, retains a depictive significance. It is a "symptom of the world itself," rather than of "the image": ibid., 163.
23 M. Foucault, *The Birth of the Clinic: An Archaeology of Medical Perception*, trans. Alan Sheridan (New York: Pantheon, 1973), 15.
24 Ibid., 19.
25 Ibid., 30.
26 J. Fernandes, "Ebola Takes to the Road: Mobilizing Viruses in Defense of the Nation-State," in *Sovereign Lives: Power in Global Politics*, ed. J. Edkins, V. Pin-Fat, and M. J. Shapiro (New York: Routledge, 2004), 191.
27 Ibid., 192.
28 Ibid.
29 A. R. Stone, *The War of Desire and Technology* (Cambridge, MA: MIT Press, 1995), 41.
30 Foucault, *The Birth of the Clinic*, 3.
31 Ibid., 38.
32 Ibid., 31.
33 Ibid., 109.
34 See J. L. Conrad and J. L. Pearson, "Improving Epidemiology, and Laboratory Capabilities," in *Terrorism and Public Health*, ed. B. S. Levy and V. W. Sidel (New York: Oxford University Press, 2003), 272. The point is not to suggest that it is politically untoward to protect people from the use of infectious diseases as weapons against populations but to note that, now that health agencies are no longer healing arts but are part of modern governance, they are subject to participating with other agencies in militarization.
35 The expression "institutional ecologies" is part of M. De Landa's analysis of the institutional collaborations involved in contemporary modes of militarization. See his "Economics, Computers, and the War Machine," in *Ars Electronica: Facing the Future*, ed. T. Druckrey (Cambridge, MA: MIT Press, 1999), 319.
36 P. Virilio, *War and Cinema*, trans. Patrick Camiller (New York: Verso, 1989), 17–18.
37 Ibid., 18.

38 The cited commentary is M. Brzezinski's in the *New York Times* Magazine section: "The Unmanned Army," April 18, 2003, on the web at: http://www.nytimes.com/2003/04/18/magazine/20Drone.html (obtained Sept. 16, 2004).

39 See the General Atomics web site: http://www.ga.com/about/aboutga.htm/ (obtained Sept. 16, 2004).

40 C. J. Hanley, "Air-Attack Robots Iraq-Bound," Associated Press account, carried in the *Honolulu Advertiser*, July 16, 2007, a-11.

41 See for example M. W. Herold, "A Dossier of Civilian Victims of the United States' Aerial Bombing of Afghanistan," on the web at: http://cursor.org/stories/civilian_deaths.htm (obtained July 17, 2007). The dossier documents between 3,000 and 3,400 civilian deaths between October 7, 2001 and March 2002 alone. It contains many specific instances; for example, "On October 21st, U.S. Planes apparently targeting their bombs at a Taliban military base—long abandoned—released their deadly cargo on the Kabul residential area of Khair Khana, killing eight members of one family who had just sat down to breakfast." By May of 2007, the Afghan president, Hamid Karzai, stated, "Civilian deaths and arbitrary decisions to search people's houses have reached an unacceptable level and Afghans cannot put up with it any longer." The estimated civilian deaths during the prior year were over 4,000. See "Karzai Anger over Civilian Deaths," *BBC News*, on the web at: http://news.bbc.co.uk/1/hi/world/south_asia/6615781.stm.

42 F. Kittler, "On the History of the Theory of Information Warfare," in *Ars Electronica: Facing the Future*, ed. Druckrey, 175.

43 Quotations are from P. R. Zimmerman, "Matrices of War," *Afterimage* 28 (2001): 29.

44 Brzezinski, "The Unmanned Army."

45 See T. P. M. Barnett, *The Pentagon's New Map* (New York: G. P. Putnam, 2004), 121.

46 P. Virilio, *Desert Screen*, trans. M. Degener (New York: Continuum, 2002), 8.

47 A. Mbembe, "Necropolitics," trans. Libby Meintjes, *Public Culture* 15 (2003): 30.

48 A. L. Myers, "Drone Aids Border Patrol Searches," *Honolulu Advertiser*, June 26, 2004, A2.

49 L. Alvarez, "Army Effort to Enlist Hispanics Draws Recruits and Criticism," *New York Times*, on the web at: http://www.nytimes.com/2006/02/09/national/09recruit.html? (obtained Mar. 20, 2006).

50 Ibid.

51 Barnett, *The Pentagon's New Map*, 95.

52 As Patricia Zimmerman points out, as "World War II was fought with cameras and guns," the 16mm camera work developed in propaganda documentaries aimed at "the home front" migrated into Hollywood's feature films to instill "a new realism to Hollywood narrative films": P. Zimmerman, *Reel Families* (Bloomington: Indiana University Press, 1995), 90.

53 For a critical ethnography of USC's ICT relationship with modern infowar, see J. Der Derian, *Virtuous War* (Boulder, CO: Westview Press, 2001).

54 B. Readings, *The University in Ruins* (Minneapolis: University of Minnesota Press, 1995), 12.

55 Ibid., 29.

56 J. Ellis, *The Social History of the Machine Gun* (Baltimore: Johns Hopkins University Press, 1975), 1.

57 See G. Viswanathan, *Masks of Conquest: Literary Study and British Rule in India* (New York: Columbia University Press, 1989).

58 V. Rafael, "The Cultures of Area Studies," *Social Text* 41 (1994): 3.

59 S. P. Waring, "Cold Calculus: The Cold War and Operations Research," *Radical History* 63 (1995): 34.

60 Quotation from F. S. Saunders, *The Cultural Cold War: The CIA and the World of Arts and Letters* (New York: New Press, 2001), 15.

61 W. H. Epstein, "Counter-Intelligence: Cold-War Criticism and Eighteenth-Century Studies," *ELH* 57 (1990): 63.

62  Ibid., 68.
63  Ibid., 83.
64  Brzezinski, "The Unmanned Army."
65  Kittler, "On the History of the Theory of Information Warfare," 173.
66  Publication of the ICT, http://www.ict.usc.edu (obtained Dec. 3, 2005).
67  T. Golden, "Voices from Guantanamo: Brash and Befuddled," *International Herald Tribune*, March 3, 2006, 1.
68  G. Agamben, *State of Exception*, trans. Kevin Attell (Chicago: University of Chicago Press, 2005), 50.
69  I saw the exhibition in Rome and subsequently discovered a feature about the exhibition's schedule in an article by R. Johnson, "Art that Accuses," *Los Angeles Times*, July 17, 2005, E 33, E 40.
70  See R. Bernstein, "A Mind on Politics and a Feel for What's Gritty," *International Herald Tribune*, February 17, 2006, 28.
71  For the report on the changes at Cannes, see J. Dupont, "At Cannes, Boring Is Out, Political Is In," *International Herald Tribune*, May 17, 2006, 20.
72  Ibid.
73  The quotation is a remark by a character in William Gibson's novel *Spook Country* (New York: G. P. Putnam, 2007), 137.
74  D. Vaughan, *For Documentary* (Berkeley: University of California Press, 1999), 9.
75  Ibid., 10.
76  The concept of the image fact belongs to A. Bazin, *What Is Cinema?*, Vol. 2, trans. Hugh Gray (Berkeley: University of California Press, 1971).
77  See M. Dillon, "Governing Terror: The State of Emergency of Biopolitical Emergence," Paper delivered at the 2006 International Studies Association meeting, San Diego, CA, p. 8.
78  W. Benjamin, "The Work of Art in the Age of Mechanical Reproduction," in *Illuminations*, trans. Harry Zohn (New York: Schocken, 1968), 122.
79  Ibid., 228.

## 2  Preemption up close: film and pax Americana

1  B. Massumi, "Potential Politics and the Primacy of Preemption," *Theory and Event* 10 (2007).
2  M. Foucault, *Society Must Be Defended*, trans. David Macey (New York: Picador, 2003), 54–55.
3  Area studies has been among the disciplines most complicit with war. As Rey Chow puts it, "area studies as a mode of knowledge production is, strictly speaking, military in its origins": R. Chow, *The Age of the World Target: Self Referentiality in War, Theory, and Comparative Work* (Durham, NC: Duke University Press, 2006), 39.
4  M. Foucault, *The Politics of Truth*, trans. Lysa Hochroth (New York: Semiotext(e), 1997), 32.
5  J. Johnston, "Introduction," to F. Kittler, *Literature, Media, Information Systems* (Amsterdam: OPA, 1997), 21.
6  G. Deleuze, *Foucault*, trans. Sean Hand (Minneapolis: University of Minnesota Press, 1986), 94–95.
7  See E. Scarry, *The Body in Pain* (New York: Oxford University Press, 1985).
8  The quotation is from J. D. Slocum, "Cinema and the Civilizing Process: Rethinking Violence in the World War II Combat Film," *Cinema Journal* 44 (2005): 35.
9  Slocum notes this cinematic grammar in *Sergeant York* (1941), ibid., 45, but that visual grammar was typical in war films well into the 1960s.
10  Scarry, *The Body in Pain*, 12.
11  The quotation is from D. N. Rodowick's analysis of Gilles Deleuze's approach to cinema: *Gilles Deleuze's Time Machine* (Durham, NC: Duke University Press, 1997), 6–7.

12 F. Jameson, *The Geopolitical Aesthetic: Cinema and Space in the World System* (Bloomington: Indiana University Press, 1992), 3.
13 Ibid., 4.
14 Ibid., 9.
15 Ibid., 10.
16 As I did in chapter 1, I put "violent cartography" in quotations because of its reference to my earlier work: M. J. Shapiro, *Violent Cartographies: Mapping Cultures of War* (Minneapolis: University of Minnesota Press, 1997).
17 J. Rancière, *The Politics of Aesthetics*, trans. G. Rockhill (New York: Continuum, 2004), 24.
18 J. Didion, *Salvador* (New York: Simon & Schuster, 1982), 77–78.
19 Jameson, *The Geopolitical Aesthetic*, 27.
20 Chow, *The Age of the World Target*, 31.
21 See A. Liptak, "Spying Program May Be Tested by Terror Case," *New York Times*, August 26, 2007, A-1, A-17.
22 See G. Agamben, *Homo Sacer: Sovereign Power and Bare Life* (Stanford, CA: Stanford University Press, 1998).
23 See *Njals Saga*, trans. Robert Cook (New York: Penguin, 2002).
24 For a comprehensive review of the program of "rendering" and its venues and torture and interrogation techniques, see J. Mayer, "The Black Sites," *New Yorker*, August 30, 2007, 46–57.
25 Judith Butler, *Precarious Lives: The Powers of Mourning and Violence* (New York: Verso, 2004), 62.
26 See Agamben, *Homo Sacer*, 181.
27 "The Deaths at Gitmo," *New York Times*, June 12, 2006, A-20.
28 J.-L. Nancy, *The Ground of the Image*, trans. Jeff Fort (New York: Fordham University Press, 2005), 16.
29 See B. Massumi's analysis of the fear-promoting strategy involved in the color alerts: "Fear (The Spectrum Said)," *Positions: East Asia Cultures Critique* 13 (2005): 31–48.
30 See V. Sobchack, *The Address of the Eye: A Phenomenology of the Film Experience* (Princeton, NJ: Princeton University Press, 1992).
31 F. Jameson, *Signatures of the Visible* (New York: Routledge, 1992), 54.
32 Ibid. For a discussion of the inconsistencies and contradictions involved in the concept of totality, see A. Badiou, *Theoretical Writings*, trans. Ray Brassier and Alberto Toscano (New York: Continuum, 2004), chapters 15–17.
33 V. Sobchack, *Carnal Thoughts: Embodiment and Moving Image Culture* (Berkeley: University of California Press, 2004), 272.
34 See M. Hirsh and J. Barry, "The Salvador Option," on the web at: http://www.msnbc.msn.com/id/6802629/site/newsweek/ (obtained June 13, 2006).
35 K. Gude, "Iraq," on the web at: http://thinkprogress.org/2006/03/02/roots-of-iraq-civil-war-may-be-in-salvador-option/ (obtained June 13, 2006).
36 Didion, *Salvador*, 103.
37 W. LaFeber, "*Salvador*," in *Oliver Stone's USA*, ed. R. B. Toplin (Lawrence: University Press of Kansas, 2000), 95.
38 B. Schwarz, "Dirty Hands: The Success of U.S. Policy in El Salvador—Preventing a Guerilla Victory—Was Based on 40,000 Political Murders," *Atlantic Monthly* 282 (December 1998): 106.
39 Ibid., 106–07.
40 See for example K. Greenberg, J. L. Dratel, and A. Lewis, *The Torture Papers: The Road to Abu Ghraib* (New York: Cambridge University Press, 2005).
41 See F. Braudel, *After Thoughts on Material Civilization and Capitalism*, trans. P. M. Ranum (Baltimore, MD: Johns Hopkins University Press, 1977), 58–59.

42 M. Mazetti, "Efforts by C.I.A. Fail in Somalia, Officials Charge," *New York Times*, on the web at: http://nytimes.com/2006/06/08/world/africa/08intel.html (obtained July 14, 2006).

43 The notable films, directed by Phillip Noyce, are *Patriot Games* (1992) and *Clear and Present Danger* (1994).

44 As noted in the Introduction, this is the essential point that Jacques Rancière derives from his reading of Deleuze on cinema. See his *Film Fables*, trans. Emiliano Battista (New York: Berg, 2006), 111.

45 This is the essence of Slavoj Žižek's insight into the functioning of ideology. See S. Žižek, *The Sublime Object of Ideology* (London: Verso, 1989).

46 Rancière, *Film Fables*, 111.

47 I treat Deleuze on Bacon more extensively in M. J. Shapiro, *Deforming American Political Thought: Ethnicity, Facticity, and Genre* (Lexington: University Press of Kentucky, 2006).

48 G. Deleuze, *Francis Bacon: The Logic of Sensation*, trans. Daniel W. Smith (Minneapolis: University of Minnesota Press, 2003), 71.

49 Ibid., 71–72.

50 Deleuze, *Francis Bacon*, 14.

51 Ibid., 6.

52 See Shapiro, *Deforming American Political Thought*, 37–38, where I designate the African-American character Professor (Antonio Fargas) as an attendant who creates the facticity of a scene, connecting the transition from childhood to the vocation of a prostitute of a young girl raised in a New Orleans bordello with an earlier case of the body as a commodity, that of slavery.

53 Hilton, quoted in A. J. Wharton, *Building the Cold War: Hilton International Hotels and Modern Architecture* (Chicago: University of Chicago Press, 2001), 8.

54 Ibid., 5.

55 The quotations are from a report: "The Sheraton Murder Case," *New York Times* archives, September 6, 1981.

56 See D. Farah, "Salvador Rebels Take Hotel," *Washington Post*, on the web at: http://pqasb.pqarchiver.com/washingtonpost/access/73912224.html (obtained Aug. 23, 2007).

57 Influenced by the philosophy of Henri Bergson, Gilles Deleuze argues that thinking is quintessentially temporal. As a result, his turn to film in his two cinema books is not to do "film theory" but to show that the moving image in film, rendered as both moving and time images, constitutes critical thinking (as opposed to mere recognition). See his *Cinema 1*, trans. Hugh Tomlinson (Minneapolis: University of Minnesota Press, 1986), and *Cinema 2*, trans. Hugh Tomlinson and Robert Galeta (Minneapolis: University of Minnesota Press, 1989).

58 H. Harootunian, "The Black Cat in the Dark Room," *Positions: East Asia Cultures Critique* 13 (2005): 140.

59 Deleuze, *Cinema 1*, 65.

60 See G. Deleuze and F. Guattari, *A Thousand Plateaus*, trans. Brian Massumi (Minneapolis: University of Minnesota Press, 1987), 260–61.

61 The quotation is from a commentary on Amiel's approach to the cinematographic body: J. Game, "Cinematic Bodies," *Studies in French Cinema* 1 (2001): 50–51.

62 V. Amiel, *Le Corps au cinema: Keaton, Bresson, Cassavetes* (Paris: Presses Universitaires de France, 1998), 2 (my translation).

63 Ibid., 7.

64 Schwarz, "Dirty Hands," 112.

65 Ibid., 109.

66 The quotation is from ibid., 107.

67 Quotations form D. Van Natta, Jr., "U.S. Recruits a Rough Ally to Be a Jailer," *New York Times*, May 1, 2005, on the web at: http://nytimes.com/2005/05/01/international/01renditions.html (obtained Mar. 20, 2006).

68 Ibid.
69 Ibid.
70 R. A. Rosenstone, "Oliver Stone as Historian," in *Oliver Stone's USA*, ed. Toplin, 26.


**3 Fogs of war**

1 J. M. Coetzee, *The Master of Petersburg* (New York: Vintage, 1999), 137.
2 See for example M. Merleau-Ponty, *The Structure of Behavior*, trans. A. L. Fisher (Boston, MA: Beacon Press, 1967).
3 The quoted concepts are from Kaja Silverman's politically oriented adaption of Lacan's approach to the gaze. See K. Silverman, *The Threshold of the Visible World* (New York: Routledge, 1996).
4 J. Lacan, "The Eye and the Gaze," Chapter 6 in *The Four Fundamental Concepts of Psycho-Analysis*, trans. Alan Sheridan (London: Penguin, 1979), 73.
5 C. von Clausewitz, *On War*, ed. and trans. M. Howard and P. Paret (Princeton, NJ: Princeton University Press, 1984), 101.
6 W. A. Owens, *Lifting the Fog of War* (New York: Farrar, Straus and Giroux, 2000), 13.
7 Ibid., 18.
8 C. J. Hanley, "Air-Attack Robots Iraq Bound," from the AP, obtained from the *Honolulu Advertiser*, July 16, 2007, B-7.
9 H. K. Ullman and J. P. Wade, *Shock and Awe: Achieving Rapid Dominance* (Washington, DC: National Defense University Press, 1996), 1.
10 P. Bonitzer, "Hitchcockian Suspense," in *Everything You Always Wanted to Know about Lacan ... But Were Afraid to Ask*, ed. S. Žižek (New York: Verso, 1992), 23.
11 D. Tanovic, "Director's Statement," DVD version of *No Man's Land* (Los Angeles: MGM, 2001).
12 B. Jaguaribe, "Cities without Maps: Favelas and the Aesthetics of Realism," in *Urban Imaginaries: Locating the Modern City*, ed. A. Cinar and T. Bender (Minneapolis: University of Minnesota Press, 2007), 101.
13 D. E. von Mücke, *Modernity and the Occult* (Palo Alto, CA: Stanford University Press, 2003), 61–62.
14 Ibid., 66–67.
15 Silverman, *The Threshold of the Visible World*, 152–53.
16 Ibid., 153.
17 W. Benjamin, "The Work of Art in the Age of Mechanical Reproduction," in *Illuminations*, trans. Harry Zohn (New York: Schocken, 1968), 238.
18 Ibid.
19 See G. Deleuze, *Cinema 2*, trans. Hugh Tomlinson and Robert Galeta (Minneapolis: University of Minnesota Press, 1989).
20 Quotation from M. J. Shapiro, *Cinematic Political Thought: Narrating Race, Nation, and Gender* (New York: NYU Press, 1999), 25.
21 S. Mehmedinovic, *Sarajevo Blues*, trans. A. Alcalay (San Francisco: City Lights, 1998), 21.
22 The quotation is from Ammiel Alcalay's "Introduction" to ibid., xv.
23 Mehmedinovic, *Sarajevo Blues*, 90.
24 Ibid., 107.
25 S. Bernardi, "Rossellini's Landscapes: Nature, Myth, History," in *Roberto Rossellini: Magician of the Real*, ed. D. Forgacs, S. Lutton, and G. Nowell-Smith (London: BFI, 2001), 53.
26 M. Foucault, *The Politics of Truth*, trans. Lysa Hochroth (New York: Semiotext(e), 1997), 50.
27 G. Deleuze, "Portrait of the Philosopher as a Moviegoer," in *Two Regimes of Madness: Texts and Interviews 1975–1995*, trans. Ames Hodges and Mike Taormina (New York: Semiotext(e), 2006), 214.

28  T. Myers, *Walking Point* (New York: Oxford University Press, 1988), 219.
29  W. Just, *American Blues* (New York: Viking, 1984), 201.
30  See R. S. McNamara, *In Retrospect: The Tragedy and Lessons of Vietnam* (New York: Times Books, 1995).
31  R. S. McNamara, J. G. Blight, and R. K. Brigham, *Argument without End: In Search of Answers to the Vietnam Tragedy* (New York: Public Affairs, 1999).
32  Ibid., 26.
33  M. J. Shapiro, *Violent Cartographies: Mapping Cultures of War* (Minneapolis: University of Minnesota Press, 1997), 151.
34  Schwarzkopf has a more thoroughgoing attempt to efface the "Vietnam syndrome" (the loss of prestige for soldiers and the nation in an unpopular war) in his autobiography: N. Schwarzkopf, with P. Peter, *It Doesn't Take a Hero* (New York: Bantam, 1992).
35  R. Ebert, "Striding through the Fog of 20th-Century Wars," *Honolulu Advertiser*, February 27, 2004, TGIF section.
36  M. Renov, "Introduction: The Truth about Non-Fiction," in *Theorizing Documentary*, ed. M. Renov (New York, Routledge, 1993), 3.
37  The quotation is from J. Hicks, *Dziga Vertov: Defining Documentary Film* (New York: I. B. Tauris, 2007); and the inner quotations are translated from a Russian source, cited by Hicks as: Vertova-Svilova and Vinogradova, *Djiga Vertov v vospominaniiakh sovremennikov*, 70.
38  The quotation is from H. Tworkov, "Interview with Philip Glass," in *Writings on Glass*, ed. R. Kostelanetz (New York: Schirmer, 1997), 319.
39  See M. Foucault, *"Society Must Be Defended": Lectures at the Collège de France 1975–1976*, trans. David Macey (New York: Picador, 2003).
40  See R. Slotkin, *Gunfighter Nation: The Myth of the Frontier in Twentieth Century America* (New York: Atheneum, 1992).
41  The quotation is from Joy M. Lynch, "'A Distinct Place in America Where all *Mestizos* Reside': Landscape and Identity in Ana Castillo's *Sapogonia* and Diana Chang's *The Frontiers of Love*," *Melus* 26 (3) (Fall, 2001), 120.
42  V. Amiel, *Le Corps au cinema: Keaton, Bresson, Cassavetes* (Paris: Presses Universitaires de France, 1998), 2.
43  See C. M. Hurlbert, "'From behind the Veil': Teaching the Literature of the Enemy," *Canadian Modern Language Review* 60 (2003), 56, and B. Readings, *The University in Ruins* (Minneapolis: University of Minnesota Press, 1995), 185.
44  E. Levinas, *Totality and Infinity*, trans. Alphonso Lingus (Pittsburgh, PA: Duquesne University Press, 1969), 39.
45  A. Roy, *The God of Small Things* (New York: Random House, 1997), 35.
46  A. Gopnik, "Headless Horseman: The Reign of Terror Revisited," *New Yorker*, June 5, 2006, 84.
47  Quotation from D. Totaro, "Hiroshima Mon Amour," on the web at: http://www.hoschamp.qc.ca/new_offscreen/hiroshima.html (obtained Sept. 20, 2007).
48  Ibid.
49  Gilles Deleuze puts this aspect of Bergsonism succinctly: "The past is 'contemporaneous' with the present it *has been*": G. Deleuze, *Bergsonism*, trans. Hugh Tomlinson and Barbara Habberjam (New York: Zone Books, 1991), 58.

**4  The sublime today: re-partitioning the global sensible**

1  See I. Kant, "Perpetual Peace," in *Kant: Political Writings*, ed. H. Reiss (New York: Cambridge University Press, 1970).
2  The quotations are from N. Bernstein, "New Scrutiny as Immigrants Die in Custody," *New York Times*, on the web at: http://www.nytimes.com/2007/06/26/us/26detain.html (obtained June 27, 2007).

3  K. D. Madsen, "Local Impact of the Balloon Effect of Border Law Enforcement," *Geopolitics* 12 (2007): 282.
4  E. Danticat, "Impounded Fathers," *New York Times*, June 17, 2007, Op-Ed section, 12.
5  N. Scheper-Hughes, "The Global Traffic in Human Organs," in *The Anthropology of Globalization*, ed. J. X. Inda and R. Rosaldo (Malden, MA: Blackwell, 2002), 272.
6  Ibid., 270.
7  Ibid., 275.
8  Ibid., 273.
9  Ibid.
10  J. Crary, *Techniques of the Observer* (Cambridge, MA: MIT Press, 1991), 10.
11  The quoted remark is from a review of the film: "The City's Secret Heartbeat," on the web at: http://www.telegraph.co.uk/arts/main.jhtml?xml'/arts/2002/12/13/bfss13.xml (obtained June 30, 2007).
12  From an interview conducted by C. Lucia in *Cineaste* 28 (2003), quoted in S. Gibson, "The Hotel Business Is about Strangers: Border Politics and the Hospitable Spaces in Stephen Frears's *Dirty Pretty Things*," *Third Text* 20 (2006): 698.
13  For a review of the various cinematic examples, see the monograph issue, Y. Loshintzky (ed.), "Fortress Europe: Migration, Culture and Representation," *Third Text* 20 (2006).
14  For the treatment of distraction, see W. Benjamin, "The Work of Art in the Age of Mechanical Reproduction," in *Illuminations*, trans. Harry Zohn (New York: Schocken, 1968), 217–52. The quotation for "the analytic of the sublime" is in I. Kant, *The Critique of Judgment*, trans. J. H. Bernard (Amherst, NY: Prometheus Books, 2000), 102.
15  Kant, *The Critique of Judgment*, 102.
16  The review is on the web at: http://www.dvdanswers.com/index.php?c'9898s'2 (obtained Sept. 18, 2005).
17  See J. Butler, *Precarious Life* (New York: Verso, 2004).
18  See Hannah Arendt's discussion of imperialism in her *The Origins of Totalitarianism* (New York: Harcourt, 1973).
19  See Rancière on film in S. Guenoun, "An Interview with Jacques Rancière: Cinematographic Image, Democracy, and the Splendor of the … ," *Sites* 4 (2000), 1–7.
20  J. Rancière, *La Fable Cinematographique* (Paris: Editions du Seuil, 2001), 22.
21  Although there are many, among the most notable is Hannah Arendt's location of Kant's politics in his *Critique of Judgment*. See her *Lectures on Kant's Political Philosophy*, ed. Ronald Beiner (Chicago: University of Chicago Press, 1982).
22  J. Rancière, "The Politics of Aesthetics," on the web at: http://theater.kein.org/node/view/99 (obtained Mar. 23, 2005).
23  J. Rancière, *The Politics of Aesthetics*, trans. Gabriel Rockhill (New York: Continuum, 2004), 65.
24  Rancière, "The Politics of Aesthetics."
25  The quotations are from Deleuze's review of the Kant- and Hegel-influenced ontological position of Jean Hyppolite in Hyppolite's *Logic and Existence*: G. Deleuze, "Jean Hyppolite's *Logic and Existence*," in *Desert Islands and Other Texts* (New York: Semiotext(e), 2004), 16.
26  Kant, "Perpetual Peace," 108.
27  These references to Jefferson's use of nature to warrant a Euro-American continental ethnogenesis are from M. J. Shapiro, *Deforming American Political Thought: Ethnicity, Facticity, and Genre* (Lexington: University Press of Kentucky, 2006).
28  J.-F. Lyotard, "After the Sublime: The State of Aesthetics," in *The Inhuman*, trans. G. Bennington and R. Bowlby (Stanford, CA: Stanford University Press, 1991), 137.
29  The quotation is from L. Daston, "Attention and the Values of Nature in the Enlightenment," in *The Moral Authority of Nature*, ed. L. Daston and F. Vidal (Chicago: University of Chicago Press, 2004), 101.

30 Kant, *The Critique of Judgment*, 117.
31 The expression "metapolitics of aesthetics" belongs to Jacques Rancière. See his "The Sublime from Lyotard to Schiller: Two Readings of Kant and Their Political Significance," *Radical Philosophy* 126 (2004): 13.
32 Quotation from G. Deleuze, "The Idea of Genesis in Kant's Esthetics," in *Desert Islands and Other Texts*, 70.
33 Kant, *The Critique of Judgment*, 119.
34 Ibid., 104.
35 Ibid., 126.
36 A recognition of the link between Kant's *Critique of Judgment* and his "Perpetual Peace" provides a deeper appreciation of Kant's politics than is offered in the typical neo-liberal readings of the latter treatise by international relations practitioners.
37 Rancière, "The Sublime from Lyotard to Schiller," 12.
38 Ibid.
39 Kant, *The Critique of Judgment*, 94.
40 Ibid., 130.
41 Ibid.
42 Ibid., 131.
43 The Deleuze position is stated in "The Idea of Genesis in Kant's Esthetics," 70, and the Lyotard quotation is from "After the Sublime: The State of Aesthetics," 142.
44 I. Kant, *Critique of Practical Reason*, trans. Werner S. Pluhar (Indianapolis: Hackett, 2002), 63.
45 Ibid., 78.
46 See I. Kant, *The Critique of Pure Reason*, trans. Paul Guyer and Allen W. Wood (New York: Cambridge University Press, 1999). And for a discussion of the delicate balance between passivity and activity in the Kantian subject, see G. Deleuze, *Kant's Critical Philosophy*, trans. Hugh Tomlinson and Barbara Habberjam (Minneapolis: University of Minnesota Press, 1984), 14–15.
47 My discussion here is benefiting from Daniel Smith's concise explication of the Kantian synthesis in his "Translator's Introduction" to G. Deleuze, *Francis Bacon: The Logic of Sensation*, trans. Daniel W. Smith (Minneapolis: University of Minnesota Press, 2003), xv–xvi.
48 The quotation is from ibid., xvii.
49 G. Deleuze, "Kant: Synthesis and Time," Lecture of March 14, 1978, trans. M. McMahon, on the web at: http://www.webdeleuze.com/php/sommaire.html.
50 Ibid.
51 See for example E. Ellis's comprehensive summary of the different approaches: *Kant's Politics* (New Haven, CT: Yale University Press, 2005), 49.
52 Ibid.
53 Ibid.
54 Deleuze, *Francis Bacon*, 14.
55 Ibid., 60.
56 Ibid., 59.
57 This section on Louis Malle's *Pretty Baby* is developed in my *Deforming American Political Thought*.
58 Giorgio Agamben, "Beyond Human Rights," trans. Cesare Casarino, in *Radical Thought in Italy*, ed. P. Virno and M. Hardt (Minneapolis: University of Minnesota Press, 1996), 159.
59 The quotation is from my treatment of Kant's geography in my *Cinematic Political Thought: Narrating Race, Nation and Gender* (New York: NYU Press, 1999), 89.
60 See Kant's "Perpetual Peace."
61 Gayatri Spivak, "*Sammy and Rosie Get Laid*," in *Outside in the Teaching Machine* (New York: Routledge, 1993), 252.

62  Ibid., 244.
63  Franco Moretti, *Atlas of the European Novel* (New York: Verso, 1998), 86.
64  Ibid., 117.
65  Ibid., 123.
66  S. M. Eisenstein, "Montage and Architecture," trans. Michael Glenny, *Assemblage* 10 (1989): 117.
67  Y.-A. Bois, Introduction to Eisenstein, "Montage and Architecture," 113.
68  F. Kracauer, *The Mass Ornament: Weimar Essays* (Cambridge, MA: Harvard University Press, 1995), 181.
69  J. Rancière, *Dis-agreement*, trans. Julie Rose (Minneapolis: University of Minnesota Press, 1999), 36.
70  Ibid., 35.
71  M. de Certeau, *Practices of Everyday Life* (Berkeley: University of California Press, 1984), 35.
72  Ibid., 37.
73  J. Rancière, "The Thinking of Dissensus: Politics and Aesthetics," Paper read at the conference "Fidelity to Disagreement: Jacques Rancière and the Political," Goldsmiths College, September 2003, 17.
74  The quotations are from D. Tomas, *Beyond the Image Machine* (New York: Continuum, 2004), 5.
75  J.-F. Lyotard, "Introduction: About the Inhuman," in *The Inhuman*, 1.
76  The quotations are from an essay in which Rancière interprets the implications of Lyotard in the inhuman: J. Rancière, "Who Is the Subject of the Rights of Man?," *South Atlantic Quarterly* 103 (2004): 307.
77  Lyotard, "Introduction: About the Inhuman," 2.
78  Rancière, "Who Is the Subject of the Rights of Man?," 304.
79  See K. Silverman, *The Threshold of the Visible World* (New York: Routledge, 1996), 152–61.
80  Ibid., 103.
81  Rancière, "The Politics of Aesthetics."
82  Deleuze, *Desert Islands and Other Texts*, 260.
83  K. Wodiczko, *Critical Vehicles* (Cambridge, MA: MIT Press, 1999), xi.
84  Ibid., 104.
85  Ibid.
86  Shapiro, *Cinematic Political Thought*, 70.
87  Wodiczko, *Critical Vehicles*, 118.
88  M. J. Shapiro, "The Events of Discourse and the Ethics of Global Hospitality," in *Ethics and International Relations*, ed. H. Seckinelgin and H. Shinoda (New York: Palgrave, 2001), 125.
89  See *Of Hospitality: Anne Dufourmantelle Invites Jacques Derrida to Respond*, trans. Rachel Bowlby (Stanford, CA: Stanford University Press, 2000), 2.
90  Ibid., 5.
91  Ibid., 83.
92  See G. W. F. Hegel, *Natural Law*, trans. T. M. Knox (Philadelphia: University of Pennsylvania Press, 1962), 94–95.
93  Derrida, *Of Hospitality*, 77.
94  P. Nyers, "Emergency of Emerging Identities? Refugees and Transformations in World Order," *Millennium* 28 (1999): 22.
95  For the traditional, state-centric "normative" approach to ethics in international affairs, see for example M. Frost, *Ethics in International Relations: A Constitutive Theory* (Cambridge: Cambridge University Press, 1996).
96  Rancière, "Who is the Subject of the Rights of Man?," 309.

## 5 Aesthetics of disintegration: allegiance and intimacy in the former "Eastern bloc"

1 S. Boym, "On Diasporic Intimacy," in *Intimacy*, ed. L. Berlant (Chicago: University of Chicago Press, 2000), 228.
2 T. T. Minh-ha, *The Digital Event* (New York: Routledge, 2006), 199.
3 F. Moretti, *Atlas of the European Novel 1800–1900* (London: Verso, 1998), 18.
4 Ibid., 70.
5 Ibid., 33.
6 Ibid., 35.
8 Ibid., 38.
9 Ibid., 40.
10 Ibid., 53.
11 Ibid., 55.
12 See M. M. Bakhtin, "Discourse and the Novel," in *The Dialogic Imagination*, trans. C. Emerson and M. Holquist (Austin: University of Texas Press, 1981), 259–422.
13 R. Doyle, *A Star Called Henry* (London: Penguin Books, 1999), 191.
14 For the sequel, see Roddy Doyle, *Oh Play That Thing* (London: Penguin, 2005).
15 Milan Kundera, *Ignorance*, trans. Linda Asher (London: Faber & Faber, 2002), 3.
16 The quotation is from A. White, *Within Nietzsche's Labyrinth* (New York: Routledge, 1990), 66. Throughout his focus on Nietzsche's Zarathustra, White offers an illuminating set of illustrations by reading Nietzsche through Kundera and Kundera through Nietzsche.
17 Kundera, *Ignorance*, 9.
18 Ibid., 34–35.
19 Ibid., 37.
20 P. Nora, "Between Memory and History: *Les Lieux de mémoire*," *Representations* 26 (1989): 8.
21 Ibid.
22 Ibid.
23 See G. Deleuze and F. Guattari, *A Thousand Plateaus: Capitalism and Schizophrenia*, trans. B. Massumi (Minneapolis: University of Minnesota Press, 1987).
24 See G. Deleuze, *Proust and Signs*, trans. R. Howard (Minneapolis: University of Minnesota Press, 2000), 65.
25 L. Berlant, "Intimacy: A Special Issue," in *Intimacy*, ed. Berlant, 2.
26 Ibid., 139.
27 Ibid., 159.
28 G. Deleuze, *Pure Immanence*, trans. A. Boyman (New York: Zone Books, 2005), 46.
29 Ibid., 45.
30 Ibid., 46.
31 D. Hume, *A Treatise of Human Nature*, 2nd ed. (Oxford: Oxford University Press, 1978), 494.
32 Ibid., 494–95.
33 Ibid., 581.
34 See P. Ayer, *The Global Soul: Jet Lag, Shopping Malls, and the Search for Home* (New York: Vintage Books, 2000).
35 S. Rushdie, *Imaginary Homelands* (London: Granta, 1991), 19.
36 Kundera, *Ignorance*, 11.
37 Ibid., 17.
38 Quoted from N. Crane, *Mercator: The Man Who Mapped the World* (London, Weidenfeld & Nicolson, 2002), in R. B. J. Walker, *After the Globe/Before the World* (London: Routledge, forthcoming).
39 Kundera, *Ignorance*, 24.
40 Ibid., 24–25.

41 St. Augustine, *The Confessions*, trans. J. K. Ryan (New York: Doubleday, 1960), 288.

42 Ibid., 290.

43 See J. G. A. Pocock, *The Machiavellian Moment: Florentine Political Thought and the Republican Tradition* (Princeton, NJ: Princeton University Press, 1975).

44 Ibid., 53.

45 Ibid., 54.

46 The quotation belongs to B. Massumi, *A User's Guide to Capitalism and Schizophrenia* (Cambridge, MA: MIT Press, 1992), 76.

47 G. Deleuze, *Empiricism and Subjectivity*, trans. C. V. Boundas (New York: Columbia University Press, 1991), 126.

48 Kundera, *Ignorance*, 140–41.

49 Ibid., 138.

50 Ibid., 143.

51 Ibid., 162.

52 Ibid., 179.

53 Boym, "On Diasporic Intimacy," 229.

54 Kundera, *Ignorance*, 155–56.

55 The study is reported in the 1999 issue of *British Medical Journal*, on the web at: http://bmj.bmjjournals.com/cgi/content/extract/319/7208/468/a?ck'nck (obtained Nov. 4, 2006).

56 The quotation is from Berlant, "Intimacy: A Special Issue," 7.

57 H. Arendt, *The Human Condition* (Garden City, NY: Doubleday, 1959), 27.

58 Ibid., 28.

59 The quotation is from L. Birken, *Consuming Desires* (Ithaca, NY: Cornell University Press, 1988), 31.

60 Ibid., 35.

61 A. Kurkov, *A Matter of Life and Death* (London: Vintage, 2006), 72.

62 See "The Director's Statement," on the web at: http://www.sonypicures.com/classics/friend.

63 See J. Derrida, *Politics of Friendship*, trans. George Collins (London: Verso, 1997), 19.

64 L. Kipnes, "Adultery," in *Intimacy*, ed. Belant, 14.

65 Kurkov, *A Matter of Life and Death*, 76.

66 The quotations are from J.-J. Goux's reading of *The Counterfeiters*: *The Coiners of Language*, trans. J. C. Gage (Norman: University of Oklahoma Press, 1996), 20. For an extended treatment of the novel and its relationship to value, see M. J. Shapiro, *Cinematic Political Thought* (New York: NYU Press, 1999), 146–49.

67 See G. Deleuze, *Cinema 2*, trans. Hugh Tomlinson and Robert Galeta (Minneapolis: University of Minnesota Press, 1989), 38.

68 J. Derrida, *Politics of Friendship*, trans. G. Collins (New York: Verso, 1997), 19.

69 Ibid., 14.

70 J.-J. Goux, *Symbolic Economies: After Marx and Freud*, trans. J. C. Gage (Ithaca, NY: Cornell University Press, 1990), 129.

## 6 Perpetual war?

1 S. Mehmedinovic, *Sarajevo Blues*, trans. A. Alacalay (San Francisco: City Lights, 1998), 54.

2 G. Deleuze, *Cinema 2*, trans. H. Tomlinson and R. Galeta (Minneapolis: University of Minnesota Press, 1989), 2.

3 D. Cave, "G.I.'s in Iraq Ready for Rest, but Hardly at Ease," *New York Times*, on the web at: http://www.nytimes.com/2007/09/30/world/middleeast/30mahmudiya.html?_r'1&oref'slogin (obtained Sept. 30, 2007).

4 Ibid.

5 G. Deleuze, *Cinema 1: The Movement Image*, trans. Hugh Tomlinson and Barbara Habberjam (Minneapolis: University of Minnesota Press, 1986), 64.

6 I. Kant, "Perpetual Peace," in *Kant: Political Writings*, ed. H. Reiss (New York: Cambridge University Press, 1970), 108.

7 I. Kant, "The Contest of Faculties," in *Kant: Political Writings*, ed. H. Reiss, 183.

8 See I. Kant, *The Critique of Judgment*, trans. J. H. Bernard (Amherst, NY: Prometheus Books, 2000).

9 M. Foucault, *The Politics of Truth*, trans. Lysa Hochroth (New York: Semiotext(e), 1997), 42.

10 This complaint can be found in M. Dempsey, "Hellbent for Mystery," *Film Quarterly* 32 (1979): 10–13.

11 This is the position taken by M. Kinder, "Political Game," *Film Quarterly* 32 (1979).

12 J. Rancière, *The Politics of Aesthetics*, trans. Gabriel Rockhill (New York: Continuum, 2004), 22–24.

13 The complaint about the late emergence of a "narrative drive" is in Dempsey, "Hellbent for Mystery," 13.

14 The quotations are from D. Tanovic, "Director's Statement," DVD version of *No Man's Land* (Los Angeles: MGM, 2001).

15 The quotation is from I.-M. Rijsdijk, "Searching for the 'Good War': The Challenge Posed by Terrence Malick's *The Thin Red Line*," on the web at: http://www.uct.ac.za/ conferences/filmhistorynow/papers/irijsdijk.doc (obtained Apr. 7, 2007). The remarks in brackets are my emendations of Rijsdijk's parenthetical remarks.

16 See T. Malick, "Translator's Introduction," in Martin Heidegger, *The Essence of Reasons*, trans. T. Malick (Evanston, IL: Northwestern University Press, 1969), xv.

17 G. Deleuze, *Proust and Signs*, trans. R. Howard (Minneapolis: University of Minnesota Press, 2000).

18 L. Bersani and U. Dutoit, *Forms of Being: Cinema, Aesthetics, Subjectivity* (London: BFI, 2004), 145.

19 Ibid., 146.

20 For another treatment that sees the deer hunt as a symbolic displacement, see F. Burke, "Reading Michael Cimino's *The Deer Hunter*: Interpretation as Melting Pot," *Literature Film Quarterly* 20 (1992).

21 See M. Komarovsky, *Blue Collar Marriage* (New Haven, CT: Yale University Press, 1987), 26.

22 The quotation is from Burke, Reading Michael Cimino's *The Deer Hunter*: Interpretation as Melting Pot," 252.

23 These observations on melancholy follow S. Žižek, "Melancholy and the Act," *Critical Inquiry* 26 (2000): 657–81.

24 Ibid., 660–61.

25 See D. Wood, "All the Words We Cannot Say: A Critical Commentary on *The Deer Hunter*," *Journal of Popular Film and Television* 7 (1980): 368.

26 J. Derrida, "Onto-Theology of National-Humanism (Prolegomena to a Hypothesis)," *Oxford Literary Review* 14 (1992): 6.

27 S. Rushdie, *The Ground Beneath Her Feet* (New York: Henry Holt, 1999).

28 Ibid., 24.

29 S. Rushdie, *Imaginary Homelands* (New York: Penguin, 1992): 15.

30 For an analysis and explication of semiosis, see Walter Mignolo's discussion of the semiotic interaction between diverse meaning systems and their material realizations during the Euro- and Meso-American encounter in the Renaissance, in W. Mignolo, *The Darker Side of the Renaissance* (Ann Arbor: University of Michigan Press, 1995), 7–9.

31 S. Rushdie, "Marvels of the World Unveiled," *Whole Earth* (1998), 7.

32 Rushdie, *The Ground Beneath Her Feet*, 93.

33 Ibid., 95–96.

34 H. al-Shaykh, *Beirut Blues*, trans. C. Cobham (New York: Doubleday, 1995).

35 P. W. Sunderman, "Between Two Worlds: An Interview with Hanan al-Shaykh," *Literary Review* 40 (1997): 297.

36 Ibid., 304.

37 Ibid., 303.

38 Ibid., 304.

39 Shaykh, *Beirut Blues*, 67.

40 S. G. Freedman, "For the Author of 'Spider Woman,' Hollywood Provided Hope," *New York Times*, Aug. 13, 2000, C-2.

41 Ibid., 3.

42 J. Rancière, "The Politics of Aesthetics," on the web at: http://theater.kein.org/node/view/99 (obtained Mar. 23, 2005).

43 Reported by D. Butler of the Associated Press: "Bush Urges Defeat of Genocide Bill," on the web at: http://www.boston.com/news/nation/washington/articles/2007/10/10/bush_urges_defeat.html (obtained Oct. 10, 2007).

44 See A. Bazin, *What is Cinema?*, Vol. 2, trans. Hugh Gray (Berkeley: University of California Press, 1971), 37.

45 See Kant, *The Critique of Judgment*, 120–25.

46 Ibid., 132–45.

47 As I note in chapter 4, in his analytic of the sublime Kant becomes less optimistic about the subject's achievement of a "subjective necessity." Here, I am indebted to Rudolph Gasche's discussion of the connection between Kant's reflections on how his analytics of the beautiful and the sublime implicate moral sensibility. See R. Gasche, *The Idea of Form: Rethinking Kant's Aesthetics* (Stanford, CA: Stanford University Press, 2002), 155–78.

# Index